Seeing the Light:
Personal Encounters With the Middle East and Islam

Richard H. Curtiss and Janet McMahon, eds.

Published by the
American Educational Trust
Washington, D.C.

Copyright 1997 by AET
All rights reserved
Published in the United States of America
by the American Educational Trust
P.O. Box 53062
Washington, DC 20009

Library of Congress Cataloging-in-Publication Data

Seeing the light : personal encounters with the Middle East and Islam
 / Richard H. Curtiss and Janet McMahon, eds.
    p.   cm.
    Includes index.
    ISBN 0-937165-06-9
    1. Israel-Arab conflicts—Public opinion.   2. Public opinion—
United States.   3. Israel—Foreign public opinion, American.
4. Propaganda, Zionist—Public opinion.   5. United States—Foreign
relations—Israel—Public opinion.   6. Israel—Foreign relations—
United States—Public opinion.   7. Islam—Public opinion.
I. Curtiss, Richard H., 1927-   .   II. McMahon, Janet, 1948-
DS119.7.S38165   1997
956.9405—dc21

97-6644
CIP

FOREWORD

This book has 74 authors. The great majority of them are North Americans, but they also include Europeans, Middle Easterners and South Asians. They are Christians, Jews, Muslims, a London-born Zen Buddhist, and others. When they wrote their articles, two of the writers were in their teens, most were in their 20s and 30s, and a few were fully qualified senior citizens.

Although some of these submissions are by professional writers, probably half are the first articles their authors ever have had published. All but one of the writers, however, have one thing in common. Their article in this collection first was published in the *Washington Report on Middle East Affairs,* between November, 1986, and April, 1997, in its ongoing "Seeing the Light" series.

The exception is the opening article by author Vincent Sheehan, perhaps the most famous war correspondent of his time, who made his first, and only, visit to Palestine in 1929. That extended visit, which involved eyewitness reporting of the notorious Hebron riots, was so traumatic that it precipitated the author's temporary nervous collapse.

As his account in this book makes clear, he was "present at the creation" of one of the many disputed events that ever since have skewed attempts in the United States to understand or even discuss rationally Palestine, Israel, the Middle East and Islam. His is an emotional account by a highly sophisticated American who felt a particular empathy with the many Jews he had known as a journalist and world traveler. The cognitive dissonance created between the general bias he brought with him from the West and his contradictory first-hand observations in the Middle East, literally shut down his mental and physical faculties for a time. When he recovered, he fled the Middle East forever. But his account sets the standard for the 73 other personal reminiscences that follow.

What emerges from the accounts by Americans is that the more they thought they had learned about the Middle East from afar, the more they had to unlearn on the spot, and the greater their chagrin at having been so thoroughly misled.

Conversely, the accounts of many Middle Easterners and South Asians reveal that they were equally misinformed about Westerners in general and Americans in particular. Based upon their observations of U.S. political policies in the Arab-Israeli dispute, they arrived in the United States expecting to encounter deep-rooted prejudice and malevolence where Middle Easterners were concerned. Instead they found almost measureless ignorance of the history and geography of the Middle East among individual Americans, coupled with a friendly willingness by those same

Americans to take what was said by Middle Easterners they met personally at face value, and even to learn from them.

The editors both had the unusual personal experiences of "seeing the light" about the Middle East before actually spending time there. One was a journalist turned diplomat preparing at the Foreign Service Institute for his first Middle East assignment during the dramatic leadup to the Suez war of 1956. He was able to contrast daily treatment of the story in the mainstream media of Washington, DC with the comments and insights of academics and diplomats who personally had lived and worked in the area. The conclusions he reached in a matter of weeks were confirmed by 40 subsequent years of living in or dealing with the area, which included co-founding the American Educational Trust, publisher of this book, and serving as executive editor of the *Washington Report on Middle East Affairs.*

The other editor's journey of discovery began with the "adoption" of a Muslim "foster daughter." Living in Oregon at the time and doing non-profit editorial work unrelated to the Middle East, she was astonished at the contrasting impressions of the child, her family, her village and her people as provided in letters from their village in south Lebanon, and the U.S. mainstream media's depiction of exactly the same people as inveterate terrorists. What began as a charitable gesture evolved into a personal search for the truth, which took the editor to the Middle East for a year at the American University in Cairo, and eight years as managing editor of the *Washington Report on Middle East Affairs,* America's leading publication in its field.

So this book, like the magazine, has an agenda. For readers who have never been to the Middle East, it is to replicate the experiences that enabled the editors to see the area and its people clearly and, as it turned out, accurately even before going there. And for readers who have been to the Middle East and seen the light, if ever so briefly, without misleading U.S. media filters, it is to reinforce those moments of clarity with the impressions of others who have shared the experience.

The Middle East gave the world the Abrahamic religions. The Arabs preserved and enhanced the wisdom of the ancient world while the West was slumbering through the Dark Ages. Islamic civilization sparked the European Renaissance that ended them.

In turn, when the contemporary Middle East began its own awakening from centuries of repression and stagnation, Americans played a key role in modernizing the area's educational and medical systems. As a result, prior to World War II, Americans were the most trusted foreigners in the Middle East. In the two generations since then, however, Americans have become the most reviled.

These personal accounts shed needed light on how this happened. They lift the veil of what author Alfred Lilienthal calls "mythinformation" about the Israel-Palestine dispute which has brought U.S.-Arab relations to their present nadir. These writers also help readers see how they can contribute to setting the record straight, just as did these 74 individuals who personally saw the light about the Israelis and the Palestinians, the United States and the Middle East, and the world and Islam. ❖

CONTENTS

SECTION VII:

SECTION VIII:

I. THE BRITISH MANDATE
1919-1947

DURING WORLD WAR I, Great Britain entered into conflicting obligations in the Middle East. For their support against the Ottoman Empire of the Turks, who were allied with Germany and the other Central Powers, the British promised the Arabs independence. With its ally, France, Britain entered into the secret Sykes-Picot agreement, which divided the same Arab areas which were being promised independence into British and French spheres of influence. And to court Jewish support in Europe and the United States, Britain negotiated and finally adopted in 1917 the Balfour Declaration saying, "His Majesty's government view with favor the establishment in Palestine of a national home for the Jewish people...it being clearly understood that nothing shall be done which may prejudice the civil and religious rights of the existing non-Jewish communities in Palestine, or the rights and political status enjoyed by Jews in any other country." Following the World War I defeat of the Ottoman Empire, the League of Nations in 1919 appointed Britain as the mandatory power in Palestine, charged with "the rendering of administrative advice and assistance...until such time as [Palestine is] able to stand alone." As these mutually incompatible goals played out, Arab resistance was suppressed in Syria, Lebanon, Iraq and Palestine. Meanwhile Jewish immigration into Palestine increased from a trickle in the 1920s to a flood in the mid- and late 1930s under the pressure of Nazi Germany's persecution of Europe's Jews. When World War II ended, tens of thousands of displaced Jewish survivors of the European Holocaust pressed to go to Palestine, legally or illegally, backed by three Jewish militias that had become active during World War II. They were the mainstream Haganah, created from a force organized by the British to fight alongside Allied forces during the war; the underground terrorist Irgun Zvai Leumi, headed by future Israeli Prime Minister Menachem Begin; and the Jewish nationalist Lehi, called the Stern Gang by the British, one of whose three principal leaders was future Israeli Prime Minister Yitzhak Shamir. Lehi had fought against the British during World War II and, joined by the Irgun, continued its campaign of assassinations and terrorism after the end of the war. On the Palestinian Arab side, members of Arab militias, which also had been organized to fight alongside the British in Italy during World War II, and remnants of anti-British Arab resistance groups which had been largely defeated by the British between 1936 and the outbreak of World War II, had largely deteriorated into local defense militias incapable of concerted effective action.

Holy Land, August 1929

By Vincent Sheean

For years before 1929 I had thought of making a journey to Palestine. I had long had an exaggerated admiration for the Jewish people, and invested them with all the characteristics of poetic insight, intensity of feeling, and loftiness of motive which seemed to me lacking in the generality of the so-called Christians. This attitude was a kind of anti-Semitism turned wrong side out, I suppose—a product, perhaps, of the extraordinary experience in which I first made the acquaintance of Jews as a freshman in college—but it was, whatever its nature, strong enough to make me gravitate toward the Jews of my acquaintance and submit with eagerness to the influences they (whether they wished to do so or not) could not help exercising...

And on a more practical plane I firmly believed in the thesis Romain Rolland set forth at length in a part of *Jean Christophe*: that the Jews of Western Europe and America constituted the one international layer of culture, through which everything good in literature, music and art spread from nation to nation and slowly tended to give the Western world a closer relationship between its parts. I was, in short, as thoroughgoing a pro-Semite (if there is such a word) as you could have found anywhere...

Forgiveness was what it seemed to me the Christians had to ask of the Jews—and the only thing they had a right to demand. The more I read of the history of the Jewish people the more I was ashamed of the behavior of the Christians. The literature of anti-Semitism was nonsense, abounding in the silliest accusations it was possible for minds clouded by hatred to invent (ritual murder, the "protocol of the elders of Zion," conspiracy of the Jews to conquer the world, etc., etc.).

The literature that recorded the facts was a different affair altogether: the story of a race forever driven and oppressed, surrounded by superstitious hatreds until it was forced to live as the traveller lives on a desert journey, alert and aware of death. Even with the decline of superstition in the 19th century, when legal disabilities were removed from the Jews in most civilized countries, a social prejudice remained, the legacy of 2,000 years...In fact, the motives that turned me toward Palestine were not altogether those of interest or curiosity: there was also a perceptible element of militancy, a desire to strike some kind of small blow against race hatred, to help, somehow or other, to *écraser l'infame*...

My old friend Hillel Bernstein was not a Zionist himself, but he knew enough of the Zionist organization to be aware that it sometimes sent writers to Palestine to contribute articles to its own publications. It was Bernie's idea that I might get some such contact, with enough of an advance on it to make a stay in Palestine possible. He pointed out that Zionism was a controversial question, even among Jews, and that it would be well to make some stipulation about it—that I would not write political propaganda, that a description of the country and the Zionist colonies would have to be enough...

By an appointment made through Bernie I went to see the editor of *The New Palestine*, a Zionist publication, and told him what I wanted to do. I suggested that I could do a series of articles on life in the Jewish colonies (my plan being to live as a colonist for a while if possible), and that these articles would have to be noncontroversial and nonpolitical, as I could not bind myself in advance to adopt any particular attitude toward the larger questions. I added that so far as I knew the problems at issue I was already sympathetic to the Zionist views, as I had been for years; but that I could not engage future opinions.

The editor was friendly and polite, but he seemed to regard all this formulation of attitude as unnecessary. "Don't you worry about that," he said. "We don't want people to write propaganda. Propaganda's no good anyway. How much do you want?"

The simplicity of the business delighted me. In 15 minutes it was all arranged...

An Arab City

Jerusalem enchanted me from the beginning...The city was beautiful, particularly when seen from above—a small jewel of a city, white roofs and domes serried in order up and down hills beneath a startlingly clear sky. By day the sky was burning blue, and by night it was so clear that the stars seemed within reach. The Austrian Hospice, where I lived...was deep-walled, silent and cool on the hottest days, peaceful in the midst of turmoil. There was a mosque just behind it, and the call of the muezzin used to wake me at unearthly hours until I grew accustomed to it. There were, in fact, mosques everywhere, and Islam's call to prayer haunted the still air of an evening, so that I could scarcely see a photograph of the roofs of Jerusalem afterwards without hearing the long cry of the muezzin as a part of it.

That was, probably, the first impression I received of walled Jerusalem in the early days: that it was an Arab city. It was as Arab as Cairo or Baghdad, and the Zionist Jews (that is, the modern Jews) were as foreign to it as I was myself. I had expected this, of course. I knew that the Old City had not been changed, that the large Zionist population of Jerusalem (an actual majority) lived in new quarters outside the walls, and that Palestine was still predominantly an Arab country. But a fact on paper has not the same effect as its physical configuration. Two days in Jerusalem gave me a clearer perception of the fact than I could have received from a volume of statistics. I had enough political experience to realize that such things as these must determine feeling and action, and from my second or third day in Jerusalem I began to wonder if all was as well between the Arabs and the Jews as I had been led to believe. I knew nothing; but anybody could see, in a half an hour, that here were the physical elements of a conflict...

When I came to Jerusalem the British had been in possession of the city for more than 10 years. The Palestine Mandate, under which Britain was to administer the country in trust for the establishment of a Jewish national home, had been in operation for seven years, but the Zionist immigration policy had slowly made progress, so that by the time I arrived in the country there were no longer 10 Arabs for every Jew, but only about six— the figures given being, roughly, 750,000 Arabs to 150,000 Jews...

For two or three weeks I made every effort to avoid the signs of trouble....I absorbed what I could, listened to everybody, and wrote (on this subject, that is) nothing. I had no intention of writing a word about the country until I had had at least three or four months to observe it. I could not foresee how agitated those three or four months were going to be.

On July 9 I had my first mild jolt. An Arabic newspaper on that day announced that I had come to Palestine and added, *carrement*, that I was in the pay of the Jews.

There were other comments, but this was the one I attended to carefully. Was I in the pay of the Jews or was I not? If not, why did the statement make me angry? And if I was, what then? It took me about half an hour to see that I must either make up my mind to be, as the Arabic newspaper said, "in the pay of the Jews," and to accept any comment that might be made on the subject, or else to break my connection with the Zionists altogether and go my own way.

My diary (which was kept very full, too full, in Palestine) records the results on Thursday, July 11, in these words:

...Although I've always said I would not allow my opinions to be influenced, how can I be sure? After all, I have already taken an advance of $500 and expect $1,500 more! All this appears under an entirely different light here. I finally decided that I couldn't do it. I wrote to Weisgal, both in New York and in Zurich, and told him I didn't want any more money and would take no engagement for any Zionist subsidiary. I made it clear that I must write and speak as I please. This relieved my feelings somewhat, although God knows how I shall get along without that money. What's worse is that if I can't write a couple of articles that will suit the Zionists' book I'll have to give back the five hundred I've already received...

In three weeks I had already acquired serious misgivings about the wisdom of the Zionist policy. I still knew nothing about the Arabs of Palestine, but I could see them all around me everywhere, and if my long experience in political journalism had taught me anything, it was that one people did not like being dominated or interfered with in its own home by another. These things seemed to me plain, beyond argument. What I wanted to hear was what the Zionists were doing...Their comments on the Arabs took a form that seemed to me invariably stupid, in Palestine or elsewhere: the form of underrating the opponent. Your ordinary Zionist would say, in so many words: "We don't have to worry about the Arabs. They'll do anything for money." I knew no Palestine Arabs, but unless they were far different from the Arabs I had known in Morocco, Iraq and Persia, this could not be the truth...

As I retrace, with the aid of my old diary, the steps by which I altered my first opinions of the Zionist experiment, I see that the thing presented itself to me throughout as a practical problem. The steps were small ones, each determined by a fact. For larger ideas—for a consideration of what the whole thing might mean—I had to wait until I had left Palestine behind; no "long view" was possible in that embittered country. I had arrived on June 25 with a genuine sympathy, however ignorant or romantic, for the Zionist effort. Between June 25 and July 9, I was a little disquieted by the physical configuration of the problem, by the sight and sound of the Arab country in which Zionism was making its effort. On July 9, I received a jolt of a personal nature, and as a result broke my connection with the Zionists and resumed my freedom: all this without consciously turning against the Zionist idea. During the next week I went to Tel Aviv and the colonies, talked, talked, talked, and listened even more. I saw Jewish islands in an Arab sea: that was what I saw. And on the whole the Jewish disregard for the Arabs seemed to me (from their own point of view) perilous in the extreme. I could not believe that the Arabs of Palestine were so different from other Arabs that they would welcome the attempt to create a Jewish nation in their country.

After July 17, therefore, I made some attempt to find out what the Arabs of Palestine were like. I remained in touch with the Zionists, visited Tel Aviv, continued to read Zionist literature and talk to Zionist friends. But I no longer tried to ignore the fact that Palestine was, by the overwhelming majority of its population, an Arab country. It seemed to me important to determine for myself what were the bonds between this population and the land it inhabited. If the bonds were slight—if the Arabs of Palestine had been mere squatters for 13 centuries—it would still be feasible for the Zionists, by purchase, persuasion and pressure, to get the Arabs out sooner or later and convert Palestine into a Jewish national home. Zionists had pointed out, in conversation and in writing, that the Arabs had plenty of land to go to all around Palestine: Syria, Iraq, Transjordan and Arabia Deserta were all Arab countries. What bound the Arabs of Palestine to Palestine?

My acquaintance with the Arab world in general suggested that the answer would be found in Islamic religious feeling...I had never known a Muslim who did not regard the central doctrines of the Islamic faith with fierce, exclusive devotion. I had to find the religious connection between the Arabs and Palestine—and found it, of course, at five minutes' walk from the Austrian Hospice in the Haram Al-Sharif.

Haram Al-Sharif

The Haram Al-Sharif, occupying the traditional Temple Area of the Jews, was one of the great holy places of Islam, ranking immediately after Mecca and Medina. It also contained, as I discovered to my delight, one of the most beautiful buildings in the world. I went there first on Thursday, July 18. On that and succeeding days I had great difficulty getting beyond the one wonderful building, the Dome of the Rock (Qubbat Es-Sakhra). The Dome of the Rock was built over the great black Rock of Abraham's Sacrifice, which once upheld the Altar of Burnt Offerings in the Temple of Solomon…

The Dome of the Rock (usually called the "Mosque of Omar" by Western Christians, because of the mistaken belief that it was built by Omar the Conqueror) was not visited by Orthodox Jews because it was regarded by them as the holiest part of their Temple, and they feared to tread unwittingly upon their Holy of Holies. But Zionists—most of whom, in my experience, were without religious feeling—used to visit it as I did, out of an ordinary aesthetic interest. The Muslims had no objection to such visits. In this and in other respects the Muslims of Palestine were less jealous of their holy places than Muslims elsewhere. I had never been allowed inside a great mosque in Morocco or Persia, but the Haram Al-Sharif, a far holier place to the Islamic world, was open to me or to anybody else all day long.

A Significance Stretching Through Time

The same was true of the Mosque of El-Aksa, once a Christian basilica, and one of the other parts of the Haram. It would be quite within the facts to say that the Haram Al-Sharif (Noble, or August, Sanctuary), in spite of the religious traditions that made it one of the three holiest spots of Islam, was treated as a public monument, like St. Peter's in Rome or the Church of the Holy Sepulchre in Jerusalem. The more I learned about the tradition of the place, the more I was surprised at this. Not only did the Prophet Muhammad visit the place by night (miraculously translated there from Mecca), and ascend to Heaven from Abraham's Rock, but he will come there again on the Day of Judgment, when the Prophet Jesus and the Prophet Muhammad guard the ends of the bridge across the Valley of Jehoshaphat. These and other beliefs, some founded on the Qur'an and some mere folklore, invested the place with a significance stretching through time from the beginnings of the Judeo-Christian-Islamic religion to the last moment contemplated for earthly existence in its philosophy. And nevertheless, so long as one took one's shoes off, it was all right to spend day after day in the place, and even to photograph it.

This being so, it was possible, at first, to assume that the Muslims of Palestine did not regard their holiest shrine with the extreme religious passion characteristic of Muslims elsewhere. The assumption fell in with the Zionist idea that the Arabs of Palestine were, on the whole, a careless and easy-going race. But I had strong doubts, just the same…It seemed to me more likely that what had happened to the Haram Al-Sharif was due to the Westernized character of life in Jerusalem: this place had fallen under so many different kinds of rule, had experienced such a mixture of invasions and such an assimilation of cultures, that its Muslim leaders were constrained by Western taste and manners to open their great sanctuary to the visits of the infidel. I did not believe that underneath this Europeanization of taste and manners was any slackening of the ardour with which Muslims everywhere regard a place sanctified by the Prophet.

Such considerations—divorced, that is, from current problems, and independently of the "incidents" that filled the newspapers every week on the subject—would have led me in any case to examine the question of the Wailing Wall.

The Wailing Wall was a segment of the southwestern wall of the Haram Al-Sharif. It was called by the Jews "Ha-Quotel ma-Aravi" (the Western Wall); by the Muslims "El-Buraq" (from the name of the Prophet's horse, which was tethered there); and by Western Christians the "Wailing Wall." It was a short stretch of wall with a pavement in front of it and had been chosen by the Jews centuries ago as a place of lamentation.

The idea of the Wailing Wall was an ancient one, but I was never able to find out why the idea was attached to this particular segment of the wall and not to any other. The idea was, briefly, this: God has seen fit to exile His people from their Temple, and has condemned them to a long period of disaster, to be ended when the Messiah comes to restore them to their rightful place; therefore His people lament and pray before the Temple wall, particularly on the high holy days of the religion, the Day of Atonement and the Day of the Destruction of the Temple.

This idea of a place for lamentation outside the desecrated Temple grew stronger with the passage of centuries and the accretion of tradition. Most religious Jews believed that the old stones of the wall were actually the stones of Solomon's Temple. This was not archaeologically correct; the oldest stones in the wall of the Haram were Graeco-Roman, of the period of Herod; but the original facts made no difference in religious belief. During these centuries the Western Wall had stood as a representation, a symbol or relic, of the Temple itself. Jews throughout the world who were unable to go there on the Day of Atonement, for instance, paid other Jews to do so for them, and for hundreds of years there had been a small population of religious Jews living in Jerusalem on *Haluka* (sacred doles, for praying).

Before the 19th century there was no record of trouble at the Western Wall; the Muslims made no attempt to prevent the visits of the Jews there, and a prescriptive right grew up, which was maintained under changing governments thereafter. The only records of an attempt to go beyond the original purposes of lamentation at the Wall were dated 1837 and 1912. In the first document the Egyptian governor of Jerusalem forbade the Jews to pave the area in front of the wall or to do anything else beyond "make their visits in accordance with the ancient custom." In the second document the Jews were forbidden to bring into the Wailing Wall area any of the "tools or instruments of possession," such as chairs, screens and the Ark (i.e., the furniture of a synagogue). The Muslim refusal to permit innovations was clearly based upon the fear that, if they did so, the Jews would soon have a synagogue at the wall of the mosque.

The triumph of Zionism at the end of the war brought a new element into the question. The Zionist Organization was not itself religious, although it possessed a religious (minority and opposition) right wing. Its membership professed a wide range of belief in such matters, from agnosticism to orthodoxy, and even included some Jews converted to Christianity; but considered as a whole it was a modern, Western, secular, political body. Still, the advantages to political Zionism of making a test case of the Wailing Wall were obvious. If the Zionists could get new rights at the Wall—better, if they could get absolute possession of the area—they could count on the adherence of a large number of religious Jews who had always been cold to the movement.

An attempt was made in 1919 to buy the Wailing Wall outright. The Zionists offered (through Sir Ronald Storrs) 80,000 pounds; the Arabs refused to sell. From that time onward, at intervals throughout the period of the British occupation and the League of Nations mandate, there were "incidents." There were "incidents" from the time I arrived in Palestine until I left, and the whole of the Palestine question (the national home for the Jews, the rights of the Arabs, the position of the British) came to be involved in them, so that the Zionist struggle was concentrated upon the Wailing Wall and the Arab resistance aligned before it. The question was no longer religious: it had become political and national as well...

There was never any question in my mind that the Jewish feeling about the Wailing Wall was profound and bitter. Jews who frankly confessed themselves to be without religious belief could not discuss the subject without getting excited. They did not think they could put petitions into crevices of the Wall (as Orthodox Jews did) and get them received by the holy spirit of the Temple; they did not want the Wall for themselves at all. But they felt that the Jewish nation in Palestine (as they conceived these minority settlements to be) ought to have possession of one holy place, the relic of the Temple (the only relic, as they somewhat loosely believed), and that the genuinely religious Jews, for the most part not Zionists, should have Zionism to thank for it. The Arabs, for whom they had contempt as an "uncivilized" race, to whom some of them referred as "Red Indians" and others as "savages," were in possession of a place that signified a great deal to the Jewish world in general. The fact hurt the pride of all Jews, I believe, but oddly enough it was the young agnostics and unbelievers who were most bitterly offended and expressed themselves most loudly. What appeared in everyday talk in Jerusalem was what the *Jewish Chronicle* in London summed up with admirable precision: "The Wall has come to be regarded as a gauge of Jewish prestige in Palestine"...

On August 6 the new door from the Haram Al-Sharif to the pavement before the Western Wall was opened, and the Jewish press and public in Palestine took on a more agitated tone than ever. Mr. Vladimir Jabotinsky's "Maccabees"—young men who followed the Zionist revisionist leader—vied with their favorite newspaper, *Doar Hayom* (the Hebrew newspaper with the widest circulation), in expressing their vehement dislike for the Muslim authorities, the Palestine government, and the more moderate authorities of the Zionist Organization. The Muslims were so angry that not a Friday passed without some kind of minor "incident" at the Wailing Wall. The temperature rose throughout the first fortnight of August—you could stick your hand out in the air and feel it rising.

I come now to a curious incident. How curious (and, indeed, how horrible) will appear later on in the story...

On the afternoon of Wednesday, August 14, I was writing in my room in the Austrian Hospice when one of our ever breathless Tyrolean servants broke in to say that a lady was downstairs to see me. I threw on a voluminous dressing gown and clattered down the great stone staircase to the door. There, to my surprise, I saw a compatriot of mine whom I knew very slightly—a Jewish-American I had met in Zionist circles...What she had to say to me, and what followed that evening are related baldly in my diary. I shall quote the entry written the next day (August 15, in the morning), calling the young lady Miss X.

Thursday, August 15. Yesterday was the Eve of Tisha ba'Av (the ninth of the Av), which the Jews of the Galut call Tishabov. Today is the actual fast itself: commemoration of the destruction of the Temple. The day is particularly associated with the Wailing Wall; and with the new Jewish Agency just formed, all the Wailing Wall propaganda going full tilt, the Arabs in a rare state of anxiety, the situation was ripe for anything. Trouble, trouble, and more trouble. There will be plenty. I knew nothing about it at all— didn't even know Tishabov was so near—when Miss X arrived at the Hospice at three in the afternoon, after yesterday's entry in this book was already written. Said she had to go to the Wailing Wall and write a telegram about it for the Times—would I go with her and help? I couldn't understand why, but she said there was going to be a "bust up." She had come up from Tel Aviv especially for this...She said the word had been passed round and hundreds of Haluzim were coming in during the afternoon and evening from the colonies and Tel Aviv, ready to fight.*

I simply couldn't believe all this. She said the Haluzim would be armed—"three-quarters of them"—and it would be a good thing if there was a row at the Wall, to "show them that we are here." I didn't believe a damned word of it: too fantastic; but I told her I'd be ready to go along at five o'clock if she would come back. She said there wouldn't be any trouble until sundown, and five o'clock would do. I went along with her when she came back. She was inconceivably cynical and flippant about the whole thing; said a row would be a very good thing for the Zionist cause, arouse world Jews and increase contributions to the new Agency. Before we reached the Wall it was evident that the police were well prepared. There were little clumps of policemen, British and Palestinian, at every turning in the road, and a force of about 20 of them on duty at the Wall itself, half in front of the Grand Mufti's house and half at the other end. There was no excitement whatever, only about half a dozen religous Jews and Jewesses (Oriental) praying and weeping against the Wall. Toward six, a little before, we went away to the Hotel St. John for a glass of beer, sat there a bit; I couldn't understand her point of view at all, and tried to find out.

When we returned to the Wall, a little before seven, everything had changed. There was a dense crowd made up chiefly of Haluzim, in the little area in front of the Wall. A Yemenite Jew was chanting the lamentations, from the Book, while four other Yemenites sat around him, weeping and rocking themselves back and forth. These seemed to me to be the most sincerely religious manifestants present—they paid no attention to their surroundings, but only to their lament. The rest of that crowd was spoiling for a fight. The crowd I was in, that is. Farther off, at the end of the Wall before the Grand Mufti's house, the service was being read by a Cantor (Sephardic, I believe) who stopped and looked around angrily at the slightest noise. Since noises were continually being made, he was continually stopping, but always had to begin again, as he discovered that the sounds came from zealous but irreverent Haluzim. The number of Jews taking part in this Sephardic group was not more than 16. I counted them as well as I could from where I stood, and am pretty sure of the number. This was at the Mufti's house; the other group was at the other end, opposite the Wall itself, sitting on the steps that go down to one of the Moghrabi houses. All the people who choked the area seemed to be either people like myself, who had come out of curiosity or interest, and Haluzim, who were—as Miss X said—"rarin' to go…"

Evidence of Preparation

Both the Arabs and the police must have been warned of this invasion from the colonies, for there was evidence of preparation. For instance, the Arabs remained invisible; the Mufti's windows were closed and shuttered at about 7:30 so that he wouldn't have to look at the mob milling around; the police were in force and vigilant. The behavior of this crowd at the wall of the mosque was, I consider, damned insulting. If I were an Arab I should be angry, very angry, and I don't for a minute think this thing is over.

X was incredibly cynical. I don't believe she's ever seen anybody wounded, or ever seen a street fight; she can't understand the awfulness of the things she said last night. We left the Wall at about nine o'clock…We went up to the Bristol Gardens for dinner. X was indescribable—apparently enjoyed the impression of horror she was making on me. Said there was bound to be trouble; if not tonight, tomorrow; "we have to show we are here"; and "it won't do a bit of harm if a couple of people get hurt." I tried to tell her, sitting there under a lemon tree, what this kind of thing meant, what it could lead to. God knows I've seen enough of it in my time. She only laughed. I think she thought I was crazy to take it so hard. According to her, it can't do any harm and will only bring in the shekels. I told her she had definitely killed any remnant of sympathy I had for the Zionist movement…

Later in the same day I added another entry to this:

…Jews parading again today. Extreme provocation, but the Arabs are doing nothing. Small army of Haluzim—these precious Maccabees—passed half an hour ago, on

their way to the Wall, with a flag, the Zionist national flag, I suppose, but I couldn't see it: it was furled. Shouts and cheers come from down there; the whole thing makes me very nervous…What an exhibition of imbecility the whole thing is! And if it weren't for the British police I think there would be terrible pogroms. My affection for Zionism has certainly reached the zero point. If this keeps up it will soon go below that and turn into an active antagonism.

This long entry (August 15, 1929) is one of the most puzzling in all the fat volumes of my diary. What did it mean? What could it mean? No sensible human being can believe that the responsible Zionists, like Sacher or Kisch, could have ordered their adherents to make such a show of force at the wall of the Haram Al-Sharif: such a thing would be madness. And yet who did tell the young men to come in from all over the country? I saw them, felt their temperature, knew that they were out for trouble. I had seen mobs and street fights from Chicago to Hankow and back again; I knew the electricity that hatred sets up in the air. And I had seen all the bloodshed I ever wanted to see in my life—all I wanted for a dozen lives, innumerable incarnations. The sight of these angry young men with their *Haluz* energy worked up to such a pitch filled me with alarm. I did not know what I could do about it, but it seemed to me…that we were in for some kind of horror far worse than the young fools could have anticipated. If Miss X was in any way typical, they did not have the slightest conception of the gravity of these issues to the Muslims.

The Jews of Jerusalem outnumbered the Arabs two to one. It was a matter of common knowledge that the Jews possessed firearms; the Arabs did not. Under these conditions, it seemed likely that the Jewish superiority in numbers and equipment, as well as their organization and centralization, would enable them to do great damage among the Arabs for a day or two if they so desired, and from what I had seen and heard the previous week I thought this was probably the wish of a good many among them.

Therefore, on the first day of these troubles the word "massacre" not only didn't occur in conversation, but never even crossed one's mind. The first casualties, we were told, had been Arabs killed by Jews; the Jews were an armed majority in the city; the Arabs were a minority armed only with sticks and knives. What it looked like, at about two o'clock on Friday afternoon, was an outbreak of murderous hatred between the two parts of the population—an outbreak that I, at least, had expected for some days; an outbreak caused by the long, exasperating controversy over the Wailing Wall, and precipitated, made inevitable, by the raising of the Jewish national flag at the wall of the Mosque of Omar. I expected the Jews and Arabs to behave more or less as Germans, Chinese, Frenchmen, Moroccans or Americans would behave under similar circumstances, only worse. In short, I thought we were in for a fight—a peculiarly revolting form of fight, in which the Jews would win in Jerusalem, Haifa and Tel Aviv, and the Arabs would probably get the upper hand elsewhere, and in which neither side would respect the rules of Western civilized murder.

I did what almost any newspaperman or ex-newspaper man would have done: went straight to the post office to send a cablegram to my old office in New York…

The answer I received from New York was: *"How much do you want for articles? Can't you send them by mail?"* At the moment I received the cablegram the terrible murders at Hebron, in which 64 Jews, including some American youths, lost their lives, were actually taking place; a crisis of the first magnitude was in progress; troops and ships were on the move; the "story," considered simply from a newspaper point of view, as an event of interest, was the most important in the world. But I was asked to "send it by mail…"

For three days I worked again as a correspondent. Even as it was, with all these delays and difficulties, mine were still the earliest full accounts of the trouble to reach the English and American newspapers. This was partly due to the difficulties under which my Jewish colleagues labored—few of them dared circulate in the city, and at the beginning none of them went to the government for information—but also to the severity of the censorship established at the beginning of the outbreak.

I cannot remember clearly the details of those terrible days. I scarcely slept at all; I was up at all hours and in all parts of the city, trying to follow the course of events for professional purposes. I went from Arab quarters to Jewish quarters and back again, through police lines and about the unguarded parts of the city…On all previous occasions of this kind I had been fully aware of the perils that threatened the curious bystander, and from the time I had first heard a bullet whiz past in the air, years before, I had retained a salutary fear of death. But in Jerusalem the intensity of nervous excitement produced, after the first day or two, a kind of daze in which I lost awareness of my own identity; I could not have been more unconscious of personal dangers if I had been invisible. Here again I had ceased to be a rational newspaper man: I was roaming the streets of Jerusalem at all hours, overworking fanatically, sleeping scarcely at all, out of sheer nervous horror. Sometimes I noticed my own existence and was surprised at it: for example, when an anxious city Arab would attach himself to me and walk through the streets, as if in protection. This happened several times as I was on my way through the Arab city. I never knew who the self-appointed bodyguards were—they were never twice the same—but I suppose they must have been some of the men the Supreme Moslem Council had sent out to try to keep order. In the Jewish quarters I neither needed nor received such escorts, for there I was usually taken to be British; but as I passed the barricades in those stricken streets I did get many a frown and a curse, for the British were by no means popular among the Jewish population during those days.

The disorders of Friday resulted in many deaths among both Jews and Arabs (the Arabs including Christians as well as Moslems), and the impulse of murder continued for a week. At the end of the terror the official roll for Jerusalem was: 29 Jews and 38 Arabs killed, 43 Jews and 51 Arabs wounded. Here, as in Haifa, the Arabs got considerably the worst of it, but it seems clear (and seemed clear even at the time) that the casualties inflicted by Jews were chiefly in self-defense. The government had undertaken to disarm the Jewish police and the Jewish special constables, to avoid giving the Arabs a chance to say that they were being murdered by Jews with official approval; but no government could have disarmed the Jewish population. What surprised me in the roll of the dead and wounded was not that Arabs outnumbered Jews, but that they did not outnumber them a great deal more.

The horrors of Friday in Jerusalem were followed by something much worse: the ghastly outbreak at Hebron, where 64 Jews of the old-fashioned religious community were slaughtered and 54 of them wounded. Hebron was one of the four holy cities of Judaism, and had had a small, constant Jewish population since mediaeval days. These were not Zionists at all; a more innocent and harmless group of people could not have been found in Palestine; many of them were Oriental Jews, and all were religious. They had had nothing to do with the Zionist excessses, and had lived in amity with their Arab neighbors up to that day. But when the Arabs of Hebron—an unruly lot, at best—heard that Arabs were being killed by Jews in Jerusalem, and that the Mosque of Omar was in danger, they went mad...

I cannot, at this late date, go through all the story of that week; it has been told over and over again. The horrors of Hebron were not repeated elsewhere, but an Arab mob attack on the religious Jews of Safad, on the following Thursday, was sufficiently terrible to be classified as another massacre. In Haifa, where the Jews were predominantly of the modern Zionist type and occupied an excellent strategic position at the top of the hill, the Arabs had much the worst of it. The same was true in some of the colonies; others were almost wiped out. At the end of the disturbances, the official British casualty lists showed 207 dead and 379 wounded among the population of Palestine, of which the dead included 87 Arabs (Christian and Moslem) and 120 Jews, the wounded 181 Arabs and 198 Jews.

The effort to be an efficient, unemotional newspaper correspondent was difficult to the point of impossibility. Living as I did, without sleep and without rest, eating little, and that at the weirdest hours, I should probably have collapsed in time simply from physical exhaustion. But there was a great deal more in it than that...Although I had spent a good part of my life amid scenes of violence and was no stranger to the sight of blood and dying men, I had never overcome my loathing for the spectacle even when it seemed, as in some of the conflicts I had witnessed, compelled by historical necessity. But here, in this miserable little country no bigger, in relation to the rest of the world, than the tip of your finger in relation to your body, I could see no historical necessity whatever. The country was tiny and was already inhabited: why couldn't the Zionists leave it alone? It would never hold enough Jews to make even a beginning toward the solution of the Jewish problem; it would always be prey to such ghastly horrors as those I saw every day and every night: religion, the eternal intransigence of religion, ensured that the problem could never be solved. The Holy Land seemed as near an approximation of hell on earth as I had ever seen...

The factors of physical strain, sleeplessness, excitement and indignation, reached a climax on Tuesday (August 27)...When I got back to the Austrian Hospice that night (it was a little after two o'clock in the morning, I remember—earlier than usual) I knew that I was finished; I could not go on. My nerves had fallen to pieces altogether, so that I could not hit the right keys on the typewriter and indeed could scarcely pick up a pencil. I had seen too many dead and wounded Arabs being carried silently through the street in front of the Hospice; my ears were ringing with the sounds I had heard in the Jewish hospitals. Worst of all, I could never get out of my head that awful conversation with the lady I have called Miss X, who had told me how desirable "incidents" would be for the new Jewish Agency. I was half crazy with nervous horror and indignation—indignation at the Zionists for bringing on such a catastrophe, at the Arabs for behaving with such ferocity, at the government for its general helplessness. All these things produced a mental derangement unlike anything else I have ever known. I sat at my typewriter all night long, making up cablegrams explaining things to the N.A.N.A. in New York and asking them to release me from further work. Toward seven o'clock in the morning (as I know only by the evidence of my next-door neighbor, the auditor of the government; for my own memory of that night vanished) I stopped trying to write on the typewriter and tumbled into bed. I did not get up again for four days...

The Commission of Enquiry

I saw the Arab leaders frequently after the troubles, as I was working on a magazine article about the Haram Al-Sharif...

I stayed on in Jerusalem—stayed for weeks longer than I really wanted to stay—chiefly because of the Parliamentary Commission of Enquiry into the Palestine Disturbances...Its purpose was to find out what had caused the outbreak of August 23 and to make recommendations for the future...

The Zionist case before the Commission of Enquiry was prepared with the utmost care. Every available typewriter in Jerusalem was in use for weeks in the preparation of their documents as I found out to my discomfort (I had to give up the machine I had rented for the period)...

The Arabs were in a position of great inferiority before the Commission. Their counsel—chosen on the advice of some of those self-appointed "friends of the Arabs" in London—were not at best the equals of Sir Boyd Merriman in ability, and were further handicapped by incompetent, dilatory, haphazard preparation. I knew something of the way they went to work, for they lived in the Austrian Hospice, and I saw them frequently...

The Arab inferiority was indeed so bad that many Arabs wished to boycott the Commission altogether. But the Grand Mufti kept his head; the better I knew him the more I realized that he was a man of remarkable character, extraordinary inner calm and certainty. He never got excited, he was always open to reason, and he never rejected an argument or a suggestion without examining it carefully. His knowledge of Western methods was limited, but he said from the beginning that if the Commission of Enquiry were really interested in getting the truth they would get it no matter what the various barristers did: and he was right...

I had agreed to testify to one thing only: the business of Miss X and the gathering at Tishabov. But I had never tried to offer evidence in a court before, and did not realize that it was impossible to say your one thing and get out...

Naiveté and Denial

What with one thing and another I was a sorry witness, but on the whole I suppose most members of the Commission must have supposed that the central fact (the point I had come there to make) did refer to something. At any rate, they called on Miss X immediately afterward—and she denied the whole thing! I was told that it was stupidly naive of me not to expect this, but the fact is that I didn't. Miss X confirmed only those parts of my testimony that could have been confirmed by other witnesses (times, movements, the stretchers at Hadassah Hospital) and denied all the essential parts, those concerned with what she had told me. She futher said that she was not a Zionist, saw few people at Tel Aviv, knew nothing about the Tishabov gatherings, and had not come to Jerusalem on that account at all. Her last and most surprising statement was that when she went to the Wailing Wall, she "generally felt pretty quiet" and did not speak much.

I did not know the details of this evidence for years afterwards. That evening in Jerusalem I only knew that Miss X had denied my evidence under oath, and I had to assume that this disposed of the matter. I had tried to put a rather important point, and if the Commission of Enquiry did not believe me it could not be helped. And in any case it made no great difference to me or to anybody else, for the Commission of Enquiry, whatever it made out of the mass of conflicting evidence before it, could not change the regime in Palestine. The regime, under which an Arab majority had to be governed without representation until such time as a Jewish majority could be pumped into the country from abroad, was regulated by the Balfour Declaration and the Mandate. And with this regime the disturbances of August 1929 were sure to be repeated from time to time whenever the Zionist policy grew so obviously aggressive as to arouse popular indignation. I was weary of the whole thing, which had never brought anything but trouble and difficulty to me; and it was with the profoundest feelings of relief that I left that wretched little country—the "Holy Land"—behind. ✦

Vincent Sheean was an international correspondent in the 1920s and 1930s and the author of numerous articles and books, including Anatomy of Virtue *and* New Persia. *The above is an excerpt from his 1934 memoir,* Personal History ©*1934, 1935, 1940,* ©*1969 by Vincent Sheean. Published by arrangement with Carol Publishing Group. A Citadel Press book.*

II. ISRAEL & THE PALESTINIAN DIASPORA
1948-1966

In November, 1947, under strong American pressure, the United Nations voted to partition Palestine between what were to be a Jewish state and a Palestinian Arab state, with Jerusalem to remain separate from either. The partition resolution gave 53 percent of the land to the 33 percent of the population who were Jews and 47 percent to the 67 percent of the population who were Muslim or Christian Arabs. Fighting broke out almost immediately, with the well-organized Jewish groups rapidly increasing the areas they occupied. Unable to cope with the bloodshed inside Palestine and the political pressure, largely generated by the United States, outside, the British unilaterally withdrew from Palestine on May 15, 1948. By then the massacre of the Arab villagers of Deir Yassin, near Jerusalem, by Jewish Irgun and Lehi militiamen already had taken place, and large additional areas that had been assigned by the U.N. to the Palestinian Arabs already had been occupied by the Haganah, which shortly was to become the Israel Defense Forces. At 6 p.m. (Eastern Standard Time) on May 14, 1948 (midnight in Palestine), the British Mandate expired. At 6:01 p.m. EST Israel came into existence, thanks to the U.N. partition plan. At 6:11 p.m., U.S. President Harry S Truman recognized the Jewish state, despite strong opposition from his secretary of state, General George C. Marshall, and U.S. diplomats. A few hours later Israel was recognized by the Soviet Union. The British withdrew on the same day, and military forces from Egypt and Jordan crossed into Palestine to halt what they perceived as a rout already in progress of Palestinian militias aided by military units from Syria and individual volunteers from Lebanon. In the ensuing fighting, which continued intermittently until the fall of 1948, the Israelis at all times had more armed men in the field than the combined forces they were opposing. When the fighting ended, an estimated 750,000 Palestinians had fled or been driven at gunpoint from their homes. Then, even after a truce was reached, the Israelis refused to allow them to return. Instead the displaced Palestinians remained in refugee camps in the Gaza Strip, occupied by Egypt; in the West Bank, occupied by Jordan; and in Lebanon and Syria. Individually, Palestinians resettled throughout the rest of the Middle East, Western Europe, and as far away as North and South America. After eight tense years Israel, which, to this day, has never defined its borders, attacked Egypt in 1956, in conjunction with Britain and France. From Israel's point of view the attack was primarily an attempt to draw Jordan into the fighting and seize the West Bank and the parts of Jerusalem Israel had not occupied in 1948. The British and French goal was to regain control of Egypt's Suez Canal. Jordan did not enter the fighting. British and French forces withdrew almost immediately from the Canal Zone under American pressure. Israel withdrew from the Sinai Peninsula early in 1957, but only after U.S. President Dwight D. Eisenhower threatened to end the U.S. tax exemption for American Jewish donations to Israeli charities.

Breaking Bread With My Enemy

By Hala Deeb Jabbour

My enlightenment did not occur in a single incident, but over many turbulent years...**1948:** I was born in Jerusalem, Palestine and was only a child when my country was partitioned and my family forced to leave. I spent most of my young adult life hating Jews, Israelis, Zionists and anyone who was on their side, and dismissed the Holocaust as exaggerated Jewish paranoia.

1973: In Beirut, Lebanon, a young married couple moved into the apartment next to mine. They were Jews. At first we just nodded, then the nods turned into whispers of greeting, the greeting became audible, we lingered in the hallway and finally stepped into each other's apartments. It was a slow process and very strange to our Arab way of life, where new neighbors ordinarily became instant family. However, the war in Lebanon put an end to our budding exchanges.

1976: The war for the control of the highrise hotels in Beirut was underway. The Holiday Inn, a sniper's nest until it was burned out, was two blocks away from my apartment. Heavily armed militia roamed our streets. Pack the bags, bundle up the children, and travel for safety to Amman. A few days. We'll be back.

In Amman I was greeted by my sobbing Aunt Aniseh. "Refugees again? Our generation and now yours? When will it end?" Unlike the previous generation of Palestinians, we did go back to Beirut. As the situation intensified, however, we left again, this time for England.

I was in London when my mother called me from her apartment there to tell me excitedly that "Pnina" had just called her and was coming to visit. Pnina was my mother's Jewish friend, about whom I had heard for years as I was growing up. They were high school friends in Jerusalem, had graduated together, married during the same year, and had their children in the same years. They lost touch, however, after the establishment of the State of Israel in 1948.

My mother loved Pnina but in my hot, angry, youthful days I had resented this woman, this Jew. She had stayed on in Palestine because she was Jewish, while my family and I had to be uprooted and exiled because we were not.

No, I did not really look forward to seeing Pnina, who had traced my mother through the grapevine, located her in London and called her from my Jerusalem to announce her impending visit. However, on the day of the visit, I went to meet her, having geared myself for a confrontation.

Pnina was wonderful. Sensitive, warm, teary-eyed as she embraced us all. We talked. We laughed. We ate. They reminisced. I loved her. I did not confront her, or my feelings. I could not deal with the fact that here I was, loving and admiring a Jewish woman! My enemy!

1982: The Israelis invaded Lebanon. Bombardment, siege, and evacuation of the PLO from West Beirut. The massacres. The fear. The whole insecurity of being a Palestinian once again. There is no backing out. One can uproot from a place but not from one's skin, one's history, one's people. The dilemmas. The sense that we had betrayed those we left behind, as we now safely dwelt in the West. Abhorrence of the West for being the cause and the prime financier of our exile and tragedy. The sense of helplessness and total incapacitation, of loss and that immense guilt.

1985: Sitting by my window in the safety of my suburban American home, missing my parents, friends and way of life, out of touch with my culture and my roots. I cried for having lived 40 years over which I had absolutely no control, a life constantly sub-jected to changing political circumstances, which dominated every level of my being.

I took up my pen and wrote, "Dear Leah," addressing an imaginary Jewish woman. I had pictured her to be of my age. I asked her when it would be over for both of us. That letter, written in utter despair, became the epilogue of a novel, my first, titled *A Woman of Nazareth*.

Writing was the best therapy for me, as I aired all of my anger, all of my emotions, over the Palestinian tragedy.

1987: I was asked to read the "Dear Leah" letter and share a stage with another Pales-tinian sister, Zeinab Sha'ath, and two Israelis, a traditionalist and a radical, at the Sister-fire Conference in Maryland. Having accepted, I could not then imagine going to the pre-conference dinner and sharing bread with my enemies. I tried to think up excuses for not going. However, I had been preaching tolerance and understanding. I had stated my views in non-erasable print. I dared myself to go, or be exposed to myself as a hypocrite.

I went and found commonalities which surprised me. The wall between me and any-thing Jewish or Israeli started to crumble. From then on it was easier to participate in di-aloguing with the enemy.

November 31, 1987: I flew to London. My father had passed away unexpectedly. Another Palestinian being buried, in exile, away from his Jerusalem. My hatred rose in oceanic waves. My anger and grief commingled into a crescendo that belied all my recent acceptance of peaceful coexistence. People would be coming to the small London flat, which did not have enough seating space. I went over to the neighbor, Theresa, and asked to borrow some of her chairs. We stood and cried together as she told me how she had been living with death all of her life. She had lost two brothers—17 and 18 years old—to the Nazi Holocaust.

December 9, 1987: The intifada. A resurgence of hope, pride and dignity. The Palestinians had taken their destiny into their own hands. Nothing more magnificent had occurred within our Palestinian national consciousness. As one, we all rose to support our intifada. Yes, we can talk now. Yes, we are paying the price of freedom with the blood of our children. Yes, we have earned our place at the negotiating table. It was a tremendous feeling.

February 1990: I participated in a dialogue conference with American-Palestinian women and American-Jewish women. It presented many dilemmas. Is it all worth it? What are the benefits of such an exercise? Will I have regrets next week, next month or next year?

Maybe. Maybe not. Maybe tomorrow, next month or next year what has been germinating within me for so many years will suddenly flower into peace.

When I saw one of the American-Jewish women fighting a battle within herself during the conference, feeling the push and pull of both sides of the coin, wanting to be objective yet afraid to betray her people by doing so, I was reminded of myself. I could see deep into her very heart, into recesses of her soul where she, herself, had not yet dared to look. I saw a Leah, responding to her Palestinian counterpart, as they both extended, though fearfully, their hands in peace. Perhaps this is seeing the light. ✦

Hala Deeb Jabbour is the author of A Woman of Nazareth.

Learning That I Didn't Know It All

By George R. Thompson

Newspaper editors think they know it all. At least I did—until I met my first Palestinian. I met him in 1954. His name was Farouk. I've forgotten his last name. That's really not as important as were his words and the tale he told: "You are an editor [I was at the time] of an historic [150-year-old] American daily newspaper. What do you know of the Palestinians? I mean, really know?"

That question was followed by a long pause. The answer, of course, was not one helluva lot.

Like many Americans in media, I thought I was reasonably well-educated, informed and aware—unlike many Americans who were inclined to ignore the fact that the U.S. was indeed surrounded by other countries. There was, also indeed, a whole world out there about which we (and, damn-it-all, I) knew nothing.

And he was asking about the Palestinians?

There I stood, bathed in abysmal ignorance, mind racing, searching for a suitable reply, until I took refuge behind the newsman's shield:

"Tell me more."

He did: "You wonder why Palestinians are concerned about the Israelis. You wonder why I and countless other Arabs are concerned that the Israelis have shed the cloak of captive for captor. Let me ask you some questions: Who flies over, drops bombs on, attacks, takes, and occupies whose land? Where are the refugees from? Who are among the largest groups of refugees in the world? Why isn't something being done to correct the situation?"

Another long pause, and he continued: "The answers are: Israel, Palestine, the Palestinians, and 'because some of my best friends are Jews.'"

The next day was spent in the library, where I learned a few things. He was right, and so many of us in the media—to say nothing of my compatriot Americans—were wrong, and continue to be so.

Since then, 43 years have passed. They have been years filled with "up-close-and-personal" experiences with Palestinians and Israelis in which I indeed have learned more.

Let me share but one of a kaleidoscope filled with memories of how much I finally did learn:

It took place on the roof of the venerable American Colony Hotel on a hilltop in East Jerusalem long before the 1967 war. A Palestinian waiter paused to look out over the no-man's-land cutting a swath of desolation between Jordan and Israel. The tears on his cheeks glistened in the moonlight.

"Is there anything wrong? Can I help you?"

"No thank you. I come up here every night at dusk when the lights go on over there. Do you see those lights there? There, on the side of the mountain? Count down three from the top. That's my house. I can see it. When the wind is right I imagine I can smell my mother's cooking from the kitchen.

"I can see it. I can smell it. But I can't touch it.

"The Israelis came one day with a note. 'Watch the mukhtar's (mayor's) house at six tonight,' it said. 'If you don't leave by six tomorrow night, your house is next.'

"At six that night, the mukhtar's house disappeared in a cloud of smoke and a big explosion. We left the next day."

I've been learning and "seeing the light" ever since. For most of us, it's been under a bushel for far too long. ✦

George R. Thompson, retired U.S. Information Agency foreign service officer, is a television talk-show host, author, and syndicated columnist for USA Today *and* Florida Today *now living in Melbourne Village, Florida.*

No Matter Where You Start, the Solution Is Equal Rights for All

By George V. Parmelee

Although Noah Kramer says "History Begins at Summer," it was five millennia later that my wife and I began to see the vexing Middle East situation in a clear-ish light, first through our personal experiences while living in the region for seven years, and then through diligent attention to what many different people and organizations said, wrote and did about the situation.

Our Middle East history began one spring day in 1953, when the director of the research laboratory where I worked in Cleveland received a request from the United Nations Technical Assistance Administration. The new state of Israel wanted someone to advise it in matters of indoor climate. Because I had been researching problems of solar radiation and building cooling, my director suggested that I accept the assignment.

I jumped at the chance to visit the country whose struggles to achieve nationhood had received so much publicity in our media. My two months in Israel that summer were preceded by seeing a bit of Europe with my wife, Freddie, and our two daughters, 10 and 12. It was our first foreign experience.

The Epitome of Naiveté

In regard to the Middle East I was the epitome of political naiveté. I had never heard of the Balfour Declaration and the negative impact upon the Palestinians of the developments which came from it. I had only a dim idea of the political maneuvers that preceded the U.N. plan to partition Palestine.

Most of the Israelis I worked with that summer had left Germany in the early 1930s, when the Nazi persecution of Jews was just beginning. I expressed a sympathetic understanding to one of the men, a French Jew, telling him that my maternal and paternal ancestors had fled France during the Huguenot persecutions and had come to America via Holland and England. Moreover, Freddie's ancestors had fled Germany because of the endless religious wars in Europe, at the same time and by the same route.

That was the extent of political discussion that I remember. The Arab presence in

Israel did not come to my attention except in a trip to survey the thermal environment in Eilat. Our group was armed and alert to possible trouble in the desolate Wadi Al Arabah bordering Jordan. I still recall, however, a meeting on my last evening in Israel at the home of the director of the weather division. There I sensed a tension that I later identified as arrogance.

Some months later, in 1954, one of the Israeli weathermen was our house guest during a study trip to the U.S. and Canada. He was surprised by the large amount of publicity and news coverage given Israel in the Cleveland papers. That has not changed much in the intervening years.

Our summer's experience gave Freddie and me a strong taste for travel, out of which was to come an intense concern over our country's role in the Middle East. Neither taste for travel nor concern about deteriorating American relationships with the Middle East were to be quenched in Freddie's lifetime, and they have continued in mine since her death a few years ago.

In September, 1955, as an air conditioning specialist, I became a staff engineer at the Arabian American Petroleum Company, Aramco. Freddie and the girls flew to Beirut, where she set up housekeeping and put the girls in the American Community School. I followed two months later, going on to Dhahran, Saudi Arabia, after a two-week briefing in Lebanon. The family followed to Dhahran a year later.

The world opened wide its doors to our inquiring minds and eyes. What were Palestinians doing in refugee camps in Beirut? How did Lebanon and Syria relate? How did our Western Christian enterprises fit into the sectarian millet system which characterized the political and social life of Lebanon?

In Arabia we met Palestinians, Jordanians, Lebanese and the other nationalities who were sprinkled among the large Saudi and American work forces. We began to acquire a much broader view of the Israelis and the Arab Palestinians as we worked, listened, read and traveled about the region.

Perhaps our first shock came during our first years, when we recommended to friends at home objective books about American relationships with the Middle East and Israel. Our friends wrote back to say that the books we named were not to be found in Cleveland bookstores. The light was pretty dim in the States then. Only recently has this subtle censorship been changing.

A small foretaste of the turmoil that has gripped Lebanon through much of two decades came in October, 1956, when Freddie, Suzanne and I landed in Beirut on a flight from Tehran after visiting Iran on our first short leave. Sally was then in the ACS boarding department. Americans were pouring in from Syria and Jordan seeking a haven in Ras Beirut (now referred to as Muslim West Beirut). They feared the spread of the fighting in Sinai, where Israel, Britain and France had teamed up to bring down Nasser because of his nationalization of the Suez Canal. How attitudes have changed! Would Americans venture into West Beirut for refuge today? What has gone wrong?

In May, 1958, Freddie, Suzanne and I spent a long weekend in Iraq visiting the Muslim Shi'i centers in Najaf and Kerbala, and Babylon and other ancient sites accessible from Baghdad. Bookstores have always been a magnet, and next door to our hotel we found Rabbi Elmer Berger's little book, *Who Knows Better Should Say So*. It shed much light on how Zionism works!

Living in Two Worlds

When we returned to Cleveland in December, 1962, so that I could accept a professorship in mechanical engineering at Cleveland State University, we began living in two worlds: America and, vicariously, the Middle East. We visited Dr. Berger in New York in 1969. Later that summer we gathered interested people at our home in Cleveland to meet with him. Such activities accelerated thanks to the Rev. Donald Powers of nearby Cuyahoga Falls, who launched the Northeast Ohio Committee for Middle East Understanding that fall.

Our involvement in spreading understanding of the Middle East became continuous. It was sparked by Freddie's well-organized enthusiasm and propelled by our continued contact with Elmer Berger and the many friends we found who shared our desire for justice and peace in the Middle East. There will be neither, I am convinced, until our country acts decisively to support for all peoples abroad, including the Palestinians, the same self-determination, human rights and fair play that we insist upon for all Americans at home. ✦

George V. Parmelee of East Cleveland, emeritus professor of mechanical engineering at Cleveland State University, is active in the Northeast Ohio Committee for Middle East Understanding, Ohioans for Middle East Peace and other groups working for peace and justice in the world.

For His Students, The Middle East Began With Edwin Wright

By Richard H. Curtiss

The year was 1956, I was 29, and it was hard to be humble. As a teenage soldier and then student, journalist, and foreign service officer, I'd seen a lot of the United States and Western Europe, and significant bits and pieces of Eastern Europe, Latin America, South Asia and the Far East. I had smatterings of two Asian and three European languages and, I thought, a pretty good grasp of the emerging outlines of what would, much later, be called "the new world order." Now, as I sat in my first Middle East orientation lecture at the Foreign Service Institute in Washington, DC, everything was working out just as I'd hoped. It was not, to my shame, America's growing political estrangement from old Middle Eastern friends that had induced me to request an assignment there. It was the archaeology and history of the area, half of whose civilizations had already vanished before the Bible, as we know it, had even been written.

Dr. Edwin M. Wright was in charge of a State Department program which included lectures by country specialists and by experts in such subjects as the millet or mosaic system of the Ottoman Empire, the World War I Sykes-Picot agreement to divide the Middle East between Britain and France, and France's continuing, ruthless, last-ditch military efforts to retain its North African colonies. Ed Wright's own historical lectures were delivered in a rapid, polished, outspoken, and highly personalized style that soon revealed him to be the very personification of an "old Middle East hand."

"It All Began At Eridu"

Born in Tabriz, Iran, in 1897 of American missionary parents, he was an ordained Presbyterian minister who, after World War I, had worked in Iraq among the Armenian, Assyrian and Chaldean refugees of that conflict, and then settled in for 13 years of teaching in American missionary schools in Iran. In 1938 he returned to the U.S. for graduate studies in Middle Eastern history and languages, and emerged speaking and reading Farsi, Turkish, Armenian, some Kurdish, and Arabic.

That was just in time for World War II, when he took his first-hand familiarity with the languages, peoples and terrain of Iran to the Pentagon. There, and back in Iran, he helped plan, negotiate and implement the incredible sea and land supply line that poured American arms, munitions, and food into the Soviet Union in time to keep the vital southern front from collapsing in the face of Hitler's all-out onslaught on Stalingrad. At the end of the war he was Lieutenant Colonel Edwin Wright of the OSS. He moved to the State Department in 1946 and helped set up the Voice of America's Persian, Turkish and Arabic broadcasts. Further desk officer work in State led to increasingly frequent lectures at the Foreign Service Institute, where he eventually assumed full-time duties, preparing literally thousands of State Department, USIA, AID and military personnel for service in the Middle East.

I vividly remember the first sentence in his first overview lecture on Middle East history. "It all began at Eridu," he intoned solemnly, and went on to describe the earliest known town in the part of southern Iraq occupied by the Sumerians, who built the world's first cities, invented the world's first writing system, recorded for the first time humankind's myths and legends, and in doing so left us the first known description of the Garden of Eden, the first recounting of the story of Noah and his ark, and the first telling of the Gilgamesh epic, describing humanity's eternal search for immortality.

It was a good 1,500 years after Eridu was founded that Abraham set out from Ur, another great Sumerian city some 20 miles away, for his journeys along the curve of the Fertile Crescent to become the patriarch figure for both Jews and Arabs throughout the Middle East today. So, as Dr. Wright emphasized day after day, civilization, writing, literature, Judaism, Christianity, Islam, and everything in modern world cultures derived from them all did, in one way or another, begin at Eridu.

I realized as these wonders were revealed in fascinating lectures by this colorful, warm and marvelously learned man that my upcoming tour of duty in Syria was going to be at least as fulfilling as anything that had preceded it. Even as we ranged from Eridu forward to Israel and from Palestine back to Abraham, however, the prospects for my tour began to fade. Israel, Britain and France launched a surprise attack on Egypt. President Eisenhower quickly broke up the invasion, and, by threatening to withdraw the tax-deductibility of contributions by Americans to Israel, eventually forced the Israelis to vacate Sinai and return to the borders over which they had suddenly lunged three months earlier. The Syrians, however, expelled most of the American Embassy staff in Damascus, and postponed the opening of the American Consulate in Aleppo, where I was to be public affairs officer.

Wright Had Both Questions and Answers

I'd been absorbing every word in the lectures about ancient and medieval Middle Eastern history. Now that current events threatened my personal plans, I found myself listening with equally rapt attention to whatever Edwin Wright, and his guest lecturers, had to say about what was happening in the Middle East that turbulent fall of 1956. Why were the *Syrians* so upset about the Israeli attack on *Egypt,* and why were they taking it out on the United States in general, and me in particular? Dr. Wright, it turned out, had some answers to these questions and I didn't like them. He seemed to be saying there were clear cause-and-effect *reasons* for what I took to be irrational, destructive, and vindictive acts by Arab states against the United States and its Israeli protégé. Afternoons I was spending among officers of my own U.S. Information Agency, many of them former war correspondents or veterans of America's World War II psychological warfare against the Germans.

"A lecturer at FSI told us today that it was only arm-twisting by the U.S. of countries that needed our foreign aid that caused the United Nations to partition Palestine, and it was that that set off the fighting there," I complained to one of them. He looked around carefully before he ventured his own strong opinion that the fellow at FSI was right. I was even more horrified to hear that President Truman's sympathy for European-Jewish refugees demanding to settle in Palestine had manifested itself clearly only after domestic political advisers told him the Democrats might lose the 1948 presidential election if he didn't push for creation of a Jewish state. Again, colleagues I respected confirmed, almost furtively, that we were backing very unwise foreign policy moves in the Middle East for very ignoble domestic political purposes.

I loved learning about the ancient Middle East, but, increasingly, whenever we came back to the 20th century there, I seethed with indignation. I was angry with Dr. Wright because he seemed to be questioning the soundness, perhaps even the morality, of our Middle East policies, which he felt were leading to a bloodbath. I was also angry with President Truman. Everyone familiar with the story seemed to be confirming what Edwin Wright was saying—that the president in whose "campaign of truth" I had eagerly enlisted had, in the Middle East, done the wrong thing in 1947 and 1948.

And now, in 1956, an even stranger thing was happening. President Eisenhower clearly was doing the *right* thing in the Middle East. His bold and decisive action to abort the Suez attack had sent a message to the French and British that the days of gunboat diplomacy were over, and to the Israelis that regardless of what we had let them do in the 1940s, they couldn't just take over a large part of Egypt on a whim in the 1950s. My old Middle East-hand colleagues were applauding Ike, but virtually all of America's media, Republican or Democratic, were attacking him. It was first the *French* and then the *British* who had plotted with Israel to attack Egypt, without a word to the United States. But the U.S. press was bewailing *America's* betrayal of its wartime allies and the breakup of the alliance that had won World War II. The media seemed to have forgotten that we'd fought World War II to support the basic premise of international law that bars the acquisition of territory by force.

I mentioned just that at lunch with a Jewish fellow foreign service officer one day that fall. We'd shared the European World War II experience separately and our first foreign service post in Indonesia together. Suddenly, to our mutual astonishment, we were shouting angrily at each other across the table. When next we met for lunch we eyed each other warily until each was sure that the other was not about to bring up the Middle East again. On those unspoken terms our friendship survived, and we've had a hundred lunches together over the 30 intervening years, but only because we've never, never seriously discussed Middle Eastern political affairs again. It's a pity that a subject so fascinating that each of us, now in retirement, lectures regularly about it to strangers is so divisive that it still cannot be discussed amicably between close friends.

In the wake of the attack on Suez, my Middle Eastern assignment was changed from Syria to Turkey. Two years there were followed by two more in Lebanon and then came Iraq, Syria, Greece, Lebanon a third time and suddenly it was 25 years later and *I* was an old Middle East hand retiring from the foreign service.

In a lifetime of Middle East highlights, however, one that stood out came at the end of a tense trip in a four-wheel drive vehicle across a stretch of treacherous desert sand separating the towering, awesome mound that once was Ur from the site of Eridu. A rifle-toting Iraqi antiquities guard accompanied me on the off chance that my arrival at the isolated site would surprise illicit diggers for gold or cylinder seals who could be dangerous if discovered. The guard was worried that the black clouds racing ahead of a rising wind might presage a dust storm that would obscure our route back through what can only be described as an empty, howling wilderness. Suddenly the dark, brooding mound we were seeking appeared on the flat horizon. Then a brilliant shaft of sunlight pierced the clouds and illuminated the utterly deserted ruins. As plainly as if he were sitting in the car beside me, I could hear Ed Wright's words: "It all began at Eridu."

Wright Touched Many Lives

It all ended for Edwin Wright October 28, 1987, when he died of cardiac arrest in the family home in Wooster, Ohio, to which he had returned when he retired from the Department of State in 1966. He had remained active, lecturing at Wooster College where he had taken his BA during World War I, and at nearby colleges and military bases. He did not shrink from controversies and, just as there had been some in Washington, several were fought out in the pages of Ohio newspapers with people who, like me all those years ago, didn't want to hear unpleasant, but indisputable, truths. The battles were lonelier after his wife, Marjorie Wilson Wright, died in the early 1970s. His son, Wilson P. Wright, and daughter-in-law, Christine, lived far away, near Chicago.

They and his two granddaughters were on hand in January, 1986, however, when Edwin Wright's friends in the Northeast Ohio Committee on Middle East Understanding held a surprise 90th birthday dinner for him in Cleveland. Friends came from all over the United States to step up to the platform and say a few words about what Ed Wright had meant to them. It was typical that his response, at the end of the evening, was the liveliest and wittiest talk of all.

My colleague, retired Ambassador Andrew Killgore, and I were among those friends and we are grateful that we were able to say what was in our hearts then, *to* Ed, instead of only now, about Ed. It meant much to us, too, to learn that at Edwin Wright's wish the considerable proceeds from the fundraising birthday party were donated to our American Educational Trust, which publishes the *Washington Report on Middle East Affairs.* It means a great deal to us now to know that it was his request that anyone wishing to honor his memory make a contribution in his name to the AET Library Endowment.

We were *his* students and he chose *us* to carry on his work of introducing Americans to the Middle East, its history, its religions, the richness of its culture, the warmth of its people, and its catalytic role at various times in our still-incomplete human transition from hunter-gatherer to civilized human being.

Edwin Wright knew that what began at Eridu will not be complete until civilized men and women everywhere work to end barbarity anywhere. He was acutely aware of the problems in the Middle East that Americans have helped create, and that will only end when Americans understand them well enough to help solve them. He defined them clearly for his students, and in doing so afflicted us with the burden he carried. But, as his final wish shows, he wanted to share that burden to the end.

For Edwin Wright, civilization began with Eridu. For his students, the Middle East began with Edwin Wright. ✦

Richard Curtiss, former chief inspector of the U.S. Information Agency, is the executive editor of the Washington Report on Middle East Affairs *and the author of* A Changing Image: American Perceptions of the Arab-Israeli Dispute *and* Stealth PACs: Lobbying Congress for Control of U.S. Middle East Policy.

POSTSCRIPT: *This article was written upon the death of Dr. Edwin Wright in 1987. Since then, with the help of many more of his "students" and of his successors at the Foreign Service Institute, the American Educational Trust, publisher of this book, has considerably expanded its activities and, its directors hope, justified his faith. Its purpose, then and now, is to enable both North Americans and Middle Easterners to "see the light" about the value to both of resuming relationships based upon the mutual respect and cooperation that once characterized their interactions.*

Unwilling to Tell It Like It Isn't

By Andrew I. Killgore

We felt a sense of satisfaction over helping to defeat the evil represented by the Axis Powers in World War II. As tough idealists we emerged from the war convinced that colonialism had run its course.

As foreign service officers we had, by preference, gravitated toward the Near East and South Asia bureau of the State Department. The Arab world, getting its independence after centuries of Turkish and European domination, offered career opportunities in an area of great economic, historical and religious significance to the U.S.

So now we were Arabists, after two years of grinding hard work learning one of the world's most difficult languages. Then members of my class were off in March, 1957, from the language school in the American Embassy in Beirut to Khartoum, Jeddah, Kuwait, Tripoli, Cairo and, for me, Jerusalem, as U.S. consul.

My Arabic was good, and I looked forward to paying back Uncle Sam's big investment in my language training by providing Washington with a true picture of the West Bank since the end of the 1947-to-1949 fighting, during which Israel was created, but the West Bank was occupied by Jordan.

I was soon to learn, however, that my natural pride in mastering a really hard language made me an object of deep suspicion among Israelis and their more fervent American supporters. The sole reason for that suspicion was that the hard language I had mastered was Arabic.

Tell It Like It Isn't—I

Probably it was the controversy over the two cemeteries that first convinced me of deliberate Israeli pressure to influence my official reporting. The Jordanians had removed a traffic bottleneck by cutting away one meter from the old Hebrew cemetery on the Mount of Olives, and three meters from Muslim and Christian cemeteries on the other side of the road. This was depicted in the Israeli and American press as desecration of Jewish graves.

We reported, factually, that old cemeteries of several religions, including the Hebrew Cemetery, had been disturbed to allow sufficient room for two tourist buses to pass each other in the street in front of the Church of All Nations without either having to stop and tie up traffic. We also reported that the largest Muslim cemetery in the entire area of the old Palestine mandate was slowly being destroyed by Israel.

This we had reason to know because on two occasions the consul general's French poodle brought into the garden old human thigh bones from the (Muslim) Mamillah Road Cemetery across the road, where Israeli bulldozers and ditchdiggers worked on most days. These embarrassing bones we tossed back over the cemetery wall by night.

With our office on both sides of divided Jerusalem, American consuls mixed daily with Jews on one side and Palestinians on the other. Sensitivity and care not to offend were essential. My relations on both sides were satisfactory before the cemeteries controversy erupted in 1957. They deteriorated in Israeli Jerusalem, however, coincident with our reporting on the subject.

Barely veiled hostile comments from Israelis about biased Arabists began to be heard at diplomatic receptions, encouraged, we were convinced, by the Israeli government. We suspected that our cabled reports to Washington were finding their way back to the Israeli government in Jerusalem, courtesy of Israeli sympathizers in the Washington bureaucracy. I interpreted what was happening to me as intimidation to halt reporting that was critical of Israel.

Tell It Like It Isn't—II

Perhaps my most painful personal experience began with a two-minute conversation in Jerusalem in the late spring of 1958 with the visiting head of Hadassah, the American Women's Zionist organization. This intense and beautiful woman, a Ph.D. from Columbia University, vehemently denounced then-Secretary of State John Foster Dulles, whom she blamed for forcing Israel in 1957 to withdraw its forces from Sinai and Gaza, which they had seized from Egypt in 1956, during the tripartite attack in which French and British troops seized the Suez Canal. I said mildly that I agreed with U.S. policy, which also had resulted in French and British withdrawals, long before Israel reluctantly withdrew. With a furious glare the Hadassah president turned and walked off.

When I returned to Jerusalem from home leave in the late summer of 1958, the consul general told me that the same Hadassah president had visited Jerusalem again during my absence. She had asked about "that tall Southerner with gray hair." When told I was in the United States, she had said, "Now there's a real anti-Semite."

Within the consulate, concern for our personal safety, inspired by this level of open hostility, was heightened when Dr. Alva Miller, the American former director of the YMCA in Jerusalem, revisited the city in 1958. He told us that, in his opinion, the American consul general in Jerusalem during the fighting that followed the U.N. decision to partition Palestine, Thomas Wasson, had been deliberately assassinated by a Jewish terrorist gunman in 1948, the same year that Jewish terrorists of Lehi, the Stern Gang, assassinated U.N. mediator Count Folke Bernadotte in the Jewish-held portion of the city. According to Miller, Wasson, whose name is carved in stone at the State Department in Washington, where he is listed as "killed by sniper—Jerusalem 1948," was shot at close range by a gunman concealed atop a small building in the consulate general compound. The killing occurred as Wasson was returning from one of his regular meetings with the British and French consuls general in the nearby YMCA building.

Wasson's death was ordered, Miller believed, because the three Western consuls general were insisting that the fighting between Jews and Arabs be halted immediately. Jewish forces, however, had the military advantage at the time, and they were using it to gain more ground in areas which the U.N. partition plan had not assigned to the future Jewish state.

With Wasson out of the way, and the consular corps in confusion, the Jewish advantage could be pursued. Not long after Miller's visit, his allegation was chillingly supported when I chanced upon Wasson's bullet-proof vest and other detritus from earlier years in the consulate general basement. Although there was no external bullet hole, the vest was completely blood-stained on the inside. Wasson had been mortally wounded through the jacket's armhole by a crack shot at short range.

Tell It Like It Isn't—III

Tensions crackled and often exploded into violence along Israel's frontiers with its Arab neighbors during my entire assignment in Jerusalem, from March, 1957, to August, 1959. The front with Syria was particularly active.

Our reports about each incident, based on first-hand investigations by United Nations military observers, including many Americans, had a perhaps unique distinction. They never agreed, not even once, with the fabricated Israeli versions of incidents reaching the American and Israeli media. These, invariably and falsely, showed Israel as the aggrieved party.

By whatever means, Israel's government officials knew that our reports to Washington always challenged their versions. U.N. observers, who had no reason not to tell the truth, were regarded by Israel with open hostility, and were sometimes threatened with violence. Open threats to our consulate general were apparently considered impolitic, but we were acutely aware of the hostility just beneath the surface.

We quietly discussed among ourselves whether at any time in history diplomats had felt so intimidated for reporting the simple truth. We were resolved, however, that basic honesty and duty decreed that we wouldn't change what we were doing.

I welcomed my August, 1959, assignment to the U.S. Embassy in Amman. Jerusalem had been challenging, richly satisfying, but also trying. The side Israel had shown us face-to-face was not the friendly visage seen from America, but one seriously disturbing, even frightening. Getting away was only an illusion, however, because Jerusalem, only 50 miles away, intruded itself twice within a few months.

First was the old cemeteries controversy. From the front page of the *Jerusalem Post* sprang the headline: "Neglected Wasteland Turned Into Public Park." Projected as a progressive municipal improvement, the ceremony dedicating the new park had been delayed to allow a visiting Zionist delegation from South Africa to be present.

The *Post* story provided only one clue by which the reader could determine what really was going on. The story said the name of the street bordering the new park had been changed from Mamillah Road to Gershon Agron Road (after a former Jewish mayor of Jerusalem).

I broke an unwritten law in the foreign service against poaching on another diplomatic mission's reporting territory by cabling Washington (and Jerusalem) that the "neglected wasteland" was in fact the Mamillah Road Cemetery, the largest Muslim cemetery in the entire mandate of Palestine, at which Israeli bulldozers had been nibbling for so long.

A friend at the State Department sent me a private note saying "bravo." He cautioned, however, that such messages were not the recommended way to get ahead.

Intrusion number two from Jerusalem came in an astonishing letter in the diplomatic pouch from our embassy in Tel Aviv. Our deputy ambassador there, a good friend of mine, apologetically explained that he was acting at the request of the Israeli Ministry of Foreign Affairs. The ministry had not liked some of my purported views, and wanted an explanation.

Supposedly, according to the letter, I had said to a visiting American journalist, who then told the Foreign Ministry, that, looking back through history, no country based solely in the sparsely populated areas between the Nile and Tigris/Euphrates valleys had lasted a hundred years, except in alliance with one or the other of those population centers.

The journalist, whom I did not specifically remember, for I spoke to perhaps a dozen visitors a day, had said I spoke dispassionately. Still, he "sensed" (the exact word employed) that I had Israel in mind, and that Israel's eventual disappearance would not disturb me.

This was my opportunity to declare myself foursquare for Israel. But instead I decided that, since I had not permitted myself to be intimidated in Jerusalem, I would not be intimidated when the same problems followed me to Amman.

So back through the diplomatic pouch to my friend in Tel Aviv went the following message: "Tell the Israeli Ministry of Foreign Affairs that I said, 'Go to hell.'" ❖

Ambassador Andrew I. Killgore, a retired career foreign service officer, is publisher of the Washington Report on Middle East Affairs.

Fighting the "Soldiers of Occupation" From WWII to the Intifada

By Russell Warren Howe

"THERE IS A GREEN HILL FAR AWAY WITHOUT A CITY WALL"

So we sang, in childhood. I never knew then that Muslims and Jews also revered Jerusalem. Did not William Blake, he of the chariot of fire, call for Jerusalem to be rebuilt "in England's green and pleasant land"? Would that the Zionists had rebuilt it at home, in Sebastopol or Kiev.

When the British press was filled, in the months before and after Hitler's defeat, with news of Zionist atrocities against Britons, both in Palestine and elsewhere in the Middle East—the murder of Lord Moyne, the lynchings of British soldiers, the IRA-style caper at the King David Hotel—Jewish friends told me that this was the work of extremists.

They were correct, of course. They could not know that some day the extremists would hold power, not without but within the city wall. I—and perhaps they—did not know that Menachem Begin and Yitzhak Shamir had trafficked in arms with the Nazis, and exploited German mistreatment of Jews to exacerbate the problem caused by European settlers in Palestine.

I think I personally was more incensed by the assassination of the Swedish United Nations mediator, Count Bernadotte, than by that of my own countryman, Lord Moyne, who was, after all, only a British politician. I knew nothing of Deir Yassin and similar holocausts.

The London writer Louis Golding and a Jewish comrade who had done RAF pilot training with me had explained about the Khazarian conversion, so that I knew that only Sephardim, "Oriental Jews," not Ashkenazim, "European Jews," had roots in the Holy Land. But this did not in itself, to me, betoken a spurious quality in the notion of a Palestinian homeland shared by Muslims and Christians on the one side and Jews on the other—although I was bothered by the separation.

When a close friend of my father's, a Russian from Nichni-Novgorod who had fled to London after the revolution, learned that his two sons had gone to Palestine and joined the Haganah, where they were fighting their fellow Britons, he hanged himself in shame. This only confirmed for me the difference between extremist Jews and decent Jews. In 1948, freshly graduated from the Sorbonne, and covering the Security Council in Paris for Reuter, I was commanded by my profession to be neutral; but my sympathy was with the apparently outnumbered proto-Israelis.

As a correspondent in Africa a decade later, I enjoyed the company of Ehud Avriel, the Austrian who had organized, in Istanbul, the underground route to Palestine of Jewish Bulgars and others. He was by then Israel's resourceful ambassador in Ghana, where I lived from 1957 to 1959. This was the Israeli age of communes and of "making the desert bloom" (also, of course, of paving over Palestinian villages and groves, Nazi-style; but this attracted little attention in the West).

So, in 1961, after a year of living dangerously in the newly independent Congo (now Zaire), I decided to take off with my girlfriend of the moment, a Jewish American working for the United Nations, and visit Tunisia and then Israel, where Avriel met us at the airport. He took us to the kibbutz to which he had retired. There was a pleasant air of the Pilgrim Fathers about the place. (Later, Uri Davis, an Israeli professor at Birmingham University in England, was to express it perfectly: "A Jewish Disneyland," he said.)

Having by then reported on South Africa, however, I was conditioned to sense, behind the facade, the extraordinary gloom and foreboding that reigns in a segregated society, and that one feels everywhere on the streets of Israel. Avriel, an intelligent man and a bosom friend of David Ben-Gurion's, assured me that yes, there was tension, but only because of the "necessary" precautions. His people, he said, wanted only to be one with the Arabs, whom they respected.

I asked why he had said "Arabs" instead of "Muslims and Christians" and he looked surprised.

"They speak Arabic."

"So do half the Jews in this country. Do you speak Jewish?"

Ehud, too honest a fellow to invent a spurious counter-argument, simply looked startled. To this day I get similar looks of amazement from American editors when I complain that one headline says "Two Jews Attacked," while another proclaims "Five Arabs Killed in West Bank." Are our press authorities afraid that "Christian Family Slain" would lift scales from American eyes?

It was after we had left the warm embrace of the kibbutz for the rest of the country that I really began to feel that I had been duped. My companion sensed my discomfort.

"Why do you want to go to Nazareth?" she asked. "There's a wonderful artists' colony at Carmel."

"Why Nazareth? Are you serious? My entire family is Christian."

"But you're a Buddhist."

"Well, that doesn't rule out exploring Jesus of Nazareth's home town, does it?"

Matters came to a head in a nightclub in Tel Aviv.

Two Jewish comics came onstage dressed as half the city's population dressed in those days—as Palestinians. And they began an Amos 'n Andy act which produced shrieks of laughter.

It wasn't just too close for comfort to Birmingham, Alabama, during the Autherine Lucy episode, or Hillcrest, Johannesburg. It *was* Birmingham and Hillcrest.

I threw some money on the table to cover the cost of our drinks and explained to my companion that we were leaving. When she protested, I asked if she, a liberal New Yorker, didn't know raw racism when she saw it.

"It's not racism, it's just fun."

I promised that when we got back to New York, I would do an act in the Village with her. I would wear a big nose and speak with a Yiddish accent, and she would be my wife Rachel, or Sadie, wearing a dress patterned with pawnbroker balls.

"It'll all be just fun," I said.

I suppose that if my companion had said: "You're absolutely right. Don't even pay the bill," I might have stayed a few more days in Israel.

In Rome on the morrow, I learned that someone (a Belgian, this time) had shot down the plane of another U.N. peacemaker, Dag Hammarskjöld, in the Congo. I called Alfred Friendly, my managing editor at *The Washington Post*, and offered to cut short my vacation and return.

However, everything in my Reuter training and Buddhist conscience told me that I should not take sides, for or against. I could disapprove of murderers like Shamir or Vorster, and bigotry like the Amos 'n Andy act, but I shouldn't condemn Israelis or white South Africans per se. I admired the kibbutzim as much as I admired the Muslim influence in West Africa, where I had lived in the '50s, and again after the Congo, for the rest of the '60s. There must, I believed, be a common ground.

In Senegal, where I was based from 1962 to 1965, as the *Post*'s Africa bureau chief, then from 1967 to 1971 as a visiting professor at the university, the Catholic president of that Muslim country, Léopold-Sédar Senghor, had his own theory. I had known him in Paris, where he had written the preface to the French translation of one of my books. He expatiated on the notion that there were three Great Victims: the Negroid peoples, the Jews and the Palestinians. They should help each other. I debated whether to ask him to include the Tibetans, then decided against it on the grounds of practicality. There were probably a score or more of Great Victims; but I could see that Senghor's Catholic soul was comfortable with a trinity. Moreover, I had no license to speak for the Dalai Lama.

To be fair, I decided, I should go back to Israel and review the case. In 1965, when Israel Finkelstein, the editor of *Ha'aretz* (The Land), whom I met at the International Press Institute conference in London, asked me to be his Africa correspondent, I got permission from Al Friendly and accepted.

In 1968, Israel's ambassador in Dakar, whose shy English wife had become a close friend of my Zimbabwean bride, finally made me an offer I found hard to refuse: I would be invited to give a couple of lectures, in either English or French, on Islam in Black Africa at Hebrew University in Jerusalem.

CHAPTER SEVEN

I was disappointed in the student audience at Hebrew University. Most of the questions were naive, the bigotry manifest. But it was 1968, the State of Israel's 20th anniversary, and Avriel had set up interviews which I wanted: David Ben-Gurion and the new "temporary" prime minister from Milwaukee, Golda Meir.

On the eve of the independence festivities, I had three hours alone with Ben-Gurion, in the flat in Tel Aviv which he used when he came in from his exile in Beersheba. The legendary figure had become David Who? in the Palestine he had turned into Israel. Nobody competed with me for his time. He talked mostly of his own country, Russia, and of his homesickness. But he was also proud of the Israel which had relegated him to oblivion. He claimed that he had asked Nikita Khrushchev: "Have you any communism as pure as our communes?" and that Khrushchev had conceded that nothing like kibbutzim existed in the Soviet Union.

"The only achievements of my country," he said, referring to Russia after the revolution, "have been military ones. One day, there will be a coup d'état."

Could there be a coup in Israel? From Russians like himself, perhaps yes, he thought, but it was not likely. He trusted his fellow Russian, Israeli top soldier Moshe Dayan. Would he have trusted fellow Russian soldiers Yitzhak Rabin and Ariel Sharon? I had never heard of Sharon in 1968, so I didn't ask.

I said I was living in Senegal, and asked why Israel didn't name Muslim Israelis as ambassadors to Muslim countries like that. They could go to the mosque on Fridays like most of the diplomatic corps in Dakar or Niamey. It would be one-upmanship on the Europeans and Americans.

"We would never trust them, the Arabs," he said.

"Why not?"

"Because they know they can never trust us."

With Golda Meir, two days later, I asked why Israel didn't do more to make itself accepted as a Middle Eastern nation.

"That's the last thing we want to be!" she thundered. "We are and must remain a European nation."

This seemed in contradiction to fleeing Europe to be Hebrews in the land of the prophets. I tried to draw her out on this.

"But I am an atheist!" the old Russian-American schoolteacher explained. Because I looked surprised—more at the admission than at the fact—she said: "Half—no, 60 percent—of my ministers are atheists, I think."

"Then what God promised you this land?"

It was her turn to look surprised, then to smile.

"You understand nothing." She went on to explain to me, patiently, that Zionism was not a religious movement, despite its name, and that Jewry was not an association based on faith, but on a common experience.

"Like freemasonry?"

"Not exactly, but yes, a bit. That's closer."

By then, I had become convinced—by events, by Ben-Gurion, by Mrs. Meir—that Israel was not a positive factor in the area: it was the problem itself. I was sure that Christians like Mayor Elias Freij and his fellow Bethlehemite, Jesus, would never be treated as equals in their country. People with Muslim names like Mahmoud or Bashir had no more chance of equal treatment than did Nelson Mandela, who was arrested in South Africa in 1962 on the day I had an appointment for an interview with him. South Africa, of course, has since made strides toward an acceptance of reality. I confess I would never have guessed, at the time, that European South Africa would prove more sophisticated than European Israel.

In January, 1974, I followed part of what the history books call "Kissinger's first Sinai Disengagement Shuttle." In Jerusalem, I dined with my old friend who had been the Israeli ambassador in Dakar and his English-Israeli wife.

We correspondents were all due to leave in the morning for Aqaba, where Kissinger would have an audience with the Jordanian king.

"You'll get some better food in your hotel tomorrow than at the King David," the ambassador, now the equivalent of an assistant secretary of state, said.

I shook my head. I was, I explained, going to "drop off the bus" and drive to Tel Aviv instead, to interview the leader of the Knesset opposition.

My hosts were shocked. Menachem Begin was a mischievous little man, they explained. If I wanted an outside view, why didn't I talk "to Ambrose" (former foreign minister Abba Eban, who came to Israel from South Africa via Oxford). I could be interviewing Begin only because I mischievously hoped he would say something outrageous, they said.

"With what other hope in mind does one interview politicians?"

"You will find him a typical hand-kissing Polish creep," said the Israeli assistant secretary of foreign affairs.

In the event, Begin, whom I was interviewing for UPITN and Channel 5, was tiresomely virtuous in his responses. He had never before had a one-on-one for American television, and was determined to sound respectable. I knew that what I was getting was so pablumesque that it would never compete with what my colleagues were getting from King Hussein and Nixon's Metternich.

My Israeli crew could see that my hook was catching no "mischief" at all. I told the field producer I wanted another can. While the cameraman loaded, I "chatted up" Begin, of whom my hostess had said the night before that "his sense of humor would disappear into the navel of a flea, and still leave room for his objectivity." Taut and nervous, he too seemed anxious to unwind.

The Father of Terrorism

The red light had come on, under the lens. Without preamble, I turned my shoulder to the camera, stared straight into Begin's eyes, and asked: "How does it feel, in the light of all that's going on, to be the father of terrorism in the Middle East?"

"In the Middle East?" he bellowed, in his thick, cartoon accent. "In all the world!" I had finally broken the ice.

Back in Jerusalem that night, I called my ambassador friend to tell him of Begin's remark.

"You see, he does have a sense of humor!"

"Russell, you have understood nothing," said the diplomat, unintentionally reminding me of being put in my place by schoolteacher Meir six years before. "He was absolutely serious when he said that."

In later years, and notably at Camp David in 1978, I was forced to acknowledge that the assistant secretary knew Begin much better than I ever would.

My late friend Narinjan Majumder, deputy editor of *The Statesman* in India, went to Israel as a government guest in the mid-'60s and was asked by his publisher to write an editorial on Indian-Israeli relations. He was authorized, if he wished to do so, to recommend that India recognize Israel.

"I thought long and hard about it," he told me. "I liked the Israelis as a people. They were kind to me. But, in the final analysis, I decided that it would be patronizing and offensive, after we had fought so long and so bitterly to get Europe out of India, if I said that it was all right for those Russians and Poles to colonize the western tip of Asia. Israel will never be anything but a European colony in Asia."

"But you recognize South Africa."

"Well, we have a consul-general there because there are seven or eight hundred thousand Indians in that country. Anyway, those European settlers have the sanctity of a few centuries behind them."

The discomfort about Israel which I felt when I saw Shlomo Amos and Yitzhak Andy in 1961 had become more severe in the aftermath of the 1967 war. From then on, and especially after the 1968 visit, my sympathies, forged in the crucible of World War II, were with the occupied people. I remembered that Winston Churchill had said then: "The only good soldier of occupation is a dead soldier of occupation."

When Israel disregarded the Third Geneva Convention, which forbids occupation forces from bringing in their families and inessential civilians, for me the term "soldier of occupation" came to apply to all Israelis in the West Bank, including East Jerusalem, as well as in Gaza, Golan and south Lebanon.

In 1980, I made a PBS documentary, "Coming of Age in Armageddon," on the Middle East conflict as seen through the eyes of the region's children. It was regarded as too evenhanded to be shown in New York or Washington. It won a Venus at the International Film Festival in Houston, and I entered it in the Jerusalem Film Festival. Israelis are far less blinkered in their views than Jewish Americans; I was confident that I would split the jury down the middle and win the bronze. Unfortunately, the festival was canceled, and I was left to battle the American inquisition alone.

David Ben-Gurion, I feel sure, would have been a friend in need.

"American Jews! I hate them! I hate them!" he said in his passionate Slavonic way, at one point in that evening in 1968. "They'll do anything for Israel except live in the place!"

Perhaps because at that time I "understood nothing," I was shocked and reminded Ben-Gurion, "They're very generous toward Israel."

"Of course," he responded. "They feel guilty. And so they should!" ✦

Russell Warren Howe is a Washington-based free-lance journalist who writes regularly for newspapers in the U.S. and abroad. He is the chief North American correspondent of al-Wasat and also the author of numerous books and articles on the influence of special interest groups on American politics. His novel, False Flags, set in Moscow and French Guiana, won the 1996 Southern Prize for Fiction.

Even an Eight-Year-Old Can Tell Middle East Fact From Fiction

By Dr. Clyde Farris

The Arab Airways DC-3 taxied to a halt at the airport in Amman, Jordan on a summer afternoon in late June, 1955. I was only eight years old at the time, but I can still remember the warm wind and the glare of the sunshine as I stepped onto the tarmac.

My father had just taken a position as an agricultural adviser with the AID program and we were moving from the state of Montana to the Hashemite Kingdom of Jordan. I had a sense of excitement and trepidation as I anticipated living in this new and strange land.

Even at that young age, I had formed the opinion that the Israelis were the "good guys" and the Arabs were somehow the "bad guys." Exactly why I felt that way, I cannot be sure, but it was probably due to a combination of factors.

I had attended the First Baptist Church in Billings, Montana with my family. I had been taught in Sunday School and Vacation Bible School that the ancient Israelites were a force for good and the ancient Egyptians and Philistines were a force for evil. Perhaps it was difficult for my eight-year-old mind to realize that a few millennia can change things considerably. Many Christian fundamentalists continue to err by applying an ancient Biblical scenario to the present-day Middle East.

The other opinion-molding factor may have been television news. Television had barely arrived in Montana, but my parents never missed the "Huntley-Brinkley Report." Back then, it was only 15 minutes in length, and I would generally watch it with them. I cannot honestly remember any specific broadcasts at that time that might have shaped my opinions on the Mideast. However, if the bias of the networks at that time was anything like it has been for the past 20 or 30 years, I suspect I was influenced in that fashion as well.

Whatever the roots of my pro-Israel prejudices, they were soon to be challenged by facts that could not be hidden by a smooth Israeli public relations machine. The Palestinian refugee camps (the ugly fruits of Israel's "War of Independence") littered Jordan in terrible squalor. The barren hillsides of Amman were covered with thousands upon thousands of flimsy shelters. Huts made of cardboard or a piece of canvas spread over a few poles would pass as a home for an entire Palestinian family. Perceptibly malnourished Palestinian children would knock on our door, asking for a piece of bread. Palestinian women would walk for miles to fetch a small container of water from the public well.

Only seven years earlier, these sad and desperate refugees had been prosperous shopkeepers, farmers and craftsmen in what had been known as Palestine before the Holocaust had descended upon them.

My "seeing the light" was not a sudden realization that I had been "conned." There was no bolt of lightning or moment of insight to reveal suddenly the dark side of Zionism to me. However, by the time my family and I returned to the U.S., my views on the Middle East were no longer black and white. The pro-Israel bias of the media was now obvious to me. The inaccuracies, half-truths, and lies that masqueraded as news on the Middle East only served to further my suspicions that Americans were being fed propaganda and not the facts.

By the time I was in high school, my previous pro-Israel sentiments had been transformed into a healthy skepticism about the basic morality of the creation of the modern state of Israel. When my high school social studies teacher told my class that pre-Israel Palestine had been inhabited by a handful of Arabs running a few camels, I raised my hand and challenged him on that point. I can still see the look of utter disbelief on his face— it was obvious that no student had ever questioned the party line before. He became flustered and then a little bit angry, but he chose his words carefully for the rest of the time we spent on the Middle East.

My experiences in Jordan had initially left me with a sense of ambivalence regarding the Arab-Israeli conflict, but this was gradually transformed into anger. I would hear someone quote Golda Meir's callous remark that "there is no such thing as a Palestinian" and think back to the misery of the Palestinian refugee camps.

I would see unrepentent Israeli terrorists, such as Menachem Begin and Yitzhak Shamir, masquerade as statesmen and accuse the Palestinians of terrorism. I would see Ariel Sharon, the Butcher of Beirut, sit in the cabinet of the same government that was staging a show trial of alleged war criminal John Demjanjuk. Israel continued to flout international law by illegally annexing land occupied by force and deporting the indigenous population.

As time went on, I felt an urgent need to tell my fellow Americans that they were being led astray on Middle East issues. I felt something like John the Baptist—a voice crying in the wilderness. I felt that the message was important for many reasons. First of all, our blind support of Israel was stupid because it was hurting America's interests. America was losing economically, and precious diplomatic capital also was being squandered. More importantly, however, what we were doing flew in the face of everything our country is supposed to stand for.

Basic principles of justice and self-determination seemed to apply to everyone in the world except Palestinians. America should have been aiding the Palestinians in their just struggle for an independent state and punishing Israel for its gross human rights violations. Instead, America was giving Israel a blank check and turning a blind eye to injustice. America prides itself as being the world champion of human rights, but its hypocritical policies regarding Israel and the Palestinians are not lost on the rest of the world.

Today, however, I am more optimistic that the Palestinians may yet receive justice in my lifetime. The slow but irresistible current of American public opinion is finally shifting away from blind support of Israel, despite crude efforts by Israel's powerful media apologists to stem the tide.

I have confidence in the basic American sense of fairness. Once the facts are known by the average American, there will be a public outcry for a just solution to the problems of the Middle East. A cowardly Congress may have to be dragged along, kicking and screaming, but eventually will have to submit to the will of the American people. ✦

Dr. Clyde Farris is an orthopedic surgeon living in West Linn, OR. For many years he has been the donor of the "Pray for Palestine" bumper stickers distributed by the American Educational Trust.

III. AFTER THE SIX-DAY WAR
1967-1973

ON JUNE 5, 1967, Israel launched what it called a "pre-emptive" strike on Egypt and Syria, charging at the time that they were about to attack Israel. (Fifteen years later, Israeli Prime Minister Menachem Begin admitted that in 1967 Israel indeed "had a choice...We decided to attack.") Jordan, bound by a mutual defense treaty with Egypt, joined the fighting. (It was on the fourth day of the ensuing "Six-Day War" that Israeli aircraft and torpedo boats attacked and nearly sank the USS *Liberty*, a "ferret" ship electronically monitoring the fighting and operated by the U.S. Navy and the National Security Agency, killing 34 Americans and wounding 171.) At war's end, Israel had occupied Sinai, East Jerusalem, the West Bank, the Gaza Strip and the Golan Heights, creating an additional 250,000 Palestinian refugees, many of whom were driven out of refugee camps in the Jordan Valley. On Nov. 22, 1967, the United Nations Security Council passed Resolution 242, calling for the "withdrawal of Israeli armed forces from territories occupied in the recent conflict" and acknowledgement of the right of all states in the region "to live in peace within secure and recognized boundaries." This land-for-peace resolution has been the cornerstone of all subsequent internationally supported Middle East peace plans, including initiatives launched by all seven U.S. presidents who have held office since 1967.

Lessons From My Son and My Grandfather

By Rachelle Marshall

Like almost all Jews of my generation, I was indelibly marked by the calamity inflicted on the Jews of Europe between 1933 and 1945. Growing up safely in New York during those years, I knew that I was alive only because my grandparents had decided to come to America. Others in my family were not so lucky. During the late 1930s there was constant anxiety in our house as my father talked endlessly on the telephone trying to secure safe passage for relatives still in Europe. The newsreel I saw in 1938 of bearded Jews on their hands and knees in a Vienna street, surrounded by jeering crowds, was a searing revelation that ordinary men and women could suddenly become savage.

So after World War II it would have been unthinkable to me not to welcome the establishment of the state of Israel. At last, I thought, the Jewish people had a safe haven. During the 1950s and 1960s, it never occurred to me that there was any inconsistency in working for civil rights in America and giving my full support to Israel. The only "Palestinians" I knew about were Jews like my Uncle Simon, who had settled in Palestine in the 19th century to escape the Czarist pogroms.

For nearly 20 years I assumed that whatever the Israeli government did was for self-defense, and thus justified. The first, imperceptible doubt arose the day after Israel's victory in the June, 1967 war. "What a triumph!" I exclaimed at breakfast after a look at the headlines. "Israel is finally safe."

Our 12-year-old son, Jonathan, looked skeptical. "Why is Israel any safer than before?" he asked. "Doesn't conquering more territory just mean making more enemies?" I reminded him that he hadn't been alive during the Holocaust and therefore couldn't possibly understand the relief that Jews everywhere must be feeling. To my shame, I accused him of being too rational.

As the days passed and I read news reports from the Middle East that suggested the conflict was far from over, Jonathan's questions occasionally troubled me. But, at the time, U.S. involvement in Vietnam was uppermost in my mind, so much that in December, 1967 I spent three weeks in jail for helping to block the entrance to the Oakland Army Terminal.

The carpet-bombing of Vietnam by B-52s and the use of napalm and white phosphorous against defenseless peasants struck me as not so different from the Nazi ruthlessness we had once condemned. When the Honeywell Corporation announced it had developed an "improved" napalm that would stick to the skin longer, I realized that the Germans had no monopoly on evil.

When I later came to read about the Middle East, the knowledge that my own country was capable of committing atrocities gave me a degree of objectivity that enabled me to accept information about Israel that I would earlier have dismissed as Arab propaganda. The learning process began a year or two after my breakfast table confrontation with Jonathan, when an article appeared in the *Stanford Daily* that harshly criticized Israel's treatment of Palestinians.

I was angry and wanted to reply, but I couldn't counter the author's facts with facts of my own. So I went to the library and began reading—starting with Christopher Sykes's *Crossroads to Israel* and Maxime Rodinson's *Israel and the Arabs*, and going on to books by Israelis and others. It wasn't until much later that I was willing to trust works by Arab authors such as Sabri Jiryis and Edward Said. I took two courses on the Middle East at Stanford and went to hear most of the speakers who came to the campus, including Muhammad Hallaj and Ibrahim Abu-Lughod. I was shocked when they were nearly shouted off the stage by members of the audience.

The light began to dawn as I learned that the Jewish haven I had welcomed was established on land the Palestinians had a right to claim as their own. I learned about the methods that Jewish forces had used to expel over 700,000 Palestinians from their homes, such as the fiery barrel bombs that burned through Arab villages, and the massacre of 250 men, women and children at Deir Yassin. I learned about Arab terrorism and about Israeli reprisal raids. From Menachem Begin's book, *The Revolt*, I learned about Jewish terrorism and of the dedication of Jewish zealots to extending Israel's borders to include the east bank of the Jordan.

The more I read, the greater my sense of betrayal. A large part of what I had been told about Israel and its neighbors was based on myth, I realized. And the myths continued to be repeated in most of the newspaper and magazine articles I read that dealt with the Middle East. But then I found that the price of challenging the conventional wisdom came high.

In the mid-1970s I began writing letters to the editor that were critical of Israel's role in Lebanon, specifically its devastating bombing of civilian villages and its support for the Phalangist forces. The printed replies (and anonymous letters) were short on factual arguments but called me everything from an anti-Semitic Jew to a communist. The nice local rabbi, a hero of the Selma civil rights march, called me in to ask me not to wash our dirty linen in public. "It can only do harm to Jews when we criticize Israel," he said.

The hardest thing was that relatives and friends expressed pain, and sometimes anger, over what I was doing. One of the guests at a family birthday party said to me in all seriousness, "You are an enemy of the Jews."

My husband and children were shocked by this reaction, but what reassured all of us is that we soon came to know, and work with, a group of Israeli and Palestinian graduate students at Stanford who believed fervently that both peoples could peacefully coexist, as equals, in separate independent states. At the time, this was a daring position for either Israelis or Palestinians to take. The sanity and humaneness of these students reinforced my own belief that a two-state solution was the only way to settle the Middle East conflict and therefore assure Israel's security.

Despite this intellectual conviction, there were times when the accusations by fellow Jews that I was doing harm to Israel by what I wrote and said made me wonder if perhaps I was a kind of traitor. Then a chance discovery about my grandfather changed everything.

He had come to America just before World War I and died before I was born. All I really knew about him was that my parents and aunts and uncles revered him, that he had founded a Hebrew-language newspaper in New York, and had helped to raise money in America for schools in Palestine. One day while I was browsing in the library, I found his name, Abraham Lubarsky, in the index of a book and learned that he had been an associate of Ahad Ha-Am.

Ahad Ha-Am (whose real name was Asher Ginzberg) was already a hero of mine. He was one of a small group of Russian Jews called "cultural Zionists" who favored the establishment in Palestine of a homeland for the Jews but believed that they had no right to rule the entire country. The Arab inhabitants, Ahad Ha-Am wrote in 1920, "have a tangible right based on generation after generation of life and work in the country. The country is their national home, too, and they too have the right to develop their national potentialities as far as they are able." (*Zionism*, Gary Smith, ed., Harper & Row, 1974.) My grandfather's entry in *Encyclopedia Judaica* says that he was "especially close to Ahad Ha-Am, whom he stimulated to write his first famous essay."

The Legacy of Cultural Zionists

It is now too late for the kind of multicultural nation in Palestine that Ahad Ha-Am and my grandfather envisioned. But their insight that Arabs and Jews would have to live together as equals in the land of Palestine if there was to be peace between them is as valid today as it ever was. The "cultural Zionists" believed the identity and survival of the Jewish people depended not on wielding power over others but on establishing a community that would preserve and put into practice centuries of Jewish teaching and tradition. Central to the Judaism they valued were the words of Amos: "Let justice roll down like waters and righteousness like an ever-flowing stream."

If they were alive today, Ahad Ha-Am and my grandfather would undoubtedly have felt obliged, as Jews, to speak out against acts of brutality and injustice no matter who committed them. And I think they would have believed, as I do, that today the Jewish people face their greatest danger not from Palestinians seeking self-determination, but from an Israeli government that is making a mockery of Judaism. ✦

Rachelle Marshall is an editor and free-lance writer living in Stanford, CA. She is a member of the International Jewish Peace Union and writes frequently on the Middle East. She also works actively on Middle East issues with the American Friends Service Committee and the Women's International League for Peace and Freedom.

Twenty Years of Learning

By T.P. Ellsworth, Jr.

Everyone knows that the Six-Day War of June 1967 was a pivotal point in Middle East history. It also happened to be a pivotal period in my personal and professional life. That was the month I started work as an intern in the office of then-Congressman George Bush. My fellow intern was Chase Untermeyer, who 20 years later became Bush's first director of White House personnel.

Even more important, however, was my marriage, which took place during the Six-Day War. My bride was of Turkish and Syrian background, and our first "marital discourse" was over the causes of that war in which Israel defeated Egypt, Syria and Jordan and occupied the lands which the U.S. now hopes it will exchange for peace with all of its Arab neighbors.

As a WASP whose middle-class family has lived in the same Connecticut River valley community since 1789, with a distant forebear, Oliver Ellsworth, who was the third chief justice of the Supreme Court, and with a Yale and Texas Law School education, I was a typical, pro-Israel American. Unless one had direct contact with people who had lived in the Middle East, and was therefore not solely dependent upon the U.S. media for information, I realize now, there was little opportunity to be anything else.

Like most Americans of my generation, my opinions about the Arabs and sympathies for the Israelis had been shaped largely by the film "Exodus," based upon the novel by Leon Uris and produced by Otto Preminger. Years later, I learned that Uris had actually been employed by a Zionist organization to write the book, and Preminger certainly had no objection to turning out a clever and manipulative propaganda film which sold Israel, and a lot of tickets, to Americans who, like me, accepted the film as history and became emotionally involved with Israel. Leon Uris and Otto Preminger were probably laughing all the way to the bank.

Between 1967 and 1980, however, my education was no longer based solely upon Zionist mythology and Hollywood history. I began reading about the area and I met many Arabs, including Palestinian Americans. One branch of my wife's family had roots in Palestine, and she has cousins living, or at least existing, on the West Bank.

Only half jokingly, they described themselves as the "Jews of the Arab World." I found them to be tough, bright and creative, with a reverence for education that resulted in a proliferation of Palestinians in the professions in the U.S., as well as in the Middle East. I began to understand that fear of competition is one of the elements in the Israeli determination to keep the Muslim and Christian Palestinians within their borders in a permanently subservient state.

My historical reading provided my first exposure to the Deir Yassin massacre, carried out in April, 1948, by Jewish underground fighters of the Irgun Zvai Leumi and the Stern Gang. Menachem Begin was commander of the Irgun, and one of the top three commanders of the Stern Gang was Yitzhak Shamir. It's time the world learns, and then never forgets, that this massacre of the men, women and children of a Palestinian village near Jerusalem was carried out under the direction of two future prime ministers of Israel, both of whom have subsequently refused to deal with the Palestine Liberation Organization on the grounds that it is a "terrorist" organization.

My internship in Congress and many campaign experiences pointed me after 1980 toward professional lobbying. As I organized a legislative coalition called the "Small Business Superfund Alliance" and grassroots supporting networks, my education on the Middle East continued. I could hardly fail to note how Tom Dine, who in 1980 became executive director of the American Israel Public Affairs Committee (AIPAC), Israel's lobby in Washington, frequently was quoted in the press describing how powerful his group is. It struck me that the heads of most other lobbies would want to avoid such publicity, particularly if it were true, as seems to be the case with AIPAC.

By now, however, it is the Palestinian intifada that has moved me, and many like me, from concern to activity, along with hundreds of other Americans, who have decided that continued U.S. subsidization of Israel's brutal occupation of the West Bank and Gaza is truly an affront to American values.

Two peoples, two states. I hope for the day when Israel can finally live with itself and its neighbors; when Israeli leaders are more interested in a real peace than forceably annexing occupied Palestine to fulfill dreams of "Greater Israel"; when Israeli leaders are willing to sit down with genuine Palestinian leaders to negotiate that peace in good faith.

Americans want the threat of war stopped, and so, I am ultimately persuaded, does President George Bush. I know that my first boss on the Hill does have deeply humane values. From 20 years of intermittent contact, I believe he will not remain inclined much longer to have our government continue to finance Israel's crushing of Palestinian rights, aspirations and lives. I believe that Americans in every congressional district must help organize support for a U.S. policy in the Middle East that reflects American values and serves American interests.

That way is the only way I know of to ensure that our government's policies reflect the interests of all of its citizens, not just the wishes of narrow special interest groups. For example, such groups, coordinated by AIPAC, have for several years blocked most major sales of even defensive arms to moderate Arab states, costing our economy billions of dollars and over half a million jobs. Likewise, the same special interest lobby persuaded Congress to increase military aid to Israel, even after it broke American laws by using American arms supplied for defensive purposes in its failed and misguided invasion of Lebanon.

By now, I think a lot of Americans have realized that this sort of disregard of American interests, values and even our laws must be stopped. I hope some of the people who read this book will decide to make their views known. If enough of us do, I suspect that many more members of Congress will also soon be "seeing the light." ✦

T.P. (Terry) Ellsworth, Jr. is president of Court Record Searches in northern Virginia. He has written a screenplay, "The Last Cry," which compares the Palestinian and Native American experiences.

A Love for One's Own Land

By Helen Overdiek

The light dawned slowly—it was not a blinding flash. My first encounter with a Palestinian was in Saudi Arabia, where I worked as a secretary for a private U.S. oil company. He was an Arabic teacher, who told me that in his youth he had lived in a small village on the Mediterranean in Palestine.

The family's neighbors, with whom they socialized, were Jewish. The two families often shared picnics by the sea. In 1948 the Palestinian teacher's family was driven from Palestine. He subsequently married. Years later, his wife and his sister were given "permission" to go to his village, since he wanted his wife to see where he had lived as a youth. His sister located the village and the house. Neither, fortunately, had been bulldozed into oblivion, as had happened to so many others.

Their knock on the door was answered by a Jewish lady, who said she had come from Yemen. She invited them in after my friend's sister explained that this had been her home. It was then that her emotions overwhelmed her, as she viewed the kitchen where she and her mother had prepared family meals, and the family garden, now so changed.

I have a fierce attachment to my own home in Minnesota, where I was born and where I now live. Even during the 28 years I worked outside the United States, my family and the land were always there, and I returned almost every year to my haven. It is not possible, I believe, to put one's self in a Palestinian's place—to really understand the depth of longing Palestinians have for their lost land and former homes—unless one has sustained a similar loss. But already I was beginning to feel a great affinity with the Palestinians, since my own attachment to the land my parents tilled is so strong.

In 1967, Americans Were Targets for Arab Rage

I was still in the Middle East in June, 1967, at the time of Israel's sudden, devastating attack on Egypt and Syria. We Americans also came under sudden attack—windows in our homes were broken, our cars were overturned and set afire. Arabs directed their rage at us as the symbols of what they perceived to be U.S.-Israeli aggression against the

entire Arab world. By then I had lived many years in the Middle East and had participated happily in the daily life of my Arab friends and associates. I was both saddened and
troubled to see the erosion of the prestige, popularity and respect once enjoyed there by
my country, just as I was disturbed at the misinformation, distortion, and stereotypical
images of Arabs promulgated in the United States. As a result of Israel's attack, and the
speed with which the reality was replaced by the myth that Israel was the victim rather
than the aggressor, Americans living in Lebanon founded Americans for Justice in the
Middle East (AJME). I became a member of the Saudi Arabia chapter, our aim being a
presentation of the facts which U.S. citizens seldom heard about what really was happening in the Middle East.

When I returned to Minnesota on vacation that same year, I found friends and relatives generally apathetic, uninterested or uninformed. Their main reaction was surprise
that I wasn't "afraid" of being "over there." Had I mentioned the West Bank, I suspect
some would have thought that I was referring to a new savings and loan institution in
that part of town. They understood little or nothing of the cause of periodic wars in the
Middle East—only that it was "dangerous" for me to be there. I responded that I felt
safer in Saudi Arabia than I did in my own country.

U.S. Gas Lines Blamed on "the Arabs"

In the fall of 1973, while I was still in Saudi Arabia, King Faisal turned off the oil spigot.
He was responding to Henry Kissinger's airlift and sealift of U.S. weapons to Israel for
use in preventing Egypt and Syria from retaking the Sinai and Golan Heights, areas Israel
had seized from them.

Later, when I was home on vacation, I found the American public angry at "the
Arabs" because of lines at the gas pump. Reasons for the cutoff didn't make the headlines, but frustrations of motorists did. I have written to a number of journalists and companies about their references to the Arab oil embargo, saying that when they wrote about
it they were remiss in not explaining to the public why the Arabs, who would prefer selling their oil to sitting on it, used a boycott as a political weapon. Few Americans realized
then or now that the boycott was an Arab protest against unconditional U.S. support for
an Israeli effort not to defend its own territory, but to keep Arab territory seized in 1967.

I had begun writing letters from the Middle East in 1968 to members of our government, editors of newspapers and magazines, clergy, and various individuals whose articles contained misstatements, downright untruths, or erroneous maps of the Middle
East. Some of these mythmakers are just ill-informed. Others appear to operate on the
principle that if they repeat an untruth or distortion often enough, it becomes accepted
as truth. Since returning to my home in Minnesota, I have continued to be concerned
about justice for Arab Americans here and for the Palestinians in the Middle East. I am
thus a member of several national and local organizations.

When frustrations threaten to overwhelm the considerable personal satisfactions I derive from my continuing efforts to help others see the light, I remind myself of author Bonaro Overstreet's lines:

> You say the little things I do will do no good.
> They never will prevail to tip the scales
> When justice hangs in balance.
> I don't think I ever thought they would.
> But I am prejudiced beyond debate
> In favor of my right to choose which side
> Shall feel the stubborn ounces of my weight. ✦

Helen Overdiek lives in Hopkins, MN, and is active in local and national organizations seeking a peaceful solution to the Palestinian-Israeli dispute and concerned with human rights, discrimination, and political action. In October, 1987, she received the Alex Odeh Memorial Award from the Minnesota chapter of the American-Arab Anti-Discrimination Committee in recognition of her "outstanding efforts on behalf of the Arab-American community."

Middle East Facts Won't Fit Into the Ideological Baggage We Carry

By Mary E. Neznek

June, 1967, marked the heady success of a supposed David of an Israeli army against a Goliath of Arabs in the "Six-Day War." There was dancing in the streets in the United States, and I found myself "celebrating" by proxy and by virtue of being in a pub in an upstate New York college town. It all seemed so stunning, with a remarkable victory for the brave Israelis against the swarming hordes of warring Arabs.

This happened at a time when the Vietnam War was beginning to take more and more hapless young American high school- and college-aged men to that mean little war in Southeast Asia. It was also a time of heightened awareness for me as an 18-year-old recently exposed to conditions in the rural South and in small-town and urban ghettos.

The Middle East war seemed like one place where good triumphed over evil. The next year I was chosen through the Earlham College Near Eastern Studies program to study in Lebanon. At first I did not make the connection between the June, 1967, war in the Middle East and conditions in Beirut. Beirut seemed like an opportunity to view the United States from a different vantage point.

At 19, according to Eriksonian developmental theories of psychology, one's values are forged and defined. Those crucial years between 18 and 21 took me to rural Appalachia in Kentucky, a black high school in then-segregated Alabama, and finally to Lebanon as one of 20 19-year-olds chosen to study at the American University of Beirut. That chance to study in Lebanon set my way of thinking apart from friends and family for many years.

Unspeakable domestic U.S. poverty and unacceptable violence in international policy first connected for me on a student orientation trip to the Palestinian refugee camp in Tyre. This was the same Tyre referred to in Sunday School biblical stories. But who were these Palestinian refugees we saw in this part of the "Holy Land," and why were they there? Why did they swarm around our tour bus and give me an uneasy feeling that they were angry with Americans?

The year was 1968, one year after the mythic Israeli victory against the Arabs. Suddenly, I had the sinking feeling that what I was learning from my new Mideast vantage point would no longer fit into the neat ideological package I had mentally prepared. That was the starting point of a personal journey toward a better understanding of U.S.-Arab relations. It wasn't just Sami Hadawi's book *Bitter Harvest*, or lectures by well-respected Arab scholars, which pierced my layers of ignorance. It was also recognition of my own careless ignorance of what really had happened between the Palestinians and Israelis that crystallized after that first searing glimpse of a Palestinian refugee camp.

That year I also made friends with men and women from a variety of non-Western backgrounds, with whom I shared classes and living quarters in Beirut. We huddled through an Israeli air raid on the Beirut airport. We broke the curfew together during successive crises precipitated by the destabilizing presence of thousands of Palestinian refugees and an American-backed Israeli army in hot pursuit.

After the end of the school year, I ventured to Israel to meet Israelis and Palestinians on their own grounds. What I found was myth and represssion. This was brought home to me on an Israeli Ministry of Tourism junket. Being short on time and traveling alone, I thought a tour bus would offer the best way to see the area. Sitting on the bus with the other "Holy Land tourists," I realized how distortions perpetuate themselves.

Our guide, a Jewish former resident of Beirut, told of persecution of Jewish citizens in Arab countries. There was little or no mention of the centuries of harmony between Muslim, Christian and Jewish peoples in the Middle East, nor that this was ended by the violent incursion of Jewish refugees, motivated by their persecution in Europe to despoil lands and lives in pursuit of a violent nationalism of their own.

For the first time I experienced what I would feel over and over—the deliberate use of untruths to justify a violation of Palestinian basic rights.

When I returned to south Lebanon in 1972 to teach for a year in a rural farming village, I was exposed to the "have nots." My students were poor Shi'i and Christian farming children whose academic year was interrupted by the cycles of back-breaking planting and harvesting of tobacco. They lived a half-kilometer away from Israel, and a few kilometers away from the teeming refugee camps in Tyre. The frustrations of all of these people were laying the groundwork for 15 years of sporadic civil war that was to explode only three years later.

In 1973, upon my return to the U.S. from teaching in the village, an Albany, NY, newspaper published an interview containing my observations on Lebanese-Palestinian political problems kept alive by unresolved grievances left from the establishment of Israel. Two Israeli academics verbally lambasted me, and the newspaper which published my interview was censured, along with my credibility, for challenging the conventional wisdom about Middle East problems.

My life reconnected with the Middle East in 1977, during the third year of the Lebanese civil war. The lack of information about its causes pricked my conscience and led me to begin my study of Arabic. I also worked with my former AUB professor, Dr. Walid Khalidi, on his book about the Lebanese civil war, which was supported through the Center for International Affairs at Harvard University. In 1978, I transferred to Georgetown University to focus on conflict resolution and theories of nonviolence.

Being in Washington has made me realize that the part played by the United States in the continuing violence in the Mideast cannot be ignored. I spent two years researching a book that looked at domestic U.S. foreign policy formulation vis-à-vis the Israeli-Palestinian conflict, and I learned still more about the use of misinformation and myth by Washington's infamous Israel lobby.

This process of insight has brought me back to Pogo's observation that "We have met the enemy and he is us." It is up to us to exercise our right to participate in political life, accepting responsibility to correct distortions. This is the only way to replace a U.S. Middle East policy based upon a military strategic myth with a far sounder strategy based upon human rights and self-determination. The only way to achieve self-determination for Palestinians in their homeland is to restore self-determination for Americans in the U.S. ✦

Mary E. Neznek is a founding member of the Presbytery Middle East working group in Washington, DC. She is a Ph.D. candidate in conflict resolution and analysis at George Mason University in Fairfax, Virginia, and executive director of Peace Links, a women's anti-nuclear network.

Ibrahim and Daniel

By Dan Bloom

I am an American Jew who shares the belief, with many other American Jews, that a just and equitable peace must come to the Middle East. I am not pro-Israeli and I am not pro-Arab. I am pro-peace, pro-justice.

I was born in 1949 and, like many American Jews who grew up after Israel became a state, I spent many hours learning about Israel, studying maps of Israel, learning Hebrew, and even sending pennies and dimes to Israel to build and plant forests in what I had been told were desert areas. Israel became for me, and most of my contemporaries, a familiar place, an idealized place, a utopian place.

Then in 1969 I visited Israel during my junior year in college, staying with relatives in Tel Aviv and at a youth hostel in Jerusalem. I visited Bethlehem and Beersheba and Haifa, too. I read the newspapers. I spoke with both Israelis and Arabs. I watched television and I read up on the history of this "land of milk and honey" from which my forebears had come 2,000 years ago.

And then in Rome, a few weeks later, I met an Egyptian student of my own age, from Cairo. We spent an entire afternoon speaking about the Middle East and about our hopes for peace there. We disagreed about some things, but we agreed about many others. A friendship was born, across cultures, across national boundaries, across religious faiths. Ibrahim and Daniel talked of many things, but the most important thing we agreed upon was that by the year 1994 there should be peace in the Middle East.

"Twenty-five years from today," we both agreed, and shook hands and embraced.

How such a peace was to be achieved, I did not know. But I have come to understand that it will not come without more informed efforts by all who care about the Middle East, including me and including Ibrahim.

I am an independent American Jew. I read the newspapers and the magazines and the history books and I make up my own mind. When Israel makes a mistake in policy or judgment, I am not afraid to speak up and say so. When Arab countries make mistakes, I also am compelled to speak up. As I said, I am for peace and justice. I do not favor any one nation over another. We must all learn to respect the rights, the cultures, the religions, and the national aspirations of each other, be we Arabs or Jews, Israelis or Palestinians, Americans or Jordanians.

Whatever happened in the past lies in the past, and we must all learn to understand it and analyze it and come to terms with it. Where there was injustice, we must say there was injustice. Where there is ethnic stereotyping, we must speak out and confront this ethnic stereotyping, be it of Arabs or of Jews. Where there is disinformation, we must seek out the correct information. Where there is propaganda and manipulation, we must seek out the truth and accept it.

As a child I brought my pennies to Sunday School to help plant forests in Israel. Those were my innocent days. Today I feel compelled to speak out for a negotiated, just, peaceful settlement of the Middle East crisis—a peace that speaks fairly and equitably to both the Palestinians and the Israelis, a peace that recognizes the histories and aspirations of both peoples.

I am pro-life: Palestinian life and Israeli life. The American-Jewish community is not of one mind on these issues, or of one voice. There are many American Jews like myself, who came of age in the '50s, '60s and '70s, and who are not Zionists and are not anti-Arab. Like me, they are pro-peace and not afraid to say so. ✦

Daniel Halevi Bloom is a newspaper editor in Juneau, Alaska.

Journalist in Mideast Turns "180 Degrees"

By Pat McDonnell Twair

My generation was mesmerized by Leon Uris' novel *Exodus*, published in the 1950s. Even as a child in the late 1940s, I saw newsreels of shiploads of Holocaust survivors turned away from Palestine by British soldiers. As a fledgling journalist in the early 1960s, I entertained the thought of sending a résumé to the *Jerusalem Post* so that I could work in the pioneering country of Israel that was "turning the desert into a garden."

I finally visited Israel in 1969—at the crest of its media popularity for, two years earlier, defeating the "Arab states who so massively outnumbered it." But, when I arrived, somehow the spirit Uris had described seemed to be missing. I was troubled, although not enough, by seeing Arabs forced at gunpoint to step out of service taxis and endure a search for arms by Israeli soldiers, while the other Israeli passengers and I were not questioned.

In September, 1970, my aunt and I traveled through Spain and Morocco and met a former member of the Syrian parliament, who had served as interpreter for the Syrian president when CIA agents Kermit Roosevelt and Miles Copeland, author of *The Game of Nations*, were in and out of Damascus.

The Syrian gentleman offered us a sightseeing trip to Fez in his Mercedes. Many things were happening at that time. Four airliners had just been hijacked to Jordan and Egypt by George Habash's Popular Front for the Liberation of Palestine. Our host, in typical Arab fashion, did not want to disturb our outing, so he did not translate the news reports on the car radio. However, he began talking about the Palestinians displaced by the Arab-Israeli conflict. I rather naively retorted that tour guides in Israel had told me the Arab inhabitants had simply left their homes of their own accord in 1948. His emotional rejection of what I now realize was my extraordinary gullibility made me wonder about his sanity.

Tragic Events of 1970 Capture Interest

When I returned to my newspaper in California, I heard of the multiple skyjackings which were the catalyst for the Black September battles between Palestinians and Jordanians, in which hundreds of civilians were killed. One week later, Egyptian President Gamal Abdel Nasser, physically and emotionally exhausted by his efforts to mediate a battle which literally pitted Arab brother against brother, died of a heart attack. The news was full of the physical devastation left by the fighting in Jordan and the psychological devastation throughout the Arab world after the death of Egypt's president, who had become the symbol of Arab unity. It captured my imagination, and I stayed in touch with the Syrian who had so generously shown me the landmarks of Morocco.

Five months later, in February, 1971, Air France offered me a trip to write travel material on Morocco. Once again in Rabat, I expressed my sympathies for the "poor, pathetic Jews in need of a homeland" to my Syrian friend. This time he made arrangements for me to fly to Beirut, with introductions to such people as Saeb Salam, a former prime minister of Lebanon, and Sheikh Suleiman Alamuddin. Alamuddin presented me with a monograph, *Bridge of Sorrows*, written by a Harvard University professor who had interviewed survivors of the massacre in the Palestinian village of Deir Yassin carried out in April, 1948, by two Jewish underground militias, Irgun and Lehi.

Before I had left California, Jewish friends insisted I read an article in a Hadassah publication describing a bloody battle in which Palestinian Arabs had fired on an Israeli medical convoy in 1948, slaughtering both doctors and nurses. Only after I had read the Harvard monograph did I make the connection. I realized the Hadassah report had omitted any mention of the massacre of 240 Palestinian men, women, and children at Deir Yassin just one week earlier which had precipitated the retaliatory attack on the Israeli medical convoy. My American friends did not know the full story, I ruminated, gullible as ever. By the morning of my third day in Beirut, I realized that it was more beautiful than either San Francisco or Paris—another truth for which I had arrived totally unprepared. That made the impressions that followed later in the day even more memorable.

Visiting a Palestinian Refugee Camp

A Red Crescent doctor offered to take me to the Palestinian camp of Tel Al-Zatar. "You select any resident you wish to interview," he told me. I recall only intense discomfort at being served tea by a family that could ill afford it and my embarrassment as I asked the questions that uninformed American journalists are prone to ask Palestinians. I already was beginning to perceive that these questions arose not from mere ignorance, but instead from a cornucopia of U.S. misinformation and prejudice.

A few days later, I flew to Jordan on what was rapidly becoming my personal quest for the truth of the Arab-Israeli conflict. I was on my own there. Peter Saleh, of the Jordanian Ministry of Information, assigned me a guide and a car. Once again, I was drawn to the miserable Palestinian refugee camps. I kept trying to rationalize why these people were living by the thousands in such appalling conditions of deprivation. The turning point was my stop at Karameh, a village of Palestinian refugees inside Jordan. Even though they were refugees in a strange land, they had begun to prosper from raising and marketing poultry. Then, in a sudden night attack, the Israeli army had wiped out the thriving community in 1968. I still have the Israeli bullet my guide picked up from the rubble and placed in my hand.

On my return to my hotel in Amman, I was fortunate enough to meet Palestinian scholar Sami Hadawi, author of *Bitter Harvest*. During that two-week sojourn in Beirut and Jordan, I met American nurses working as volunteers with the PLO. Their dedication to what I had been led to believe was a virulently anti-U.S. terrorist organization led to my first serious questioning of Washington's unconditional support of Israel. I was confused by Lebanese Maronite hairdressers and taxi drivers who told me they sympathized with the Israelis and did not consider themselves Arabs. Above all, I didn't understand why the PLO people I spoke to in Beirut lived like prisoners in guarded mini-fortresses. After all, I reasoned, why should Palestinians be so cautious in an Arab country?

When I attempted to interview a wounded Fatah commando, he turned me away with one curt statement: "Why do you want to speak to me? People are dying in Vietnam from American armaments. Speak to them."

I wondered why, if what was taking place in the Middle East was comparable to what was happening in Vietnam, Americans were so ignorant of one war and so sensitive to the other.

When I returned to Morocco, my Syrian friend pretended to be amazed. "You have turned 180 degrees," he exclaimed in mock astonishment. I realized he had known all along that any decent American would undergo the same "conversion" upon meeting the Palestinians at first hand.

Back home in California, I published a few stories about what I'd seen and promptly lost my job. I decided right then to commit the rest of my life to informing my fellow Americans about what is truly happening in the Middle East. Not because I've been brainwashed or become "pro-Arab" or even because I'm one of the "fighting Irish," but because as a 10th-generation American, I deeply resent having my country support policies that shame all Americans abroad, and conditions that no decent American would tolerate at home. ✦

Pat McDonnell Twair was an award-winning journalist with the Tucson Daily Star *and* Long Beach Press Telegram *before returning to UCLA for graduate studies in archaeology. At present she is a Los Angeles-based free-lance writer on both Middle Eastern and archaeological subjects.*

IV. AFTER THE OCTOBER WAR
1973-1977

FOLLOWING THREE YEARS of fruitless peace overtures by Egyptian President Anwar Sadat, the armies of Egypt and Syria launched a combined attack on Oct. 6, 1973, aimed at retaking the lands occupied by Israel since the 1967 war. The attack on the Jewish high holy day of Yom Kippur took Israel by surprise and saw initial victories by the Arab forces, including the retaking of the Suez Canal. With its seeming invincibility badly shaken, the Jewish state turned to the U.S. for help. With President Richard Nixon embroiled in the Watergate scandal, Secretary of State Henry Kissinger responded to Israel's plea with a massive resupply of American weapons and equipment, thus ensuring Israel's continued occupation of Arab lands. The oil-producing Gulf countries responded with the "Arab oil boycott," revealing that the West had a vulnerability of its own.

After Growing Up Together, When My Friend Chose Death, I Chose Life

By Victor Ostrovsky

As I walked slowly into the yard, the sun was halfway to its zenith, and the temperature was rising fast. I kicked the hot sand with the tip of my shoe and stared at the group closing around me. They were scanning me with their eyes, wondering who I was. I lowered my hand and felt the cold metal of the gun at my hip. "Hands up!" I shouted, pointing my gun in a lightning draw. They stepped back, staring puzzled at one another. They didn't understand, and I couldn't speak a word of Hebrew.

I was five years old, and a newcomer to Israel. It seemed they didn't play the games we did, back home in Canada. The year was 1955 and nobody in the kindergarten had heard of television, hot dogs or comic books. I had come to live with my grandparents, who couldn't speak English either. I can't remember how long it took me to adjust. All I remember is that the following year, 1956, when the sirens were howling during the Sinai campaign, I was scared in Hebrew.

The state of Israel was only a year or two older than I was. I felt like we were friends, growing up together. I was proud of our achievements, my new friend and I. It was a common feeling among Israelis at the time.

There was harmony and unity of spirit. We were realizing an ancient promise made to our ancestors. To those whose names were etched on the marble monuments, who had provided the "silver platter" upon which independence had been handed to us, we vowed to build a place that would be worthy of their sacrifice. It was to be a beacon of justice, and hope, for all.

In time, the reality of living under siege sank in, and the hope for peace disintegrated. Being mostly secular, we created a religion unto ourselves. Mainly we wanted to distinguish ourselves from the Jews of the diaspora, for whom we had little respect. They lacked the courage and conviction to join us in the struggle, preferring the "fleshpots of foreign lands, and the palaces of Aisave to the tents of Jacob."

Then, as now, their role was to send their money and keep their opinions to themselves. As a newly resurrected nation, we drew our legitimacy from our linkage to the

Bible. Our heroes were the biblical warriors, from Barak ben Avinoam and Deborah and on to the Maccabees. To that list, we added the names of new heroes, fresh links in the chain that validated our claims. We worshipped at the altar of Trumpeldor, whose dying words at Tel-Hai (our Alamo) were, "It is good to die for our country." A "new Jew" with a plough and a rifle.

At Rosh Hashanah, the Jewish New Year, the cards we sent each other were not imprinted with the traditional religious symbols. They were depictions of soldiers, tanks and fighter planes. We accepted that there would never be peace and that we would have to defend ourselves forever.

To reinforce our conviction, we embraced the tragedy of Masada where, 2,000 years ago, a small group of Israelites besieged on a mountain top by Roman legions committed suicide by hurling themselves off the bluff rather than surrender. In that act we saw the embodiment of everything we stood for as a people. We did not realize we were worshipping death, not life.

Purposeful Arrogance

Instead, we felt we were unique and strong. We expressed this feeling with purposeful arrogance. Everything we did as youths was in anticipation of joining the army and becoming a part of the power that had miraculously bonded our diverse nation.

Almost all of our information regarding our neighbors came from a well-oiled government-sponsored media apparatus. The only portrait of the Arabs available to us was that of bloodthirsty mobs, chanting in unison, "death to the Jews." We learned that for us there was nowhere to run and no choice but to stand and fight.

We would not be like previous generations of our people, led by the millions to the slaughter, like sheep. We would fight. Then, with the trial of Adolf Eichmann, we learned in detail the horrors of the Holocaust. In a way that awed us all, we thirsted, collectively, for revenge. "Never again," we said, and dug in our heels at the top of Masada.

With the Six-Day War of June, 1967, came exhilaration. We had proved we were the best, that no one could match us. Jerusalem was reunited, and the borders were no longer so close that you could see "abroad" from every high building. Books were printed showing our victories, songs sung in praise of our leaders. And, of course, more monuments were erected and more fields hallowed by the presence of our dead.

After 1967, however, for the first time, we saw our enemy up close—not as prisoners of war or captured terrorists, but as civilians, ordinary people. We had to look into the eyes of those we had dispossessed, in whose houses we had lived while they were refugees.

We hated them for placing the mirror so close to our faces. We knew that we were better than they. We had the proof. We had won! Weren't they just a tiny patch of tranquil waters we had walled off from that hostile sea of enemies, chanting that they wanted us dead? We owed them nothing. They had set out to destroy us and they had lost. There was nothing more to be said.

In fact, as a superior and chosen people, our mere presence as a benevolent occupier was, in and of itself, a benefit for them. We allowed them to be a source of cheap labor for us, and felt it was a fair exchange. They were lucky to be employed and their presence gave us the freedom to pursue our higher calling.

To any who objected, we were ruthless and brutal from the start. When asked about peace, we would say cynically, "Sure we want peace, a piece of Jordan, a piece of Lebanon."

Instead of searching for solutions in Damascus, Cairo and Rabat, we accepted our status in the Middle East as final. We searched the world for friends, but those we found in Paris or New York could not solve our problems with our neighbors. We offered ourselves to the West as "a fortress of stability, in a sea of uncertainty and communist subversion." We became merchants of death, offering weapons to any and every dictator who could afford them.

We made the name of Israel synonymous with oppression. Yes, we lived by the sword, and were proud to die by it and have our names added to the long lists on the cold marble slabs.

Cold reality penetrated our euphoria with the Yom Kippur War of October, 1973. We were not invincible, and the idea first paralyzed and then polarized us. It frightened some of us into searching, for the first time, for a solution, and others into renewed fervor for further fortifying "fortress Israel."

A Profound Reorientation

The changes taking place around us, however, were more than attitudinal. They involved a profound reorientation of our political vision. The oppressed minority of Sephardic Jews, who had come to Israel from the Arab countries, had become a majority. They were a factor in toppling the Labor government, which they felt, correctly, had treated them badly over the years by favoring the Ashkanazi Jews from Europe.

With the right-wing Likud party came a prime minister I had learned to regard in my youth as a terrorist whose followers were thugs. Menachem Begin's Likud had at its core a smaller party called Herut. It was the political manifestation of the Betar movement whose anthem spoke for its ideology, "With blood and sweat we will build a race, benevolent, majestic and cruel."

By the next elections, the changes were becoming visible throughout Israel. What we believed to be a "working democracy" was slowly disappearing, one bit at a time. If you dared to place a bumper sticker for the Labor or any other so-called liberal party on your car, chances were that you would have your car window smashed. And now there were new "Zionist movements" that wanted to annex the territories and spoke of establishing "greater Israel" on all of "the promised lands." The murderous Kahane movement that originated in the United States found fertile soil in Israel.

Suddenly this gathering darkness was penetrated by a ray of hope. Unbelievably, a brave man we had regarded as a monster came from Cairo and turned out to be human and more. What followed the Camp David Accords and the peace with Egypt, however, seemed even more unbearable than what had gone before. We saw settlers from the fundamentalist, right-wing, messianic parties fighting physically with our soldiers, who were evicting them from the Jewish settlements they had established in the Sinai.

Then, in 1982, for the first time we saw clearly an Israeli government entering a war that it had the choice to avoid. Leading that war was the worst of the thugs surrounding the prime minister. I saw Defense Minister Ariel Sharon lying to our allies and to the world when he said he planned only a limited policing action along our northern borders, while I, as a lieutenant commander in the Navy at the time, was planning the assault on Beirut.

Seeing the Lies Up Close

Like seeing the faces of the Arab "enemy" up close, seeing the lies accompanying our wars up close started the erosion of my personal convictions. My country's big lie was followed, again, by a heavy toll of the lives of my countrymen.

By now, however, our youth wanted more than just the expectation of having their names etched on the marble slabs. They wanted life, hope and a future. The Peace Now movement had started in Israel, and it seemed to represent a revival of the pioneer spirit for a time.

By then, however, I was in the Mossad, Israel's foreign intelligence service, seeing firsthand the cold and cynical way in which the course was being charted for the country I loved. My new superiors, having seized much of the control of the ship of state from the politicians, were steering it from behind the scenes to a future their warped instincts told them was good.

Now I became, for the first time, truly terrified, knowing nothing was being done to turn Israel from the disastrous course her self-appointed protectors had set for her.

When Israel was created, it was to be a safe haven for Jewish people anywhere who felt themselves in danger. Yet today, led by still another ex-terrorist, it has embarked on a course that puts its own citizens in great danger.

Yitzhak Shamir's own LEHI terrorist organization, which became known to its British opponents as the "Stern Gang," had requested an alliance with Nazi Germany early in World War II. Its rationale was that since both Israel's revisionists and Hitler's Nazis were fighting the British, their goals were compatible.

Shamir and his followers, from their short-sighted embrace of Nazi Germany to their rejection almost two generations later of the Camp David agreements, have placed the people of Israel in greater danger than any other Jews anywhere else in the world. Shamir's antipathy to peace and his aversion to a just solution based upon U.N. Security Council Resolution 242, again will bring war into the region in the very near future.

To comprehend the kinds of weapons that could be deployed by both sides in such a war is to understand the level of stupidity involved in the taking of such chances with the fate of whole peoples. It becomes meaningless to say that Shamir will be held responsible, as will all of the others who knew better but remained silent.

No Need for More Names

The marble monuments are full. There is no need for more names, and no purpose for more dying. The peace we sought is attainable at last, but our new leaders reject it. Nor is it easy for the Jewish communities in North America to contemplate halting their blind support for Israel. It is not easy for them, even though Israel behaves in ways they would find unacceptable from their own governments. It is not easy for them even though every Jew in the United States and Canada knows that calling a halt is the only way to save Israel from the stranglehold of those who, by actively torturing and abusing the Palestinians, ensure the enmity of all of Israel's Arab neighbors, whose lands these Israeli expansionists also covet.

It is not easy, but it is absolutely necessary, for the Jews in the diaspora to say stop if the expansionists are to be halted. Israel's new leaders know this and they are counting on the diaspora Jews to avoid taking that collectively hard decision, just as they avoid taking the individually hard decision to come and participate in the difficult life of the country they profess to love. My greatest fear for Israel is that the Jews in the diaspora will leave its fate solely in the hands of the hard-eyed expansionists who rule there now. I know what Israel's current rulers still want, and I know what they will do to get it because, for too long, I was one of them myself. ❖

Victor Ostrovsky is a former Mossad case worker who now lives in Canada. He is the author of By Way of Deception *and* The Other Side of Deception, *detailing his experiences in the Mossad, and since leaving it.*

Middle America
Meets Middle East

By Dale Dermott

guess you could call me a stereotypical American guy: I am a WASP, born in Lamar, Missouri—the birthplace of Harry S Truman—and I was raised on meat and potatoes, sports and Christianity. I am a baby boomer and a college graduate. So why do I have a fixation on the Middle East and why do I see things there so differently than do my government and many Americans?

To me, growing up in Middle America, the Middle East meant the Holy Land—Israel—where Jesus lived and walked. I knew of two religions: Christianity and Judaism. People not belonging to either were heathens. I guess that was the essence of the Sunday School lessons I learned as a child.

In 1974, when I was 20, a professor friend of mind—Dr. Robert Cooley—invited me to go on a group study tour of Egypt, Jordan, Syria and Israel. I liked the idea and miraculously came up with $1,300 for the six-week trip. I remember feeling some sort of allegiance to Israel at the time, but I also liked King Hussein of Jordan, because he had an attractive, young American wife, and he was a ham radio operator, like me.

In the Damascus airport one night, I found myself very much drawn to the Syrian people I saw there. They were so joyous, beautiful, and loving. I did not know their language or anything about them, but I wished I could go home with them.

One other night during that trip, a Christian Arab from Haifa spoke to us at our East Jerusalem hotel. He told us how he lost everything when the Israelis kicked him out of his house in 1948. At that point, previous answers were no longer adequate. New images were raised in my mind. A Palestinian could be a Christian; there were people and families in the area before Israel came into existence; I had met a Palestinian who was not a terrorist. All this seems naive now, but it was disturbing new information for me then.

After returning to the United States, I did not meet any more Arabs for several years. I did meet a number of Israeli leaders when, as a radio reporter, I covered news conferences at local Jewish community centers. Like my fellow reporters, I grew weary of asking the succession of Israelis different questions, only to get the same, predictable answers.

My news career took me from Missouri to Oklahoma and eventually, in 1984, to Jacksonville, Florida. One of the first things I do upon moving to a new city is adopt a "hole-in-the-wall" breakfast restaurant, where Dad, Mom and the whole family are all involved in the operation. Such a place in Jacksonville is the Brunch Break. On my second or third visit to the restaurant, owner/cook Karim Hassan came to my booth to greet me. He said he was from Ramallah, Palestine—the very town where my group had dug at an archaeological site in the summer of 1974!

Karim, his family, and the other Arabs I met through him in Jacksonville are the most loyal, giving, and compassionate people I have ever encountered. Recently, when Karim had a heart operation, 57 people were in the waiting room to greet him as he was wheeled out of surgery.

If there is any lesson to be learned from my gradual absorption of Middle East realities, it appears to be this: people make the difference in the way I view the region. I have read thousands of stories and seen hundreds of television reports from the Middle East. When it comes down to what I believe, however, I base my opinions on my face-to-face meetings with people who live or have lived there.

For this reason, I believe that Arab Americans can make a difference. But they must take time and have patience with American friends, who are really attracted by Middle Eastern hospitality, generosity and openness, but who know literally nothing about Arab history or culture, or current Palestinian and Lebanese problems.

I am speaking not just as an American who has "seen the light," but also as a member of the American media: Yes, there is some validity to the charge that U.S. media coverage of Jewish and Israeli affairs is excessive in proportion to their true importance in the world and in the United States, but it is because many Jews seek careers in the media and work hard at being good journalists. Conversely, I have met few Arabs who are journalists or who want to be journalists. While it's nice to have sons and daughters who are doctors or lawyers, why not encourage Arab-American children who want to be journalists? What better way to help Middle Americans like me to understand the real Middle East? ✦

Dale Dermott is a former director of publications for the Arab American Institute in Washington, DC.

Accepting My Ethnicity Meant Applying American Standards Equally

By Nagla El-Bassiouni

or a while I led a double life. My "Arabness" was something of a secret life, away from my school and friends. Other than my weekly lessons in Arabic and Islam, my Arab side was limited to a number of two-week trips to Egypt, my parents' homeland. Somehow, that side of my life was constantly under attack. Value-laden words such as "terrorist" and "fundamentalist" were often equated with being Arab or Muslim.

All of my trips to Egypt followed the same painful pattern. I would get reacquainted with my relatives, fall in love with them, and then have to leave. Heartbreaking as it was, I became used to the routine. But one trip stands out in my mind the most.

It was August, 1974. I was seven years old, and my biggest dilemma was how to get the courage to pull out my semi-loose baby tooth to make room for the new tooth that already had begun to grow in its place. Since I was unable to solve this problem by myself, my parents took the matter into their hands. One of my Egyptian relatives was a dentist. I was to go to her office first thing in the morning.

A Trip to the Dentist

I remember walking down the road in front of my grandmother's house. The heat of the sun made the dust in my sandals turn to mud. I was told that this veiled woman I was accompanying was my aunt. Even though she dressed differently than my mother, their resemblance to each other made me less skeptical. I clutched her hand tightly as we walked across the tram tracks on the way to her dental clinic.

We finally reached the building and made our way up several floors to her office, the heat following us every inch of the way. I sat in the patient's chair while my aunt cleaned her dental equipment. Then a strange man walked up to me and began to talk. I could tell by the way he was dressed that he, too, was a dentist. He smiled at me and asked what seemed like a million questions—what was my name, how old was I, what grade was I in? I could understand his Arabic, but my delayed responses revealed that I wasn't a native speaker.

"You're not from here, are you?" he asked. "Where do you live?"

"America," I responded with a proud smile.

"I don't like Americans," he said. "They're bad people."

I was stunned by his accusation and, with an air of defensiveness, I asked if he had ever been to America. When he said no, I began to regain my confidence. I told him he was wrong. And, if he could meet my friends, he would surely change his mind. He didn't seem convinced. Without a word, he unbuttoned his shirt, revealing a deep scar on his chest. It looked as if someone had thrown a bowling ball at him, leaving a con-cave indentation on his chest.

"This is what Americans did to me in the war!"

I was very frightened by the sight of the wound and asked him if he was sure that it was Americans who had done that to him. He said he was sure. It wasn't until much later that I realized he was referring to the U.S. resupply of Israel in the war of October 1973.

I don't remember if I cried that night, but I think I must have. I don't know what hurt me more—the awful sight of the scar or the accusations that this colleague of my aunt had made. Definitely he affected the way I looked at things, but I would be exaggerat-ing if I said I became "aware" at that point. The only things I was aware of were Satur-day morning cartoons. Still, I never forgot that man.

At different points in my life, this dentist has meant different things to me. More often than not, his story made me defensive in the face of anti-American sentiment in the Arab world. It was humanness, not fundamentalism, that formed his feelings. Any dentist from Jordan, Syria, Lebanon, Iraq or Palestine could have had a similar experience.

In 1989, I spent a year in Cairo researching the Egyptian feminist movement. Aside from the intellectual challenge presented by that topic, my real problem that year was in facing and accepting my own identity. Before spending this year in Egypt, I had inter-nalized the contradictions involved in being an Arab American. Very quickly, I realized that I could not fool myself or fool others into thinking that I was Egyptian. My biggest mistake had been to try to separate, rather than accept, my hyphenated ethnicity.

A Changed Perspective

As a result, my perspective on the Middle East has changed. As a member of American society, I refuse to be defensive about my cultural background. Instead of going into ex-planations or apologetics when the subject of terrorism or fundamentalism arises, I have decided to reverse the argument by questioning our use of such terminology.

All Americans, myself included, should examine critically the path of our foreign policy. Too often, debates on Middle East policy get sidetracked, and American values of political, social and economic freedom are forgotten. For example, the Palestinian-Israeli conflict rarely focuses on the basic issue, which is the right of the Palestinian people to self-determination in their own land. That our nation debated and eventually decided not to talk to the PLO is an excellent example. Such a policy is based upon arrogance, racism and hypocrisy. The message our policy gives to the Palestinians is that 1) the U.S. knows what is best for Palestinians; 2) the U.S. thinks Palestinians are incapable of choosing their own leadership; and 3) until Palestinians allow their Israeli occupiers and the U.S. to choose their leadership, they cannot exercise any of the basic national and human rights we insist upon for ourselves.

The principles of freedom and democracy incorporated in our constitution clearly reject the notion of choosing another people's leadership. Yet, we allow our government to act as if it had that right in the Middle East. For this reason, we owe it to ourselves to subject our own actions, and those of all of our "allies," to the same critical scrutiny we so readily apply to peoples and nations who do not enjoy that status. The situation at home is not so perfect that we should be criticizing others.

It is true that as an Arab I feel a sense of commitment to and compassion for the peoples of the Middle East. However, it was as an American that I questioned spending billions of dollars supporting one brutal occupation in Palestine, and billions of dollars fighting another in Kuwait. It was also as an American that I rejected the hypocrisy of providing housing funds for Soviet Jews in Israel at the same time we ignored the homeless problem in our own country. Finally, it is as an American that I am searching for the response I was unable to deliver to the Egyptian dentist: Why is U.S. policy so anti-Arab? ❖

Nagla El-Bassiouni holds an M.A. in Arab Studies from Georgetown University.

A Lone Voice on a Foreign Beach Now Finds a Thousand American Echoes

By Lawrence S. Helm

If, in the course of an argument, you tell an intelligent person he is slow and ignorant, he will cock an eyebrow and carefully examine your premise. If he can, he will successfully rebut your evidence and finally indicate with a grin, "You see, I am neither slow nor ignorant."

If you make the same observation to someone who is indeed slow and ignorant, he will become frustrated and angry. Having neither the knowledge nor the verbal skills to disprove your statement, he will strike back with hard words or fists. I believe this is the drama that is beginning to be played out in the United States.

I faced this challenge on a beach in Crete in 1976. At 25 years of age, I was very well-informed and politically aware. I read the newspapers every day, whether at work or on holiday. I had read many books concerning geopolitics and the projection of American power.

Then, while soaking up rays, I met a man my age who introduced himself as a Palestinian. I had always enjoyed political discussions because they provided me an opportunity to show people how smart I was.

So when he engaged me on the topic of Palestine I expressed my joy that the Jews finally had found a homeland, and how serendipitous it was that when they arrived the land was virtually uninhabited. He did not accept my judgment. Instead, slowly but relentlessly, he began to deprogram me.

At first I was very offended. Here was an Arab presuming to instruct me about a subject upon which I considered myself especially well-informed. After all, I'd read *Exodus* twice. However, perforce, since we both were there to enjoy the sea and sand, we met every day for about a week. He spoke to me firmly and patiently, as if he were housebreaking a puppy. At the end of the week I realized that I had been fooled—totally. My government was on the side of the bad guys.

The methods used by our own media to trick us are insidious. An Israeli is never killed. He is slaughtered or murdered. We learn his name and details about the family members he leaves behind. Palestinians, however, are shot while throwing stones at "settlers." We see pictures of stones as big as pumpkins that can smash a car and cause its driver to lose control.

Our knowledge of the Holocaust in Europe is encyclopedic. Any American school child has learned that six million Jews were killed in World War II. None know how many American soldiers died in the same war.

We are orchestrated to identify with Zionism starting in Sunday School, and this continues throughout our school years. It is an effortless transition to reading newspapers or watching television as an adult and seeing images of poor put-upon Jews trying vainly to live in peace with malicious and violent Arabs. But now everything is changing for the American public, just as it did for me in 1976.

Once a person with any compassion at all understands the truth about the dispossession of the Palestinians from their homeland, and the motivation behind the great lie invented to obscure this reality, he or she can't leave it alone. I've been in the trenches ever since I saw the light on that sun-drenched beach in Crete. After I returned, no newspapers ever printed my letters, nor did I receive responses from my representatives in Congress. "Normal" people I met casually at parties undoubtedly considered me an obsessed fanatic or a vicious bigot.

Sometimes over the years I got tired of bumping up against the silent walls of indifference and considered giving up. "What's the use," I would think. You can't educate a sack of potatoes.

Then I would read or hear of the bulldozed homes, uprooted orchards and children living briefly and dying violently under occupation. I figured if they could go out for another day to face bullets with stones, I could sit down and write another batch of letters. So I did. But I operated in a vacuum, not knowing that there were other Americans who believed as I did.

It was not until the 1980s that I saw former Congressman Paul Findley on the "Today" show. They wouldn't put the American Educational Trust's number to call for his book on the screen, so he had to say it quickly before he was cut off. I sent for the book, which I'd never heard of and which wasn't available in any bookstore. After I received it, I wasn't alone anymore.

The Trickle Becomes a Flood

Now in the '90s, the trickle of information getting through or around the national media to the American public has become a flood. My letters are regularly printed in the local paper, though I doubt they would be in New York or Washington, DC. Congressmen reply now with half-hearted explanations of why they are spending my money to finance an occupation of which we both disapprove. When Israel or Palestine comes up in conversation, people stop and listen to what I have to say. I shake a copy of the *Washington Report on Middle East Affairs* in the face of anyone who asks me questions.

We will win. But when the giant awakens and is told how long he has been slow and ignorant, will he cock an eyebrow to show he's alert and indicate with a wry grin that he's caught on? Or will he lash out in anger? Those who began this struggle, meaning the *Washington Report*, Paul Findley, and others, bear a special responsibility to prepare for V-Day, giving recognition to the brave Jews who, as individuals or as members of peace groups, sought to dissuade their American co-religionists from the folly of supporting ethnic and religious discrimination and bigotry in Israel. The last thing the rest of us grunts desire is to have to return to the trenches to help a new group of victims of ignorance and bigotry begin a new search for peace and justice in the world. ✦

Lawrence S. Helm is a former Defense Department contractor who now lives in Belfair, Washington.

V. CAMP DAVID AND THE EGYPTIAN-ISRAELI PEACE 1977-1981

"I AM READY TO go to the Israeli parliament itself to discuss peace," President Anwar Sadat said on Nov. 9, 1977. Ten days later he arrived in Tel Aviv to meet with Israeli leaders and address the Knesset. Israeli Prime Minister Menachem Begin made a reciprocal visit to Cairo on Christmas Day. In the ensuing months, however, Begin's intransigence resulted in a stand-off, which American President Jimmy Carter attempted to resolve by calling for a summit at the isolated presidential retreat in Camp David, Maryland. On Sept. 17, 1978, the three leaders signed the Camp David accords, in which Israel agreed to withdraw from the Sinai but refused to make any concessions on Jewish settlements or withdrawal from the West Bank. Egypt, meanwhile, had been isolated by the rest of the Arab world, which objected to a "separate peace" with Israel. The presidency of Jimmy Carter ended with his 1980 election loss, under the cloud of American hostages held in Iran following its 1979 Islamic revolution.

Grandfather Sparks
Interest in Debate
Over Zionism

By Sheldon L. Richman

I have vivid childhood memories of collecting money to plant trees in Israel. I recall as well the frequent accounts provided by Hebrew school teachers of Jewish heroism and devotion in the midst of a hostile sea of Arabs. And I'll never forget the day my school mates and I were taken downtown in 1960 to see the eagerly awaited movie "Exodus."

Mine was a childhood that in large part revolved around Israel. Ben-Gurion, Moshe Dayan and Golda Meir were heroes. My parents, Conservative Jews, were not Zionists; moving to Israel, or seeing their children do so, was unthinkable. But they were loyal Israelists, committed to the Jewish state as necessary for the existence of Judaism and the victims, present and future, of ubiquitous anti-Semitism.

I have another memory, which stands in sharp relief to these pro-Israel images. It is the memory of my paternal grandfather, Sam Richman, a joyous, tolerant Lithuanian Orthodox Jew and a *shomos* (sexton) at a little synagogue. Every Saturday afternoon, after Shabbat services, we'd visit Zadie and Bubby at their apartment. The conversation often would turn to the Middle East. I would sit quietly and listen. There, and only there, did I hear criticism of Israel. I think this became particularly pronounced after the Six-Day War in 1967.

"The Jews in Israel are causing all the trouble," he would say repeatedly. "The Arabs want peace."

My father would counter: "How can you say that? Israel wants peace. It is one little slice of land. The Arabs have so much, but they won't sit down and talk." He would suggest that my grandfather visit Israel and see the situation for himself.

Zadie wouldn't budge. "I will never go," he'd say. Each year, as he led our Passover seder, when he was supposed to say "next year in Jerusalem," he'd improvise with a smile, "next year in Philadelphia." The family always regarded Zadie as the venerable patriarch. But on this issue he was treated as uninformed and stubborn. It was confusing. Little did I know then that he represented an important position in the original

Jewish debate over Zionism. To him Zionism was counterfeit Judaism and the Zionists charlatans. His Orthodox belief held that the re-establishment of Israel was a matter for God in the messianic future. He would have agreed with Yehoshafat Harkabi, a former chief of Israeli military intelligence, who said, "The Jews always considered that the land belonged to them, but in fact it belonged to the Arabs. I would go further: I would say the original source of this conflict lies with Israel..."

At the time of the Six-Day War I was 17 years old. Aside from this one dissenter, I never imagined there was another side to the Israeli-Arab dispute. As I understood it, the Jews had a Biblical and legal right to the land and were eager to live peacefully with the Arabs. But the Arabs hated the Jews because they were Jews. So there was no peace. I don't think I'd heard the word Palestinian.

My parents and teachers sincerely believed what they taught me. They bore no ill will toward the Arabs. But like many of us, they were too busy with their lives to research the question themselves, so they relied on the people they trusted, namely, the Jewish and Israeli leaders, who were Zionists.

In the early 1970s I had stirrings of dissatisfaction with what I had been taught. By then I had adopted the philosophy of classical liberalism (or libertarianism), which sees individual property rights as central to human liberty and justice. I began to wonder how European Jews came to own land in Palestine when an indigenous population lived there. My teachers said the Jews bought the land. That satisfied me at first. Meanwhile, I made two trips to Israel, during the 1973 war and a year later. By this time I was a journalist looking for adventure. I put my reservations on hold.

In 1978 I began hearing the land question discussed and for the first time I came across the argument that most of the land bought by the Zionists was sold by absentee feudal landlords, whose "tenants" were then run off by the purchasers. In my view of property this was illegitimate. According to John Locke, a father of classical liberalism, land is justly acquired by mixing one's labor with it, in the case of unowned land, or by purchase or gift from a legitimate owner. The Turkish and Arab feudal landlords who sold large tracts to the Zionists had acquired the land by conquest or political favor. They were not the real owners and thus they could not transfer title to anyone. The real owners were the people actually working the land: the homesteaders, the Palestinians.

Since my libertarianism puts me on the side of the victims of the state, no matter who they are, I began to understand that the Palestinians were the latest in a long line of groups oppressed by political power. Jews of course have been similarly oppressed in many places; now some Jews, the Zionists, were in the role of oppressor. My childhood view of Israel was unraveling.

I belatedly began investigating the real story of the founding of Israel. I read Elmer Berger's *Memoirs of an Anti-Zionist Jew* and the writings of Alfred Lilienthal, Noam Chomsky, Edward Said and others. I revised my views on the relationship of Judaism and Zionism, on the Arab-Israeli wars, and on the Zionist agenda for Eretz Yisroel. I "discovered" the Palestinians. I became satisfied that what my parents and teachers told me (with the best of intentions) was mistaken and that what Zadie had said was right.

He died in 1974. I'm painfully sorry I didn't know before then what I know now. When I see Palestinian kids beaten and shot by Israelis in the occupied territories, or their homes blown up, I wish I could talk to him. He was a wise man, a prophet unsung (in this matter) in his own land. ✦

Sheldon L. Richman is vice president of policy affairs at The Future of Freedom Foundation in Fairfax, Virginia.

POSTSCRIPT: *As I think about my grandfather today, I marvel at how close our views are on Israel. But our ultimate reasons are opposite. His views were motivated by a religious literalism I do not share. Mine are similar to the Reform rabbis who opposed Jewish nationalism as a distortion of Judaism and a betrayal of liberal values. On religion itself, our views could not be further apart. He was devoutly Orthodox; I am a complete secularist. His authorities were Maimonides and Rashi. I prefer Voltaire and Mencken. Nevertheless, I remain inspired by his passion and his courage to reject the conventional wisdom. He remains a genuine hero.*

Living Among "Typical Israelis"

By Alison J. Glick

How can anyone break the legs of a two-year-old? Or throw tear gas into a maternity ward? Or shoot dead a schoolgirl? Each time I am confronted with questions such as these in conversations about living the past two-and-a-half years in the Israeli-occupied territories, my mind returns to my own experiences in Israeli society.

I lived in Israel for three months in 1980 as a foreign exchange student with what the exchange program promised was a "typical Israeli family." That summer, spent swimming in the Mediterranean and exploring the endless beauty of the country, made for many happy memories. So many years later, however, there are other experiences that also stand out in my mind.

One sticky summer afternoon my "host mother," returning from her job in the industrial sector of Haifa, began complaining about how hot and dirty she felt every day after work. I vividly recall sitting with her at the dining room table, sipping iced coffee together as she explained that there were showers for the workers, but she didn't like to use them.

"Why not?" I asked.

"Because the Arabs use them," she replied quite matter-of-factly, wrinkling her nose in a gesture signifying displeasure, if not disgust.

Hearing her reply, I remember feeling my stomach tighten in a knot. Even as a naive 17-year-old, I recognized racism when it reared its ugly head. Somehow this aspect of Israeli society had been left out of all that I had read and all the newscasts I had watched about Israel, in what I thought was a thorough preparation for my stay.

Later that summer, sitting with neighbors who were listening to a radio news broadcast, I noticed one of them respond quite enthusiastically to a news report in Hebrew, which I could not follow.

When I asked what had happened he informed me, "Four Arabs were killed in a car accident today." Seeing my unenthusiastic response, he explained, "That's good!"

Again I felt my stomach knot.

These comments came not from Kach supporters or other right-wing ideologues, but from middle-class Israelis who were proud Labor Party supporters and who certainly considered themselves moral, upstanding citizens of the state. I was living, as the program had assured me, among typical Israelis.

I have seen that racism against Arabs is an integral part of Israeli culture and society. It provides, in part, the ideological framework for the atrocities committed against Palestinians that the world is just beginning to recognize. One can crush the bones of a child or beat the abdomen of a pregnant woman when one has internalized the prevailing sentiment that the object of your violence is not really human. For a frightening and, I fear, increasing number of Israelis, Arabs are not only not to be showered with; they are, as former Prime Minister Menachem Begin has described them, "beasts with two legs."

Once again, living near the same sea in which I swam as a teenager during that formative and educational summer, I think often of the family with whom I stayed and the "typical" Israelis I met. I think about how I've changed. I wonder if they have changed, and if so, how. I wonder if one day while stepping aside for an army patrol I'll see anyone I recognize. I wonder if they would recognize me. More often, though, I wonder if the Israelis I knew then would recognize themselves now. ✦

Alison J. Glick, in addition to her summer as an exchange student, spent six months in an Israeli kibbutz. She is now the director of International Services at the University of Dayton in Ohio.

Linking the Holocaust and Israeli Abuse of the Palestinians

By Gene Knudsen Hoffman

In 1980 I was walking in London when I saw a huge sign which read: "Meeting for Worship for the Tortured and the Torturers." It was sponsored by the London Quakers. I was astonished. As a Quaker pacifist, I believed that I should have no enemy and care for the wounded on all sides of every battle. But put the torturers on the same level as the tortured? I'd never thought of that.

The thought opened a whole new chapter of my life. I began to wonder why people tortured others. I reasoned that if I could know the answer, it might open new possibilities for peacemaking and reconciliation.

In that same year, I worked on both sides of the Israel-Palestine Green Line, moving back and forth interviewing both Israeli and Palestinian peace people. Though there was no intifada and no stone-throwing children, the suffering of the Palestinians under Israeli occupation was horrifying. What was being done to them seemed madness. I began to wonder whether the brutal treatment of the Palestinians by the Israeli government, the Israeli military, and even many of the Israeli people themselves had anything to do with Jewish suffering during and after the Jewish Holocaust in Europe.

I began reading everything I could find on the subject. As the years went on, I also learned about post-traumatic stress disorder (PTSD)—a tragic condition which can affect soldiers even years after they emerge seemingly unscathed from battle. Triggered by terror from a catastrophic event "outside the range of normal human experience," it can produce a variety of symptoms. These may include depression, isolation, withdrawal, convulsions of rage, emotional numbing, alienation, intrusive thoughts, horrifying flashbacks, a form of hypervigilance akin to paranoia, and more.

Many veterans have used alcohol or drugs to blot out terrifying memories. Many revert to violence when they feel threatened. By now, there may have been more suicides among Vietnam veterans than there were soldiers killed in that long and tragic war.

In the hope of understanding the Israeli-Palestinian conflict more deeply, and of being able to feel compassion instead of anger and despair, I joined an American Friends Service Committee trip to the Middle East in January, 1992. On that trip I learned that there is a new consciousness of the long-term effects of the concentration camp experience on Jewish survivors, for whom there were no healing processes available at the time they were released. Some people are beginning to call it PTSD. Like combat veterans, Holocaust survivors experience both fear of surfacing memories and fear "that it will happen again." Many Israelis appear to be affected by a "siege mentality," which is understandable. Throughout our trip there was no way of forgetting we were in a "war zone."

The suffering of Palestinians is deep and wide. They see the land they call their homeland shrinking and their children dying from malnutrition, disease, and bullets. Many Palestinians are homeless, jobless or both. Palestinian schools are most often closed; there are imprisonments, beatings, killings, daily disappearances. Like soldiers, or the concentration camp inmates of World War II, Palestinians live lives of rage and terror.

Dr. Jan Bastiaans, a Dutch psychiatrist, is an authority on the Holocaust syndrome, and has treated many survivors. In 1973 he wrote, "In recent years the Ka-tzet (concentration camp) syndrome has suddenly received general recognition…This concept is concerned with…pathological processes that occurred after the war in former concentration camp prisoners…The Ka-tzet syndrome is the expression of a permanent, chronic obstruction of sound human relationships. The victims are not free from the concentration camp…Behind their adaptation façade continues to live the child or adult of [that time] in all fear, in all misery, in all powerlessness."

Dr. Haim Dasberg, an associate professor of psychiatry at the Hebrew University and medical director of the Ezrat Nashim Jerusalem Mental Health Center, has written extensively on PTSD and the Israeli army. Now living on the outskirts of West Jerusalem in an apartment pleasingly filled with books, paintings, and Oriental rugs, he resisted conversion efforts by the Christian couple in Holland who adopted him after his father was put into a Nazi concentration camp and his mother went into hiding.

As a therapist for the Israeli military, he encourages battle-shocked soldiers to return to the front because he believes there is no cure for PTSD except the return to community and belonging. "If you leave your comrades in war, you are exiled and cannot function again," he writes.

Dr. Dasberg and three colleagues have written thoughtfully on the psychological disintegration that can follow severe trauma, explaining: "The trauma forces the opening of boundaries [in the sufferer]. This forced, open state and the inability to terminate it is accompanied by intense emotions, immense fears. The usual supports…have been drastically destructured. The final realization is that the rules which define reality are not operational anymore and the individual loses the capacity to function and collapses."

An American-born Israeli, Rabbi Jeremy Milgrom, heads Israel's Clergy for Peace. A tall, slender, compassionate young man, he explains: "The Holocaust has left Jews so scarred we believe powerlessness is a sin. We feel the whole world is hostile to us. This is sick behavior. Our political agenda is irrational because of the Holocaust. Our Jewish state has been implemented at the expense of the Palestinians [partly] because spiritual Zionism changed to statehood after the Nazi persecution. Our agenda is corrupt because we're not permitting the Palestinians to reunify. We Jews feel guilt toward the Palestinians and we're unwilling to have a dialogue with them because it will be so unpleasant."

An Israeli psychiatrist, who wished to remain anonymous, warned me that "It is very dangerous to suggest that our people in government still suffer from the Holocaust. They are our government, our leaders—they cannot be crazy." Pressed as to whether these leaders "suffer from PTSD," he responded, "Holocaust survivors do not suffer from PTSD. But they have similar symptoms."

Chaim Shur, the generous, gentle editor-in-chief of Israel's liberal *New Outlook* magazine, explained: "The Holocaust is the worst trauma in Jewish history. The whole world was killing us. No one did anything to prevent it. The Holocaust syndrome invades a large part of our life. Five hundred thousand people in Israel are Holocaust survivors and now there is a second generation..." The editor demurred, however, when asked, "Do survivors suffer from PTSD?"

"PTSD is not a scientific diagnosis," he said. "I have a daughter-in-law who comes from Holocaust survivors. I don't accept it."

Dr. Eliezer Witztum, senior psychotherapist at the Ezrat Nashim Hospital, who wrote a book entitled *The History of PTSD and the Israeli Army*, said PTSD was denied in every Israeli war, including the 1973 war, and all PTSD data was edited out of psychological papers.

"PTSD sufferers were treated as cowards," he explained. "Officers and mental health workers were told that if they recognized this phenomenon, they should not encourage it...But, in 1973, 30 percent of the casualties were PTSD sufferers and the military began to admit this was a problem. However, in 1982, they withdrew their admission and cut the budgets for psychiatrists."

Dr. Witztum said that although Israelis generally felt "the Holocaust was a Pandora's box and it was better not to talk about it," he believes there is a direct connection between the Holocaust and much of the subsequent tragic Israeli political behavior regarding the Palestinians. He spoke of Israel's loss of her spiritual connection and believes it must be regained before healing and peace can take place.

Today some of the most cogent voices about PTSD and the Holocaust are coming from the United States. In Rabbi Yonassan Gershom's article "Breaking the Cycle of Abuse" in the February, 1992, issue of the *Washington Report on Middle East Affairs*, he writes, "On a conscious level the Israelis are not purposely punishing the Palestinians for the Holocaust...But it is also true that people who have been abused will, when they come to power, abuse others because they do not have healthy models for exercising power. Abuse is passed down from generation to generation...unless there is some kind of therapy to teach new ways of coping with frustration and anger."

In an article entitled "Terrible Knowledge" in the November-December *Networker*,

Jeffrey Jay extends PTSD not only to Holocaust and war survivors, but also to survivors of severe child abuse and uncontrollable rage and violence in some families.

"Some great individuals like Martin Luther King Jr., Elie Weisel, and peace activist Thich Nhat Hanh lived through brutalization and drew from it visionary insights that have moved whole populations to greater compassion for human suffering," Jay writes. "These exemplars…suggest the possibility of return from exile for victims of trauma… Their terrible knowledge is a message few can afford to refuse."

Thomas Greening, editor of the *Journal of Humanistic Psychology*, writes: "The moral, philosophical, and religious context in which [a trauma's] meaning is interpreted by the sufferer is very important. Viktor Frankel wrote of his concentration camp experience in 1963: 'Human values are sometimes sustained and recreated in dehumanizing conditions.'"

I believe that America's Henry Wadsworth Longfellow summarized best what, challenged by that sign in London in 1980, I have learned from my own exploration of the link between the Holocaust and Israel's brutalization of the Palestinians: "If we could read the secret history of our enemies, we would find in each person's life sorrow and suffering enough to disarm all hostility." All efforts at finding a solution to the Israeli-Palestinian dispute, I have concluded, will be more fruitful when the parties come to see peacemaking as a healing process. It is as necessary to traumatized peoples and nations as it is to individuals subjected to fear, rage or pain "outside the range of normal human experience." ✦

Gene Knudsen Hoffman, author of four books, holds an M.A. in pastoral counseling. She has created a Compassionate Listening project which takes groups to areas of conflict to listen to all sides of the dispute and, in conjunction with The Fellowship of Reconciliation, plans to take a group of American Jewish leaders to Israel/Palestine in October, 1997.

A Commitment to Truth

By Glen Allen

My first inkling that there are groups in this country that abuse the political process regularly whenever the interests of Israel are concerned came nearly 20 years ago, when I was a teenager growing up in Grand Junction, Colorado. Our congressman at that time was James Johnson.

In the late 1960s, as I recall, Johnson incurred the wrath of certain local Jewish groups for not voting as they wished on some issue that affected Israel. Spearheading the local attack was novelist Leon Uris, who lived in Aspen. I understood the issues only dimly, but I understood the emotions that followed very well. Johnson, half-apologetic if somewhat diffident, sought by all means to avoid the label "anti-Semite." Uris, rancorous and aggressive, attacked on behalf of Israel with a vehemence that seemed clearly disproportionate for one who, after all, was a citizen of the United States, not of the country whose interests he was advancing so stridently. That incident started me thinking.

Another thing happened about then, too. An interview with an alumnus was part of the application process for Colorado College, which I later attended. My interview was with a highly respected local banker in Grand Junction. During that interview the conversation turned to the major topic on all university campuses at that time: the war in Vietnam. The banker, in an offhand way, remarked upon how patently inconsistent it seemed to him that many of the same groups actively opposing the Vietnam War simultaneously supported Israeli military actions in the Middle East. Initially, I was appalled at the comparison. Yet, as I thought about his remark off and on for the next decade, I came to see that the man was right.

There is perhaps a lesson in this. Sometimes our remarks on controversial questions may seem to have no effect on our listeners. And yet, if our remarks contain truth, like dormant seeds they may take root and grow long afterward.

The progress of my thought in this area for the next decade was a classic case of cognitive dissonance. It is odd that a person can believe that pro-Israel organizations present a false picture of the Middle East, intimidate critics, in essence bribe Congress, and set a pernicious self-serving example for other American ethnic groups, and yet simultaneously believe that Israel is a valiant, peace-loving democracy surrounded by bellicose

Arab fanatics, that it shares and supports American values and is a true ally. But this described my state of mind. It also, I believe, describes the state of mind of a great many Americans today.

Cognitive Dissonance

My cognitive dissonance began to be cured about 1981, when I first learned of the USS *Liberty* incident. If any day ever deserves to live in infamy, it is June 8, 1967. I was convinced then and I am even more certain now, after having studied the matter, that the Israeli attack on a virtually defenseless U.S. Navy vessel in which 34 Americans were killed and another 110 wounded was deliberate, and the subsequent U.S. government cover-up was undertaken with the knowledge that the attack was deliberate.

The USS *Liberty* incident opened my eyes once and for all to the distortions present on many critical issues, especially those involving the Middle East, in the major American media. This realization imparted a degree of unreality to my subsequent law school studies. Perhaps this new clarity with which I approached the theory and practice of law in the United States is one reason that I did very well in law school. I studied First Amendment doctrine with great care. When I compared the law with its real life application, it reaffirmed my conclusion that, in the real world, First Amendment principles are subordinate to the biases of major advertisers, who may withdraw their advertising if a newspaper or television or radio network or station does not properly tailor its news and views.

Most Americans—including most law students—have yet even to recognize these problems, much less cope with them. We must cope with them, however, if freedom of the press and of expression are to retain any real meaning. No truly free people let themselves be lied to by their government, or manipulated by their major media. Supporting independent publications such as the *Washington Report on Middle East Affairs,* I am convinced, is one positive step we can take. Seeking out truly independent candidates prepared to lead rather than follow the dictates of special interests is another.

My instincts are basically patriotic, but ever since leaving the army, I have been unable to suppress a large measure of cynicism whenever any political figure invokes patriotic symbols rather than discussing real issues.

Maybe Dr. Johnson was right when he exclaimed, "Patriotism is the last refuge of a scoundrel." I am today convinced that no true patriot—and no honest American—can avoid speaking out against the increasingly despotic grip of pro-Israel special interest groups on American foreign policy in the Middle East. ✦

Glen Allen practices law in Baltimore, MD.

An Interest in Middle East Events Turns Into a Quest for Truth

By Laura Drake

It was January, 1981, at the climax of the Iranian hostage crisis. The release of the hostages seemed imminent, the voices of the nightly newscasters euphoric. Bright yellow ribbons displayed on the antennas of thousands of cars around the nation symbolized the shared outrage at the Iranian action, and the shared American hope that the hostages might finally come home.

In the middle of all this, a new president was about to be inaugurated to take the place of the unfortunate Jimmy Carter, whose re-election campaign had been crippled by an aura of impotence in dealing with Iran's relentless ayatollah. At age 16, these events were enough to transform me from an apathetic high school student into an individual suddenly interested in the world around me.

After the hostages returned physically unharmed, my interest in the region not only did not subside, but grew stronger. As I watched the nightly television news, I began to observe variations in how the news was selected and reported. Reports and pictures filled our screens of oppression by tyrannical regimes—in South Africa, the Philippines and, of course, Iran. People seeking freedom were being harassed, imprisoned, and tortured, by the cruel, self-important dictators under whom they lived.

Two Sides to Every Issue—Except Palestine

But then there was Palestine. To me, the situation there seemed similar to that in many other parts of the world. Yet our news media, without exception, depicted Palestinians not as oppressed, but as terrorists. For some reason I did not yet understand, Palestinians were being treated differently by the news media. These were the same media which acknowledged that there were two sides to every issue—except the issue in Palestine.

Israeli government actions, which struck me as analogous to those of any other repressive government, were instead portrayed as part of the heroic resistance of a tiny nation under a constant state of siege. Israel's enemies were barbaric Arab states, populated by faceless, bloodthirsty terrorists. The state of Israel had been proclaimed in 1948, but our media gave the impression that it had endured senseless, incessant warfare since biblical times.

It did not take me too long to discover that the modern state of Israel was in fact created on land stolen from an Eastern people in order to right a wrong that had been committed by one Western people against another. My own sense of justice, however, could not accept punishing one party for the crimes of another. It slowly dawned on me that the U.S. media has delegitimized the Palestinian-Arab liberation struggle by attaching to it a label that inspires universal horror and condemnation: terrorism.

I set out to learn why. By the middle of my senior year, after many long hours in the city library, I had not only "seen the light," but found myself obsessed with the idea that the truth must come out. To symbolize my personal commitment, I made a Palestinian flag out of cardboard and hung it in my locker at school. At this point I was 17 years old and only one event away from becoming a political activist.

From Knowledge to Political Activism

That event was the Israeli invasion of Lebanon. I graduated from high school on June 5, 1982, the day before the invasion. After the ceremony, I went home to watch the news reports of Israeli troops massing on the Lebanese border. Three days later I was at my first demonstration. A month later I was on public radio denouncing the invasion, and reporting news for the Arab Radio Program in San Francisco.

My horror at U.S. inaction during the initial weeks of the invasion was only exceeded at summer's end. Then, after the PLO evacuated Beirut under a pledge of U.S. protection for the families they were leaving behind, Israeli forces moved into West Beirut and provided cover for the massacres by Lebanese militiamen of those same Palestinian families at the Sabra and Shatila refugee camps.

I began to dream of going to Jerusalem in order to better understand the Palestinian situation. Two years later, on a hot, humid summer evening in 1984, I stepped off a plane onto the tarmac of Ben-Gurion airport in Lydda. It was, without question, the most emotional moment of my life.

My year-long stay in Palestine just confirmed what I already believed—that the Palestinian people have the right to be free and independent in their own country and to combat the Israeli effort to erase the Arab character and identity, and even the people themselves, from that land. I witnessed the daily humiliations faced by the Palestinians who are allowed to live in their own country. I felt their sadness at the fact that the greater number of their compatriots continue to live in forced exile.

I even experienced personally a small dose of Israeli repression. I was awakened from a sound sleep by four Israeli soldiers at my doorstep. From my apartment I was taken to the Moscobiyyah detention center in Jerusalem, where I was made to stand in blazing sunlight along with dozens of Palestinians to find out why they had taken me.

All I had to show them was the paper the soldiers had given me, stating my name and religious status—in their words, "minority." I was told I had been summoned by the military government. Then I underwent a half-day interrogation by a man who said he was from the Shin Bet and had come up from Tel Aviv. I was threatened with physical harm and with deportation, and was finally released at about 4 p.m. For the rest of my stay I was subjected to various forms of harassment, ending with a humiliating four-hour search at the airport on the day of my departure.

Since then, I have earned an M.A. in international affairs and have spent time in several Arab countries. More than ever, I am driven to work for a change in U.S. public opinion. The children of the intifada, through their courage and sacrifice, have begun this process, enabling thousands of Americans finally to "see the light." I believe that it is the duty of each of us who has finally penetrated to the truth of this matter to help our fellow Americans complete the same journey. When they do, the Palestinians can be liberated from tyranny, and Americans from the falsehoods that sustain it. ❖

Laura Drake is a Middle East specialist in Washington focusing on the strategic affairs of the Levant and northern Gulf.

My Second Visit to Israel Made a World of Difference

By Tom Kinsolving

Probably the first introduction I had to the Middle East's most contentious issue was in 1966, when my parents took me to see the film "Cast a Giant Shadow." It was one of those blockbuster films, like "Exodus," designed to promote the Zionist cause. Israelis were portrayed as valiant warriors struggling against bloodthirsty Arabs.

Years later, in a library, I came across a little book entitled *Myths & Facts*. It was the annual propaganda manual published by the American Israel Public Affairs Committee (AIPAC) that provided all the "answers" to questions on the Arab-Israeli conflict. Like "Cast a Giant Shadow" and "Exodus," the reality of the diaspora—Palestinian, that is— was glossed over with clever rationale:

The Jews who suffered the Holocaust were desperate for their own state. Instead of compromising, the Arabs attacked. The Jews defended their ancient birthright and won. As for the existence of Palestinian refugees, Arab intransigence bore sole responsibility.

It was convincing. Then.

In 1976, when I was 19, I visited Israel for the first time with my father, a journalist. Our three-day visit was brief, but it left a vivid impression. As official guests of the Israeli government, we were given the red carpet treatment.

The Lebanese civil war was in full swing. With the PLO embroiled in the fighting in and around Beirut, Israel's northern border was quiet. Our guide, an Israeli officer, took us to see "The Good Fence," situated on the Israeli-Lebanese border.

"The Good Fence," he said, featured a mobile hospital to serve suffering Lebanese civilians. I saw women and children being attended by Israeli military teams. My predictable reaction: How nice of Israel to help the people of Lebanon.

Another vivid recollection of that first trip was a statement by our Israeli guide. Conditioned by the media's myopic reporting of the Palestinian struggle, I had asked why the PLO resorted to terrorism (I neglected to probe the issue of Israeli terrorism). The Israeli gave an answer worthy of print in *Myths & Facts*.

"They have little regard for human life."

Certainly.

Five years later, in 1981, I returned to Israel for two months. This time I was not an official guest of the Israeli government, but was there as a journalist myself. I spent a month living on a kibbutz near the Gaza Strip. In late December, I left the kibbutz to celebrate Christmas Eve in Bethlehem.

Cold, windy and rainy weather, military checkpoints, inebriated tourists, and heavily armed Israeli soldiers everywhere were not conducive to spirituality.

I was accompanied by a British friend, Eammon, whom I had met on the kibbutz. After attending a service at a little Jesuit church called the Milk Grotto, we began walking up one of the narrow Bethlehem streets that would take us back to a bus for Jerusalem. We turned a corner and witnessed a dramatic juxtaposition. There standing in line on a sidewalk was a small group of Israeli soldiers, aiming their automatic rifles in the air. Simultaneously, a group of six nuns appeared, walking single file along the same sidewalk.

Eammon tore open his knapsack, digging furiously for his camera. As the soldiers continued to aim their guns toward a Bethlehem rooftop, the nuns began to pass by, stoically, one by one. Eammon got to within yards of the scene and was about to get an incredible photograph when one of the soliders broke rank and rushed toward my friend.

"NO PICTURE!" growled the Israeli soldier. Though he spoke little English, he sensed Eammon's defiance.

Eammon refused to back down. The Israeli was becoming enraged.

"PASSPORT!" demanded the Israeli.

Yes, it was a bit different than being an official government guest, this trip. I began to understand the helplessness of Palestinians under harassment and occupation.

The soldier scrutinized the British passport, and, after a lot of glaring, released us. Had we been Palestinians, we might have been subjected to far rougher treatment.

Although, upon my return to the United States, I published an article about that night in Israeli-occupied Bethlehem, I still did not fully comprehend the essentials of the Palestinian-Israeli conflict—until I was able to study them in graduate school in California from 1983-1986. By the time I completed my master's thesis on the 1982 Israeli invasion of Lebanon, I had learned, among other things, about the following:

•During the British Mandate, between 1922-1939, the Jewish National Fund purchased over 383,000 acres of land in Palestine. Palestinian tenants and workers were consequently evicted from this acreage which, under Jewish National Fund rules still valid today, could not be resold to any Arab, nor could it be used to provide employment for non-Jews. The Palestinians were disinherited.

•When the United Nations approved the Palestine Partition Plan in 1947, the Muslim and Christian Palestinians outnumbered Jewish residents by two-to-one, and the Jews owned less than seven percent of the land. However, the partition proposal gave the Jewish one-third of the population 53 per cent of the land and placed nearly a half million Palestinians under Zionist rule. The Palestinians were disenfranchised.

•In April, 1948, the Palestinian village of Deir Yassin, near Jerusalem, was attacked by a contingent of Irgun and Stern Gang Jewish terrorists, whose leaders included future Israeli prime ministers Menachem Begin and Yitzhak Shamir. More than 250 Palestinians, nearly half of them women and children, were murdered. When the news of the Deir Yassin massacre reached other Palestinian communities, a panic ensued, causing mass flight. The Palestinians were terrorized out of their country.

With all of this in mind, is it any mystery that some Palestinians have resorted to terrorism? Forty-one years after their diaspora began and after 22 years of Israeli military occupation, Palestinians continue to struggle for their rights, so unjustly denied.

Yes, it is incumbent upon the civilized world never to forget the Nazi Holocaust and the suffering of the Jews. Nevertheless, it is no less imperative that we recognize that using the Holocaust to justify dispossessing and persecuting the Palestinian people is morally reprehensible.

Cast a giant shadow—of shame. ❖

Tom Kinsolving is the advertising representative for the Manassas Journal Messenger, *a daily newspaper in northern Virginia in existence since 1869.*

POSTSCRIPT: The U.S. government responded justly to repel the aggression of a brutal Iraqi attempt to subjugate and destroy the Kuwaiti nation. The tragic irony is that this same government that so loudly abhors such aggression continues to subsidize—with our tax dollars—the ongoing oppression of the Palestinian nation. U.S. Congress members should be ashamed of themselves.

If Terrorists Ran All the Governments, What Would Become of Us?

By Marianne Snowden

My first visit to the Holy Land was in 1981, and I went as a Charismatic Christian filled with teachings about the "miracle" of the re-birth of Israel. The preachers had, and have, much to say about this "fulfillment of prophecy." I believed it. I believed that the only people to be considered in this matter were the Jews.

I have been told by my Christian Arab friends that the Jews were indeed the chosen people. "They were chosen to bring the Messiah, and they have done that," these Christian Arabs said. "Now it is we who are chosen." Meanwhile, over several years, I made repeated visits to the Holy Land, although I could never be there much longer than a month. Muslims and Christians took me into their homes and welcomed me as a friend. To my surprise, I concluded that the Christians now are the most persecuted people in the Holy Land!

In the spring of 1988, just before and during my stay there, two Anglican churches were desecrated and burned (one of them twice) by occupying Israeli soldiers. One church is on the West Bank, the other is in Jerusalem. I saw the newspaper article posted at St. George's Cathedral.

Back home, besides worrying about my friends, I think about the fact that the headwaters of the Jordan, and subsequently the Galilee and the Dead Sea, originate in land Israel has seized from Syria. These waters later flow through parts of the Israeli-occupied West Bank. Israeli Prime Minister Yitzhak Shamir is currently demanding annexation of "certain strategic places" before considering any peace talks.

I would be surprised if the "strategic places" do not include these headwaters, which encompass a waterfall that challenges Black Water Falls in West Virginia for beauty and drama. It is Banias, in the Golan Heights, a favorite hiking area of the Israelis.

In the desert areas of the world, whoever holds the water source has the power. One way our friends are being subjected is by being denied the use of sufficient water. As the water table drops, they are not allowed to deepen their wells. If they try, their wells are destroyed.

My closest friend in the Holy Land was the Palestinian guide we had on my first visit. I went back 18 months after the pilgrimage that had taken me there the first time. When I met him on the street and he recognized me, I was delighted and surprised. He introduced me to his sister, now one of my dearest friends. As time went on, I met more of his family and friends, and I came to know a group of people who are lovely, hospitable, friendly, helpful, kind, and fun to be with. I came to know both worlds, the men's world and the women's world.

I think my most shocking discovery in 1981 was that the Anglican hospital in Nablus was waiting for a shipment of surgical instruments and other medical supplies which had already arrived in Israel. However, the hospital couldn't come up with the required customs duties Israel had levied on these supplies, so they could not be delivered. When the Turks ruled the area, I was told, they did not tax medical supplies.

On my second trip to Jerusalem, I stayed in a one-star hotel outside the Old City, and knew only the land agents and people I'd met on that first trip 18 months earlier. We were barely acquainted but they remembered me. My new friends love Americans, but they are deeply hurt by the lack of consideration they receive from our government.

I firmly believe that our government ignores the fact that Christians and Muslims are not accorded the same human rights as Jews in all of the Holy Land because our political leaders are afraid of the Israeli government. I also believe that our fundamentalist preachers have caused this. These preachers say that we must not turn "against" Israel, or we will be doomed along with the rest of the world!

Of course we all feel somewhat guilty about the Holocaust. How can you fail to, when you have been told over half your life that we deserted Europe's Jews in their hour of need? Forget that we knew nothing about it. We were and are guilty. It seems the whole world is kept in thrall with that accusation of collective guilt. But now apparently the same crime is all right when the former victim becomes the persecutor. Are all the rest of us eventually to be accused of guilt for letting this happen again?

I call the neighbor of my friends nearly every week just to find out if they are all right. I believe that the stonethrowing will be permitted only so long, and then I fear there will likely be a bloodbath instigated by Israel's extremist leaders. The late Meir Kahane, Ariel Sharon and Yitzhak Shamir are three reasons I have no use for the Israeli government. If terrorists ran all the governments in the world, as they do in Israel, what on earth would become of us all? ✦

In 1989, Marianne Snowden was a secretary in Maryland.

Discovering the Palestinians

By Deane Tack

"**A**nd who are the Palestinians?" This was the question I asked an Arab-American acquaintance over 10 years ago after he had explained that he was a Palestinian. I had ambivalent feelings as he told of his people being driven from their homeland by the Israelis, who massacred entire villages and appropriated their land. Surely the Western world would have heard of such atrocities had they actually occurred. We were only aware of the heavy role of the Palestinian "terrorists," who received sufficient headline coverage and TV exposure to persuade the American public of the pervasive violent nature of all Palestinians. Most of us had accepted the terms "Palestinian," "PLO" and "terrorists" as being synonymous.

Since I don't condone violence as a solution to any problem, I asked my friend to provide some information that would be helpful in reconciling my mixed concepts of the Palestinians, and my skepticism at his accounts of such monumental injustices that it seemed impossible that they could have occurred in my lifetime without coming to my attention.

"Haven't you ever heard of Deir Yassin?" he asked incredulously.

I had to admit I was totally unfamiliar with the small Palestinian Arab village which he explained as being symbolic of the martyrdom of Palestinians by the Israelis. The details of this particular massacre of some 250 men, women and children on April 9, 1948, were so appalling and repugnant that I had a tinge of doubt regarding their authenticity.

A Search for the Facts

Only if I researched the situation and discovered the bare, unvarnished truths for myself could I actually accept them. I was chagrined to realize that I, a retired schoolteacher, was relatively ignorant of issues involved in the Middle East conflict.

As I began researching the subject in 1981, I found that scarcely any books were available in the public library to provide the enlightenment I sought. After writing to Arab-oriented foundations and individuals to whom I was referred, I soon acquired a sizeable, well-documented resource of books, magazines, pamphlets and journals.

As I delved into the fascinating, yet incredible, fund of information, I was impelled to share it with everyone I knew. When I tried to explain that the Deir Yassin massacre was carried out by two separate Jewish militias, one organized by and responsible to Menachem Begin, and the other by Yitzhak Shamir, both of whom subsequently became prime ministers of Israel, I met with skepticism similar to that with which I had at first reacted. The only way to break through the resistance of the American public, I concluded, was to write a suspense-filled novel which supplied documented statistics and authenticated circumstances through the dialogue and dynamics of fictional characters. After three years of research and writing, the epic of an oppressed and homeless nation emerged as a novel, *The Palestinian*, subsequently published by Amana Books.

In my empathy for the Palestinians, I gave the characters of my novel the human dimensions of love, passion and loyalty, as well as hatred, thereby balancing the stereotyped version usually shown. The friendship of the Palestinian protagonist with a Jewish family in the U.S. serves to depict the central conflict as being between the Palestinians and Zionists, not with Jews per se.

With the expansion of my understanding of the Middle East conflict and its background, I have sought to share my information by appearing on radio talk shows and speaking to church groups and literary clubs.

The Other Side of the Coin

So that readers may see "the other side of the coin," I have also donated 12 books to our local library, including *They Dare to Speak Out, Journey to Jerusalem* and *Assault on the Liberty*.

Although I'm a non-Arab, I am contributing as much as I can toward disseminating truth about the Palestinian dilemma. Reader response to my novel, to my surprise, has been rewarding, rather than hostile. Through it and through the many resulting contacts and activities, I am seeking to stimulate the open-minded response and further desire in others to search for equity and peace in the Middle East. I know, whatever the initial reactions, this is possible because that response and that desire were awakened in me by one individual who took the trouble to "share the light" only six years ago, and in doing so changed the whole focus of my life. ✦

Deane Tack was a retired schoolteacher living in Oregon when he wrote his novel, The Palestinian, *which is available from the American Educational Trust Book Club. He died in November, 1996.*

Taking a Second, Informed Look at Israel's Tribulations

By William Lord

I f the Israelis had lost the Six-Day War of June, 1967 against the Arabs, I would have
shed tears of anguish. Jews, I believed, deserved a homeland. In World War II, two
members of my infantry intelligence and reconnaissance platoon were Jews. They
were brave and trusted soldiers and we were together when, at war's end in Europe, a
rabbi came to our barracks and described the ruthless work of the Nazi death chambers
as we listened in horror.

Back home, I completed my final two years of college on an urgent schedule that allowed "no time for anything but classes." I was proud of the U.S. role in the creation of
the state of Israel in 1948. We Americans remembered the Holocaust.

In 1960 I saw the movie "Exodus." I marveled at the courage of the Jewish fighters
and their compassion for the defeated Arabs as depicted in the film. "Please come back,"
an Israeli said to a group of Arabs fleeing their country.

I read a review of the movie and was angered that the writer referred to it as shameless Israeli propaganda. I accepted without question the pro-Israeli bias of our media to
which the reviewer was referring.

In June, 1967, like most Americans, I cheered the valor and pluck of tiny Israel. Small
wonder since, as the U.S. media depicted it, Israel had successfully turned back a combined Arab onslaught.

I'm certain, however, that my attitude would have changed had I realized that it was
Israel, not Egypt and Syria, that had launched the surprise attacks on June 5 and had President Johnson acknowledged, and our media reported, the hour-long Israeli attack on the
USS *Liberty* on June 8, killing 34 crewman and wounding 171. Many Americans are just
now becoming aware of the true stories, so long subjected to cover-up and fabrication.

In 1973 the Yom Kippur War initiated by the Arabs against Israel rather surprised me.
Why wouldn't the Arabs let tiny Israel have a homeland? I didn't read in the U.S. media
the statement by the presidents of Egypt and Syria that they were fighting only on their
own Israeli-occupied territories in Sinai and the Golan Heights, and that their goals were

solely to recover these lost territories, not to attack Israel.

Then a Jewish friend asked me, in exasperation, "How long do we have to keep fighting these wars?" Although I nodded in sympathy, his use of the pronoun "we" in reference to Israel and its tribulations surprised me.

Where did his primary allegiance lie? If it lay with Israel, was it possible that some of my fellow Americans, with similarly divided loyalties, were presenting a slanted or biased picture of Israel's seemingly unending problems with its Arab neighbors? Were "Exodus," the book and the film, in fact "shameless Israeli propaganda," as that reviewer had suggested in 1960?

I began to consider the Arab side of it. They, too, believed they were fighting for their homeland. If the Arabs were living there when the Israelis arrived, was it possible that it wasn't just the Israelis who had "made the desert bloom"? And, in that case, whose land was it, really? I was beginning to see the light.

In 1974 Yasser Arafat addressed the U.N. He described a vision for a future Holy Land where Jews, Christians and Muslims would live in peace and equality. It reminded me of Martin Luther King's "I have a dream" speech made in 1963, beneath the shadow of the Lincoln Memorial, where he envisioned children of all races and creeds walking hand in hand.

The media hailed Reverend King as an American prophet of peace and tolerance. Arafat was reviled as a Palestinian terrorist.

If I needed a clincher for my about-face on the Middle East, it was the 1982 Israeli invasion of Lebanon, and the mass slaughter of defenseless Lebanese civilians in their towns and cities and of Palestinians in their refugee camps.

I now see Israel as a Zionist creation that has only succeeded in transplanting Jews from other countries by displacing an equal number of native Palestinians. The Zionists have twisted the horror of the Holocaust in Europe into a rationale for their own seizure of other people's lands and homes and even their nationality in the Middle East. Now, as Israel negotiates to keep as many of those lands and homes as possible, I hope that fewer and fewer Americans will offer their blind and mindless support, as I once did.

Instead, let there be increased dialogue in the media about the wisdom of U.S. aid to Israel, which, it appears to me, is not an incentive to make peace, but a subsidy for a brutal military occupation. And let Americans finally call to account the members of Congress who for so long have abused their constituents' trust by condoning this flagrant misuse of American political and financial support. ❖

William Lord, a retired veterinarian, is a member of the Council for the National Interest from Pittsburgh, PA.

The "Israel Can Do No Wrong" Attitude

By John P. Egan

I first became aware of the "Israel can do no wrong" attitude when I attended hearings before the Senate Foreign Relations Committee in the summer of 1981. I was an intern at the State Department at the time, and although I had no specialized knowledge of the Middle East, I noticed that developments in the region were featured more or less consistently on the front page of *The Washington Post*.

Throughout that spring, Syrian-Israeli tensions mounted, culminating in a series of Israeli attacks against Syrian missile batteries in Lebanon. In early June the Israeli air force destroyed a nuclear reactor in Iraq, claiming that it was nearly ready to produce nuclear weapons for use against the Jewish state. Shortly thereafter, Menachem Begin's Herut Party won re-election in Israel. And in July the Israeli air force bombed some residential areas of Beirut, killing scores of civilians. When the PLO responded by shelling northern Israel, the Israeli air force increased its bombing raids in Lebanon. The carnage and death were only stopped when President Ronald Reagan dispatched Philip Habib, his special envoy, to the Middle East to broker the cease-fire between Israel and the PLO that lasted until the Israeli invasion of Lebanon one year later.

During that fateful summer of 1981 I occasionally went to Capitol Hill, eager to walk in the famed "corridors of power." On this particular day, I found the Senate Foreign Relations Committee hearing room and settled in for what I hoped would be an interesting afternoon: testimony was to be given on Israel's bombing of the Iraqi nuclear reactor.

I don't remember much that was said that afternoon—many of those testifying were scientists, and they disagreed over whether the Iraqi reactor was designed primarily for peaceful uses, or as a factory for nuclear weapons. However, I do remember that one senator—later I would learn that it was Alan Cranston of California—seemed particularly prominent throughout the hearing. He had brought several witnesses to testify, and he asked each to discuss, often at great length, the potential military uses of the Iraqi nuclear reactor. Eventually, contending that Iraq had spent billions of dollars building the reactor to manufacture nuclear weapons for use against Israel, Cranston announced the

Iraqi President Saddam Hussain was to blame for Israel's attack. After all, if Iraq hadn't built the reactor, Israel wouldn't have had to destroy it.

When I returned to college, I took courses on Middle East history and politics. I was particularly intrigued by the PLO and the history of the Israeli-Palestinian problem. Very early in my research I found that a wide-ranging consensus on the Israeli-Palestinian conflict existed in the U.S. print media, stretching from ostensibly "liberal" publications like the *New Republic* to the conservative *Wall Street Journal*. Both publications, and more or less everything in between, were deeply hostile to the PLO and strongly supported Israel and the Zionist movement.

This tendency revealed itself more clearly the following year, when Israel invaded Lebanon. With only a handful of exceptions—including an important op-ed article in *The New York Times* by Israeli journalist Danny Rubinstein—the mainstream press didn't ask why Israel invaded Lebanon. Instead, there was much talk of "hot pursuit" and the need to "cleanse terrorist nests."

Those who pointed out that Israel was killing civilians with U.S.-supplied arms were vilified by Israel's supporters in America. Norman Podhoretz, editor of the American Jewish Committee's magazine *Commentary,* and Martin Peretz, editor of the *New Republic,* turned reality on its head by charging that the Palestinians were to blame for their fate: if they weren't in Beirut, then they wouldn't have been killed by Israeli soldiers. Although the U.S. government said it "deplored the continuing cycle of violence in Lebanon," it vetoed U.N. Security Council resolutions designed to halt the Israeli invasion.

Nevertheless, night after night that bloody summer, the television news shows presented horrifying film footage of Israel's siege of West Beirut. As one who had waited for such coverage of what was really happening in the Middle East, I was astonished to hear, from Israel's partisans in America, that such network news presentations were part of the "new anti-Semitism."

Finally, there was the massacre at the Sabra and Shatila refugee camps, carried out by Lebanese Maronite militiamen after Israeli troops occupied West Beirut, where the camps were located, and prevented the camp occupants from escaping. Some people remember exactly where they were and what they were doing when President John F. Kennedy was killed; I will always remember the fund-raising events I attended when those terrible massacres were first reported. The photos from Sabra and Shatila made me physically sick: how could human being carry out such atrocities, I asked somewhat naively. And, how many more times must Palestinians be massacred before the U.S. acknowledges their right to a homeland of their own? ✦

John Egan is editor of The Energy Daily, *a Washington, D.C.-based trade newsletter covering electric utilities, oil and gas companies, energy policy developments and the Clean Air Act.*

Bitter Harvest at the Moshav

By Charles Fischbein

There weren't many Fortune 500 companies recruiting graduate students with advanced philosophy degrees in 1972. So after spending months looking for "philosopher wanted" ads in the Sunday classified section, my career choices boiled down to teaching or accepting a position as an assistant director for the B'nai B'rith Council of Greater Chicago.

Little did I know that the choice I made would lead me down the road to becoming what the B'nai B'rith Anti-Defamation League would call "one of the highest level defectors from the Zionist executive ranks."

It took 11 years of work on behalf of Israel and the international Zionist movement before I finally realized that I was supporting a government and movement that was, at the very least, blatantly racist, and at its worst genocidal.

During the first eight years of my career I moved from B'nai B'rith to serve as director of the Trades and Professions Division of the United Jewish Appeal of Greater Washington, and finally to the position of executive director of the politically sensitive Washington regional office of the Jewish National Fund.

It was not until I came to the JNF that I realized that the Zionist movement was overtly racist, and that the United Nations declaration of 1975 equating Zionism with racism was indeed quite correct.

I began to see the light while preparing to spend a sabbatical in Israel. The executive vice president of the JNF suggested that I spend my year as a resident at Moshav Tomer Yosef. Since my wife and I had a background in farming, we were looking forward to our time on an Israeli communal farm. A few months before I was to take sabbatical leave, I traveled to Israel to look over the moshav and meet its members. The leaders of the moshav were elated at the idea of having a JNF executive as a member of their community for a year, and offered us the best housing available. There was only one formality left before I was to be an official member of the moshav: that was a vote of the other families in the community to accept me and my family.

The night before the vote was to take place, the moshav held a party for me and I was assured that I would be accepted unanimously as a member. A woman who ran the local school innocently asked to see photographs of my three children. I proudly showed her pictures of Jason, my son; Madra, my daughter; and David, my adopted half-Black, half-Vietnamese son.

That one incident—showing my children's pictures to a school teacher in Israel—changed everything for me.

As soon as she saw the picture of David, the teacher excused herself and summoned three senior members of the moshav and left the room.

About an hour later I was asked to go to the main office of the moshav. I was told bluntly that the members did not want my son David to come to the moshav, and it was suggested that my wife and I send him to boarding school at home for the year we were to be in Israel. I was told that Israel had enough problems with Arabs, and did not wish to deal with Blacks, even though David had converted to Judaism.

The next morning I called the office of the world chairman of the Jewish National Fund, Moshe Rivlin, and told him I was coming to Jerusalem and had to see him right away.

When I arrived, I learned that Rivlin had already received a call from the moshav and was aware of the situation. He took me out for tea and told me that I should go back to the New York office, where I would receive a check for a year's pay in advance, and that I should forget the sabbatical in Israel and study or travel in the U.S. I was warned that if I made trouble I would be fired from my post at the JNF.

Upon my return to Washington, I decided to postpone my sabbatical and attempted to work on behalf of change within the JNF.

Then came the Israeli invasion of Lebanon in June of 1982. A major backlash had developed within the Jewish community in the United States, and, in an attempt to stop the criticism of Israel from within the American Jewish community, the JNF summoned all its executives to go to Israel and Lebanon to "see the facts for themselves."

Upon our arrival in Israel, we were met at the Knesset building by Prime Minister Menachem Begin, who told us that he was upset by the adverse reaction to the invasion of Lebanon from within the Jewish community in the United States. As JNF executives, Begin said, we were expected to do whatever we could to change public opinion at home and gain support for Israel and its actions in Lebanon.

Shortly after the briefing, we were put on Israeli Air Force helicopters and flown to the northern border village of Kiryat Shimona. After landing we boarded buses with armored vehicles as escorts and went to the outskirts of Beirut.

During our drive north, Dr. Samuel L. Cohen, executive vice president of the Jewish National Fund of America, warned us that upon our return to the U.S. we were expected to support completely the Israeli invasion of Lebanon. He added that if we couldn't do so we would have to take early retirement or resign at once.

As my bus drove through towns and villages in Lebanon I exchanged glances with survivors of the Israeli invasion. They knew the bus carried Zionist agency executives and they knew that we were just as responsible for the death and destruction brought upon their villages as the Israeli army. Raw hate welled up in their eyes, hate that cut through the heavy plate glass windows on the bus, with a look that said, "If I could only kill you, I would."

I found myself fervently praying that my children would never be blamed for the violent deaths of innocent people, and then have to look into the eyes of the families of the victims.

Flying back to New York, I kept writing figures on paper. The numbers represented my car payment, my mortgage payment, my children's tuition, food, etc. I knew what I had to do, and I was trying to determine how long I could make it on severance pay.

When I left my position as executive director of the Washington office of the JNF, I dedicated my life to helping the millions of Jews throughout the world learn the truth about the racist and un-Jewish movement that has deceived and manipulated them, while exposing them to the horror and hatred I saw reflected in the eyes of its Lebanese and Palestinian victims. ✦

In October, 1987, Charles Fischbein was a Washington, DC-based writer specializing in Middle East issues.

VI. BETWEEN SABRA-SHATILA AND THE INTIFADA 1982-1987

WITH EGYPT NEUTRALIZED by its separate peace with Israel, Israeli Prime Minister Menachem Begin and his extremist defense minister, Gen. Ariel Sharon, turned their attention to Lebanon, scene of an intermittent civil war since 1975. Sharon launched a series of provocations designed to goad PLO forces in southern Lebanon into breaking a U.S.-brokered cease-fire that had kept Israel's northern border quiet for 10 months. Finally, Israel seized upon the excuse of an assassination attempt on its ambassador to London to launch a carefully planned invasion of Lebanon on June 6, 1982. After a devastating two-month siege of the Lebanese capital, a cease-fire was initiated on Aug. 3, and a plan for the evacuation of PLO forces from Lebanon under the protection of U.S., French, Italian and British troops was reached on Aug. 11. PLO forces departed by land and sea on Aug. 21 after the U.S. guaranteed the safety of their families and unarmed Palestinians remaining behind in West Beirut. When the evacuation was completed, U.S. and other forces left. On Sept. 15, Israel broke a cease-fire to occupy West Beirut. Israeli troops surrounded the Sabra and Shatila refugee camps, refusing to let anyone leave, while Lebanese Maronite militiamen massacred camp residents for 36 hours. President Ronald Reagan returned U.S. Marines to Beirut as peacekeepers, but gradually their neutrality became compromised. On Oct. 23, 1983, a suicide bomber struck at the Marine barracks at the Beirut airport, killing 241 American troops. The following February, U.S. forces "redeployed" from Lebanon. The ensuing years saw plane hijackings, the taking of American hostages in Lebanon, the Israeli occupation of southern Lebanon and its continuing occupation of and settlement in Arab lands occupied in 1967.

Israel's 1982 Invasion of Lebanon: When Outrage Failed

By Ralph McCallister

As a student at the University of Chicago 60 years ago, I became aware of the great moral and ethical contributions of the Liberal, Reform, Conservative and Humanistic branches of one of the world's great religions, Judaism. I was so appreciative of the brilliance and oratorical power of some of the rabbis that at every opportunity I would attend religious services at their synagogues in different parts of the city. I was particularly impressed with the contributions they were making to the articulation of the ideals of freedom, equality and justice for all, without respect to race, creed or ethnic background. They and their congregations seemed to me to be on the cutting edge of America's realization of its promise as the new Jerusalem, where the words of the Declaration of Independence and the Constitution meant what they said for all Americans.

Because I count this experience as a rich and significant part of my education, I realize now that I was far too long a blind supporter of the state of Israel. I made no serious attempt to distinguish between its good and bad policies, or its moderate and intransigent leaders.

I was jolted out of this unthinking acceptance by a totally unacceptable Israeli action: the Begin-Shamir-Sharon-Yaron attack against the Palestinians and other Arabs in Lebanon, which began in 1982, and which by now has killed at least 10,000 men, women and children, and maimed more than 50,000 others with technology made largely in America. I found the complicity of the United States in this Israeli action, so reminiscent of Nazi "Blitzkrieg" attacks against small, neutral states of Europe, a devastating blow to my esteem for my own country.

Following the unrestricted bombing of Beirut by American-made Israeli warplanes, causing the destruction of schools and hospitals and the denial of medical care to the thousands of dying and injured in the city, I realized that thoughtful Americans must insist that their government withdraw all support for such modern barbarism, and help to restore the devastation to which our support of Israel had contributed.

I expected to hear, first and foremost, the voices of the moral and ethical leaders in the American-Jewish community. Jewish leaders would make this imperative American action a unifying rather than a divisive one at home. Except for a few courageous individuals, however, Jewish voices were virtually silent. The large "mainstream" Jewish organizations were not only silent, they even sought to justify or defend the slaughter.

This quiescence among mainstream American Jews, in contrast to the outrage which I had expected of Jewish leaders, is profoundly disappointing to me. It does not, however, justify silence on my part. As a Christian and a concerned human being, it has become a passion with me to help restore American humaneness and fairness in our relations with people everywhere. To do this, we must disengage U.S. Middle East policy from domination by a country which, although its population does not exceed Denmark's, has used more than $38 billion poured into it by American taxpayers, and perhaps another $20 billion in private, tax-free contributions, to become the terror of the Middle East. Its iron-fist policy, including 30-to-1 reprisals against the Palestinians, Lebanese and Syrians who have been dispossessed or made second- and third-class citizens in their own land, is Nazi-like in both tactics and effects. I am assured by Middle East friends that the Star of David painted on American-made aircraft has become as much a symbol of terror as the terrible hooked cross of the Nazis to Europeans in the 1930s and 1940s.

I have been asked pointed questions and have received unpleasant comments in my own community as a result of my published articles and letters making this point. It is a shock to realize that I am subtly being accused of anti-Semitism. The purpose, I suppose, is to stun me into silence. When that fails, I suppose it will be followed by attempts to discredit me so that I will find editorial pages closed to me.

Until that happens, however, I will continue to encourage Americans who understand but fear to speak out to curb the excesses of Israel's propaganda and lobbying organizations in the United States. Directors of these organizations are, I believe, suborning our Congress through illegal coordination of the political campaign donations of somewhere in excess of 80 separate political action committees. This is a serious charge, since suborn means illegally subordinating a government agency. The best indication that this is true, however, is the reluctance of Congress to investigate activities which virtually every congressman knows, from his own experience, are taking place.

It's time for ethical and moral individuals of all religions to raise their voices against the killing and degrading of the Palestinian people. Do Yitzhak Shamir, Ariel Sharon and Meir Kahane see eventual extinction of the Palestinians as an Israeli "final solution"? If so, we should alert Elie Weisel now to save a place in the Holocaust Memorial in Washington for the Palestinians, so that the world may not forget! ❖

Ralph McCallister, a former director of the Learning Center of North Carolina and vice-president from 1944 to 1961 of the Chautauqua Institution in New York state, died in 1988.

CHAPTER THIRTY

One Thing You Still Can't Do in Miami Is Criticize Israel

Mark C. Dressler

Growing up Irish-Catholic in suburban Philadelphia is probably not much different from growing up Italian-American in Boston or Polish-American in Chicago. Since I was of neither Jewish nor Arab background, I was more comfortable when discussions of the history and politics of the Middle East were interpreted by others. Any discussion of Israel and its conflict with the Palestinians was clouded with misunderstanding, and it included a heavy dose of defensiveness and guilt. I soon came to accept the analysis of the Middle East put forth by my Jewish-American friends and acquaintances: Israel was a tiny nation beleaguered by Arab hostility and Soviet machinations.

Israel: Sacred Cow in American Politics

My suburban Philadelphia high school had a large Jewish population. The Vietnam War was just as unpopular there as Israel's role in the 1967 Arab-Israeli war had been popular. As a teenager, I opposed the Vietnam War, and in 1972 I volunteered to work as a door-to-door canvasser for George McGovern's Democratic presidential campaign. When I spoke to local Jewish Americans about McGovern, I found they were not particularly interested in his pledge to end the Vietnam War; instead, these voters wanted to know what McGovern would do for Israel. When I replied that McGovern supported Israel so strongly that he was willing to commit U.S. troops to defend Israel should the need ever arise, I was told that answer wasn't good enough, and I was asked to leave a majority of Jewish households.

The inconsistency of the campaign rhetoric gradually dawned on me. McGovern, the "peace and anti-intervention candidate" in 1972, opposed U.S. involvement in Southeast Asia. Yet his platform supported an aggressively pro-Israel U.S. Middle East policy, which could have included intervening militarily on Israel's side. This was my first inkling that Israel was a "sacred cow" in American politics.

In retrospect, I realize I suppressed such thoughts for fear of being called "anti-Semitic." This charge was once a powerful means to denounce those who hated Jews, but the term now has been stripped of virtually all meaning by some of Israel's supporters in America. These Americans—Jewish and Gentile—insist on labeling as "anti-Semitic" any and all opposition to Israel's policies, even when Israelis themselves object to the same policies.

Fear of "Anti-Semitism" Label

In current usage, an "anti-Semite" is a non-Jew who criticizes Israel or who also discusses the internal contradictions and problems of the American Jewish community. Not the least of these contradictions is the unwillingness of mainstream American Jewish leaders to confront their own deeply ingrained political chauvinism and callousness vis-à-vis the Palestinians, who were dispossessed when Israel was created in 1948.

Dr. Israel Shahak, the noted Israeli civil rights scholar and activist, has pointed out that "the chief reason why Jewish chauvinism is so virulent in the USA is, simply, because almost no one dares to say in the USA that Jewish chauvinism exists."

My pilgrimmage toward understanding the Middle East continued in 1980. After graduating from college in Philadelphia with a degree in journalism, I moved to Miami. For two years I worked with Latin American and Haitian groups concerned with human rights in their respective countries. There wasn't much time for the Middle East.

But in 1982 Israel invaded Lebanon, and much of Miami's Jewish community jumped to Israel's defense. I wrote a letter to the *Miami Herald* criticizing the invasion. Soon I began receiving harassing phone calls concerning my letter. I was angered because for two years I actively opposed U.S. policies in Central America, but I was never harassed by Miami's large conservative Cuban community. However, after *one* letter to the *Miami Herald* criticizing the Israeli invasion, I was besieged with harassment the likes of which I had never before experienced.

Still later, I lived in Washington, D.C., where I wrote news and feature articles for the Arab American Institute, and occasionally contributed articles to the Dearborn, Michigan Arabic/English weekly *Sada Alwatan.* It took a long time for me to see the light on the Middle East, partly because I feared being called an "anti-Semite," but also because the mainstream U.S. media wasn't telling the American people both sides of the Middle East conflict. If we do our homework, we can help an entire generation of young Americans better understand Middle East realities. ✦

Mark C. Dressler is a staff writer for the Castro Valley Forum, *a bi-monthly community newspaper in Alameda County, CA.*

POSTSCRIPT: *I've written several dozen articles about a variety of subjects since my "Seeing the Light" article appeared. I'm still of Irish-Catholic background, and I fit into neither Jewish-American nor Arab-American culture (for examples, I don't speak either Hebrew or Arabic). So I don't have a stake in promoting either cause.*

However, I am an American, not in any flag-waving sense, but in the sense that I have a profound grasp of American history (and now American law). During the past five years, both with AAI and since, I have learned a lot about how the American electoral system works.

My efforts toward understanding the Middle East have been a kind of "pilgrimmage." This pilgrimmage is far from over, however, because my personal understanding won't affect U.S.-Mideast policy. Only large numbers of Americans with similar understanding can do this. Perhaps this article, and the book in which it appears, will help.

To Palestine, Via Iran

By Andrea Wright

I t's possible to spend the better part of a decade in the Middle East and still know nothing about the Palestinian issue. I arrived in Tehran in October, 1964. An early winter
chill was sweeping down from the Elborz Mountains, and snow was expected within
a few days.

Snow in the Middle East! I had traveled to Iran to join my fiancé, and although I had
spent some time in the U.S. researching Iran, the information I brought with me was
scanty and outdated. A letter written home that first year showed my culture shock: "No
matter how much I might have read, I couldn't have been prepared. Mother was right:
I'm in a different world." Different indeed! At dawn I heard the *muezzin* call the faithful to prayer. Although I was studying Farsi, I could not converse with the Iranians I met.
I was stared at wherever I went, and there was always talk of "the foreigner." Nevertheless, I loved Iran, and winced at some of the queries from home: "Do you have any
electricity? How do you get your bath water? Please send us a picture of your house, or
whatever it is you live in."

While it took some time before I began to feel "at home" in the Middle East, it took
even longer for some of the political realities of the region to sink in. Although I was a
reporter for the *Tehran Journal*, my editor was only interested in local feature stories.

I was still largely oblivious to the gathering tide which was someday to sweep Americans out of much of the Middle East when, two months after the 1967 Arab-Israeli war,
I had a brief layover in Tel Aviv. I remember that my friends from Iran and Texas had applauded the fury of little David meeting and beating the Arab Goliath—everyone I knew
smugly cheered the perceived underdog. In retrospect, I see that I was only one of many
Americans, including those then conducting the Johnson administration's foreign policy,
who underestimated the momentous problems that would follow the 1967 war.

Shuffling between the U.S. and Iran for the next decade provided me with a chance
to reflect more critically on America's policy toward the Shah's Iran. Like most Americans, I naively believed our leaders knew what they were doing in the Middle East, and
that their Iran policies were designed as part of a larger regional strategy. By the mid-
1970s, however, when those of us close to the heartbeat of the Iranian people felt with

certainty the winds of chaos stirring, we watched with dismay as American leaders made one misstep after another. The way U.S. leaders responded to Iran's revolution made me question their awareness and acumen. Gradually I came to realize that my native country was following a disastrous policy in Iran, or, even worse, no policy at all.

I was in Tehran when a truly revolutionary page in Iranian history was written: the Shah was overthrown, ending what he, at least, sought to depict as Iran's 2,500-year-old monarchical tradition. There seemed to be almost as much chaos in Washington, however, as American officials sought to explain the revolution and to evade personal responsibility for pursuing American policies which had become out-dated years before.

Perhaps because Iranians and Arabs tend to distance themselves from one another—a monumental mistake in my opinion—it took Israel's invasion of Lebanon in 1982 and the ensuing massacres at the Sabra-Shatila refugee camps to focus my attention on the festering wound that is the Palestine problem.

Journalists like to consider themselves generally well-informed. Thus, as a journalist who had by 1982 spent over eight years in the Middle East, it was particularly embarrassing to admit I had a blind spot regarding the Palestinians. As a journalist I considered myself a merchant of information, but in reality I was a victim of disinformation.

As I increasingly wrote on the Palestinian issue and American policy toward the Israeli-Palestinian conflict, I found that my pile of rejection slips began to grow. Like many other writers, having discovered the unpleasant truth about U.S. policy toward the Palestinians, I wanted to share my insights with American readers. I started to notice, however, that most of the U.S. analyses and editorial commentaries on the Middle East had a more or less explicitly pro-Israel viewpoint. For example, Israeli officials often published articles on U.S. Middle East policy in America's "newspapers of record," but those newspapers rarely if ever gave the same space to Palestinian or Arab voices.

However, from the responses to my published articles, I am convinced of two things: that the American people are hungry for more information on the Middle East, and that only through a spirit of unity among all peoples in the Middle East will distorted views and stereotypes be dispelled here in America. ❖

Andrea A. Wright is a Texas-based free-lance writer. Her story of her experiences on two trips to Iran is included in Tasmania on Tuesday: An Anthology of North American Women's Travels Abroad, *published by New Rivers Press.*

Four Palestinians

By William Scanlan, Jr.

When abstract perceptions change, it is usually the result of meeting the flesh-and-blood people concerned. In my case, it took only four of them. I met them all in the spring of 1983, while my wife and I were on a one-month tour of ancient sites in the Middle East. A few months earlier. we had almost cancelled our long-planned Middle East trip as we, like most Americans, watched with mounting disbelief the televised destruction and slaughter that accompanied the Israeli invasion of Lebanon and the bombing of Beirut. Nonetheless we made the trip.

Abu Sultan

We met our first flesh-and-blood Palestinian in Amman. He bore little resemblance to the ogre of U.S. media stereotyping. Instead, he was helpful, friendly and charming. As we got to know Abu Sultan, however, one point became very clear. Although he was born in Amman, he didn't view himself as a Jordanian. His home was in Jaffa. He acknowledged that he had only seen it in photographs and he might not live long enough to see it in person. But he was convinced that, God willing, his children would have the opportunity to return to their Palestine.

Maha Elias

In Amman we also had our first experience with the legendary Arab hospitality. One of my solemn commitments was to return from the trip with Boy Scout patches for my son from the places we had visited. I explained this to a young Palestinian woman, Maha Elias, at the hotel guest relations desk. After making numerous calls, she informed me that the man who had Boy Scout patches was out of town. She said, however, that her nephew was a scout. Since we were leaving for Jerusalem at 7 the next morning, I told her not to worry about it any longer, and my wife and I went to dinner.

When we returned, under the door to our room was a small envelope containing a used and obviously much-loved Jordanian Boy Scout patch that had just been removed from the nephew's uniform.

As the trip progressed, the more Palestinians we met, the more we realized that, like us, all had their own goals and aspirations. But, among their aspirations, there was always Palestine.

Robert

It is less than 50 miles from Amman to Jerusalem as the crow flies, but the overland trip can easily take most of the day. The geographical part of the problem is a descent into the Jordan Valley, followed by an ascent up the escarpment to Jerusalem. The political part of the problem is much more serious, and involves a long wait between descent and ascent for Jordanian security checks to exit, and Israeli security checks to enter.

On the bus trip down to the Jordan River I sat next to a young man with an obvious Australian accent on his way to Jerusalem. He asked what I knew about the Israeli security checks. I said it was my understanding that for Westerners they shouldn't be any problem.

The Australian, Robert, responded: "I will probably get special treatment. I'm a Palestinian." I pointed out that he was traveling on an Australian passport. He explained that he was born in Jerusalem.

We crossed the Jordan and began the lengthy Israeli security check. Across the way from where I was being inspected, there was another large building. There Arabs were inspected. Up to that point, all of the passengers on the bus had been kept more or less together. But suddenly, as I turned to say something to Robert, he was nowhere to be found.

I never learned what happened to him, but I expect that he had been whisked away to the other building for his own private humiliation, out of sight of the Italian nuns and the American Bible Lands Tour Group members on his bus.

Musa Kamar

Once again it was the search for Boy Scout patches that led to new insights, this time in Arab Jerusalem. In the Christian quarter of the Old City we had run across the familiar Boy Scout fleur-de-lis insignia. A young man there, Musa Kamar, assured us that if we returned the following day, he would have some patches for us.

The following day in his office he handed us some patches from the Arab Catholic Scouts of Jerusalem. The insignia and inscription, he noted, had been adopted when Arab Jerusalem was part of Jordan, and it was still being used. I asked if this inscription was satisfactory. No, he replied, he would much prefer a Palestinian patch. Then why, I asked, don't you design one?

With a dramatic gesture, he clapped his wrists together, palms facing, and said: "We would all be imprisoned. It is illegal under Israeli law for a Palestinian to wear any symbol of Palestinian nationalism."

That day in Jerusalem, I reflected on the incoherence of U.S. Middle East policy:

American taxpayers had given Israel nearly $60 billion in aid since 1948, yet our Middle Eastern "strategic asset" is not only unable to help us in the Persian Gulf, it lives in fear of a symbol that a pre-pubescent boy might wear on his Boy Scout uniform. ✦

William Scanlan, Jr. is an attorney in San Antonio, TX.

Work Camps: Seeing Is Believing

By Roberta Coles

To explain how my views on the Middle East evolved, I must address both Middle Eastern issues and feminist concerns. I first began to learn about the Arab-Israeli conflict from a Jordanian who later became my husband. I was soon finding out just as much about prejudice and stereotyping in the United States, particularly among evangelical Christians like myself. Some of my friends didn't want me dating a critic of Israel, and a Muslim at that. One Japanese-American friend, whom I expected to be more sensitive to stereotyping than most, solemnly told me Middle Easterners "look deceptive." Jewish friends suddenly were no longer friends, and a Jewish relative said she "thought I could do better."

When I wrote my master's thesis on the 1979 U.S.-Iran hostage crisis, one of my male advisers said, "You must be dating an Iranian, right?" The message I heard in that question was that women think only with stars in their eyes and man feeding the information into their heads.

Even today, when male or female friends and colleagues learn that my initial interest in Middle East issues was awakened by my husband, the exchange of views often stops with a look that says, "Well, that explains it." I'm dismissed as no longer an unbiased source. All my research, and I have done a lot, becomes irrelevant.

I had always been interested in international and intercultural affairs, though mostly related to Western and Eastern European issues. I am embarrassed now to admit that I had thought Israel had existed "since time immemorial," not just for a relatively brief span a couple of millennia ago. All I knew of the modern Middle East was that little Israel seemed always to be battling for its survival, and that all these events were supposed to be happening "according to God's plan."

Shortly after I met my husband, he showed me a map of the Middle East and pointed out Israel. "Right," I said, "but where is Palestine?" I still remember the look of gentle amazement in his eyes. I soon discovered that Palestine was there, all right: Under the rubble, under Israel's Canada Park, and under the "blooming" desert.

After my first few discussions with my husband-to-be, and with other Arabs whom I met in graduate school, I still did not believe that my country could possibly be a part of what happened, and still is happening, to the Palestinians. So, I seized every chance in the international development courses I was taking to learn about the Middle East. I must have read at least 50 books by Arabs, Israelis, and Americans that first year alone. Because I still felt more trusting of familiar Christian sources, the two books most convincing to me were Frank Epps' *Whose Land is Palestine?* and A.C. Forrest's *The Unholy Land.*

In 1983, skeptic that I am, I decided to see first-hand if what I was reading was true. I traveled with a varied volunteer group to the Middle East to work in refugee camps in Jordan and the occupied territories. I was able to cross the border from Jordan to the West Bank uneventfully, but a Palestinian American traveling with us was not so fortunate. Everything she owned was dismantled, from clothes to toothpaste. She was almost held back because in her suitcase she carried a broken gold necklace in the shape of the map of Palestine. Only when a sympathetic Jewish American in the group made a ruckus did the Israeli officials allow the Palestinian American through.

We arrived in Jerusalem during a strike. Two Palestinian students had been shot in a demonstration, and all of East Jerusalem was closed. Steel doors rolled down over the storefronts made it look like a city of garages. At a roadblock on the way to Birzeit University, we, as foreigners, were pulled off the bus and questioned as to why we would be visiting a Palestinian educational institution.

At the refugee camps where I was to work, I met a retired Danish woman dentist who carried a letter of introduction from a Palestinian in Denmark to a refugee family living in Jelazoun camp. The Danish woman planned to spend a couple of days with them. The morning after she left for the visit I saw her walking back into our camp, looking as if she had been through a war. She had had a pleasant dinner and conversation during the evening with the family she was visiting, then retired to bed. (I speak loosely here. In a refugee camp, a bed frequently means a mat on a dirt floor in a crowded room under a sheet-metal roof secured by rocks.) In the middle of the night, Israeli military vehicles roared into the camp. The soldiers made all of the residents come out of their homes, line up in the street under the glare of the headlights, and watch while two houses were bulldozed. Her hosts, who were used to such intrusions, were able to go back to sleep. The Danish lady was too shaken to sleep, however, and at dawn decided to return to the relative safety of our work camp.

I had many experiences of my own that left lasting impressions of that trip: Meeting Bassam Shakaa, the mayor of Nablus, whose legs were blown off by a car bomb set by Jewish extremists who, when caught, were treated like heroes and given the mildest possible punishment; trips to the beach where Jewish "settlers," as well as Israeli soldiers, walked around toting machine guns; the demonstration in which two Israeli peace activists, one a woman in her 50s, were beaten and two of our European campers were held and interrogated; and the refugee camp with no sewer system, where I became deathly ill.

When it was time to return to Jordan, a friend and I hailed a Palestinian cab, which is distinguished from an Israeli cab by its license plate, to take us to the border. This is a mistake if you're looking forward to an easy crossing. While the Israeli cabs are allowed to reach the Allenby Bridge swiftly, the Palestinian cabs may be waved to the side of the road to wait in line until Israeli border guards are in the mood to let them pass. When we made a fuss, our driver had his identification papers confiscated. He told me that if he was caught without his papers, he would be without work and in jail. After some begging by us and flourishing of our American and European passports, Israeli guards finally returned the driver's papers and let us pass out of the occupied territories and back into Jordan.

My first two trips to the Middle East were taken without my husband. He was with me on my third visit, because we were moving to Jordan to teach there. Our stay in October 1986 was cut short by a car accident that took his life. Back in the U.S., I find old friends gently probing to see if I have buried my interest and views in the Middle East with my husband. They don't understand that now that I've seen the light, I can never again hide in the dark. ❖

Roberta Coles lives in Madison, WI, where she is a teaching assistant while working on her Ph.D. in sociology.

The Peace Stone

By Rabbi Yonassan Gershom

I am a rabbi—a rabbi who believes Israel should trade land for peace, and the Palestinians should have their own state. I could give you all kinds of historical and political arguments why this should be so, but I'm not going to do that, because academics really has nothing to do with my stand. I'm a storyteller, not a politician, and the tale I am about to share is deeply personal.

It all began in 1984, with a dozen peaceworkers sitting in my living room, their eyes glued to the television. "Don't see this film alone!" the publicity had warned. Now we were glad we hadn't, because our hearts were filled with unspeakable anguish as we watched "The Day After," a graphic depiction of the stark reality of nuclear war. With one breath we gasped as The Button was pushed; with one pair of eyes we saw the bombs explode; and with one set of tears we wept for the death of Planet Earth.

When the program ended, we all sat in shocked silence, then slowly formed a circle and chanted *shalom*—peace. Candles of hope were lit, prayers from many religious traditions were said, and some people, including myself, renewed vows of nonviolence. Then we shared stories and prophecies about world peace from our various cultures.

The Day After "The Day After"

On the day after "The Day After," I awoke with a sense of wonder at even being alive, as if I had narrowly escaped the Angel of Death. Everyday objects—a flower, a sparrow, a fallen leaf—seemed filled with miracles. But there was also a terrible sense of foreboding. What if we really did push The Button? Was there no hope for peace in this troubled world?

That evening I pulled a knitted cap over my *yarmulke*, donned a plaid flannel shirt and jeans, then went to sit anonymously in a circle of people sharing their feelings about the film. As part of this process, we were each asked to write a letter to someone who mattered to us, expressing concern about the nuclear threat and offering personal skills for peace. Next, following an American Indian tradition, we passed a "storytelling stone" around the circle. Each person held the stone while reading their letter, then passed the stone to the next person on the left.

I wrote my letter to the Prophet Elijah. Now this requires a bit of explanation. In Jewish folktales, the Prophet Elijah is mentioned more often than any other individual—even Moses. The Bible says that Elijah never died, but ascended to Heaven in a flaming chariot. Therefore Elijah still lives, and periodically descends to earth to test the hearts of the faithful and reveal inner secrets to the mystics. In addition, as the forerunner of the Messiah, Elijah also comes to see if the world is ready.

But Elijah does not come openly as Elijah—if he did that, of course everyone would honor him, and how then could he get an honest impression of the world? So he comes in disguise, perhaps as a homeless beggar, to see how he will be treated. In most of the stories, the seeker does not even realize that he has met Elijah until the "stranger" simply disappears. Therefore, Jewish tradition teaches, one must treat every person as if he or she might be Elijah.

The storytelling stone was passed to me. I held it for a moment in silence, savoring the smooth, dark surface, naturally rounded by the waves of Lake Superior. Then, slowly and softly, I began to read:

Dear Prophet Elijah:

I am writing this letter to you to say that I know you periodically check up on Planet Earth, and are probably just as worried as I am right now...To be honest, I am not sure which road to take, but am going to leave it up to God to open a door this week to some kind of peace work where I can be useful. My biggest concern is bridging the gap between the Jewish community and other peoples. So I think I would like to begin opening communications between myself and my Muslim neighbors. I may not be able to solve the Middle East crisis, but I can begin some one-to-one communication with people in my own neighborhood..."

When I finished reading my letter, someone handed me a button with "Peace" in Arabic, Hebrew and English. Then, with a big hug, he wished me luck on my quest. I felt embarrassed, because I had never met any Muslims, and had no idea how I could possibly keep such a promise. Now that I had read the letter out loud, it sounded presumptuous. Thank goodness I had come here anonymously!

When the sharing circle ended, the woman who had led the ceremony handed me the storytelling stone. "I somehow sense that this belongs to you now," she said.

The smooth stone felt warm to the touch, from all the hands that had held it that evening, and this somehow comforted me. Thanking her, I slipped it into my pocket with the letter to Elijah, then pinned the trilingual peace button on my coat and left.

The Palestinian

Three days later the blizzard came, burying Minneapolis in deep snowdrifts. On Franklin Avenue, where I was walking, the sidewalks were icy and treacherous, flanked by huge piles of snow left behind by the plows. In some places, people had shoveled only a narrow trail, barely wide enough for one person to walk or for two to pass sideways. It was at just such an impasse that I met the Palestinian.

"Jew!" he shouted in anger, recognizing my religion because of my beard and side-curls. "I am not Hitler! You are Hitler! You Jews killed my family! My wife and son are dead because of you!"

The confrontation took me by surprise, and I was very frightened. This man was a total stranger—I certainly had not killed his family or anyone else. I felt like a cardboard target with "Jew" written all over it. Had the sidewalks been clear, I would have run. But there we were, face-to-face between four-foot piles of snow. Like it or not, I had to deal with this situation.

After a few deep breaths and a silent prayer, I conquered my fear long enough to begin listening to the man's story. He was born in Jerusalem but had fled to Beirut, only to lose his family during the Israeli bombing in 1982. He then fled to America and had ended up on the streets. Now he was hurt and angry, like so many of the people in this poor inner-city neighborhood.

And then it hit me—he really was no different than anyone else I had met. This Palestinian was just another human being, grieving the death of his loved ones. I could understand that, because I, too, had no family. He was exactly like me.

When the man ended his story, I silently pointed to the button on my coat. "Peace," it said, in Arabic, Hebrew and English. Then I said to him, "I grieve for your family, and wish there were peace. I support the rights of all peoples, and I am against war, all war, even Israeli wars. We are all one human family."

His face softened and our eyes embraced. Then, clasping hands, we both turned sideways to help each other pass. Just two human beings, walking on a very slippery trail.

I had taken only a few steps when, tucking my hands into my pockets, I suddenly felt the storytelling stone and the letter to Elijah. A chill went up my spine as I turned and looked back. The Palestinian had vanished!

Was he really Elijah the Prophet, come to test my sincerity? I will never know. But the encounter was a turning point in my life. No longer could I see Arabs as "the enemy." From that moment on, I could empathize with the suffering on both sides, and realized that the real enemy was the war itself.

Over the years, I have carried the storytelling stone to many gatherings, sharing this experience and praying for peace. Somewhere along the line, my little rock was dubbed the Peace Stone. Like the proverbial swords into ploughshares, it has been transformed from a potential weapon into an instrument of human understanding. At Sabbath celebrations, Passover seders, folklore gatherings and protest rallies, literally thousands of people have passed the Peace Stone from hand to hand, expressing their hopes for Planet Earth.

I know that this alone will not bring peace, that we need negotiations and treaties, and that the process will be long and difficult for both sides. That is for the politicians to work out. But there is a deeper peace that goes beyond the absence of war, and that is the inner peace between the hearts of fellow human beings. In order to reach that level, we need to stop seeing each other as depersonalized targets, and realize that beyond all the differences in culture, language and religion, we are members of the same family, sharing the same Planet Earth. I would like to think that by sharing the story of the Peace Stone, I am helping us take one more step toward that goal. ✦

Rabbi Yonassan Gershom explains that while the story he relates "may sound a little bit like mystical fiction, it is absolutely true" and was "a turning point in my personal growth and was also the moment of decision for my current support of a two-state solution to the Palestinian-Israeli conflict." Rabbi Gershom was born in Berkeley, CA, grew up in the Philadelphia, PA, area, received his B.S. degree from Mankato State University in Minnesota, and was ordained by Rabbi Zalman Schachter-Salomi the B'nai Or Rabbi. He is the author of two books and numerous articles.

POSTSCRIPT: *Storytelling often works where polemics will not, because it bypasses our intellectual defense mechanisms to reach the heart and soul. It is for this reason that Jewish preachers have long used parables to get their point across. The early Hassidic masters were frequently able to bring about a sincere change of heart by telling a story about "someone else" in exactly the same situation. Both the rabbi and the listeners knew what the real agenda was, but by couching it in a story, the "teller of tales" made repentance possible without publicly humiliating the offenders and thereby compounding the problem.*

"The Peace Stone" has all the elements of just such a traditional Hassidic story, because while it is a true encounter between myself and a Palestinian, it is also a mirror which allows the listener to examine his or her own attitudes in a non-threatening way. A Jew and a Palestinian, meeting face-to-face on a narrow trail where neither can pass unless they help each other—what a clear metaphor for the entire Palestinian-Israeli conflict!

Jewish audiences invariably gasp at the point when the Palestinian stranger "dumps" his anger on me. Based on past experience, most Jews fully expect the incident to escalate into anti-Jewish violence with only two alternatives: run or get into a fight. The nonviolent resolution of the conflict comes as a surprise, and serves as an opener for discussing ways to break the shame-blame-abuse cycle which has trapped us all in a vicious war.

One time after I told "The Peace Stone," a woman in the audience expressed the opinion that the Jews were dumping their anger about the Holocaust onto the Palestinians. My first reaction was to say no, that can't be happening. But, not long after that, I attended a workshop on dysfunctional family systems, and as the speaker diagrammed the abuse cycle on the blackboard, I suddenly realized that I was looking at a psychological picture of the way Jews and Arabs often react to each other.

On a conscious level, Israelis are not purposely "punishing" Palestinians for the Holocaust; the very suggestion of such a thing is horrifying to most Jews. We sincerely see ourselves as basically ethical people who, after all, gave the world the Ten Commandments. And didn't we collectively vow that "never again" would such a thing as a Holocaust happen? True. But it is also true that people who have been abused will, when they come to power, tend to abuse others because they do not have healthy models for exercising power.

It happens all the time in dysfunctional families. Abuse is passed down from generation to generation. What a person experiences as a child, she in turn does to others as an adult, unless there is some kind of therapy to teach new ways of coping with frustration and anger. Without conscious effort to change behavior patterns, the dysfunctional coping mechanisms learned in childhood will take over during times of stress. This is why people who grew up in abusive families suddenly find themselves beating their children, often using the same verbal epithets that their own parents used, even though they vowed as children that they would never do that when they grew up. It is as if the brain somehow switches into "automatic," mindlessly falling back on old behavior patterns when the stress level gets too high.

What is true of individuals can also be true of nations. As someone once said, "Revolution means going in circles." It is relatively easy to overthrow a government, but far more difficult to oust the internalized oppression which causes us to "demonize" others. For example, the early Christians were persecuted by the Romans, and their own leaders no doubt exhorted them to forgive and forget. But when the Church later came to power, it ended up hunting down Jews, Muslims, and pagans with the Inquisition. In the same way, the Germans felt humiliated by the treaty of Versailles after World War I, so they scapegoated the Jews in order to make themselves feel powerful again.

The Jews of Europe, who were abused by both the Chruch and the Nazis, dreamed for centuries of a utopia in the Holy Land. Unfortunately there was no "40 years in the wilderness" between Nazi Germany and the founding of the State of Israel, and, without consciously realizing it, many Jews have indeed carried their unresolved rage against Hitler into Palestine.

At times it seems to me as if the entire Jewish community suffers from a collective case of Post-Traumatic Stress Disorder. Every Palestinian act of violence toward Israel triggers a group flashback to the Holocaust and all of the anger connected with it. This, in turn, causes Jews to react to Palestinians with a mixture of fear and rage, seeing them as Jew-hating Nazis rather than occupied people with legitimate grievances.

Today the oppressed Palestinians also dream of having their own country, with liberty and justice for all. But the sad truth is that, unless there is some way to break this vicious cycle, when the Palestinians do get a state (as I believe they eventually will), they are just as likely to end up abusing whatever minorities dwell within their borders.

Why? Because a whole generation of Palestinian children has grown up knowing only the humiliation of military occupation, where war and violence seem "normal." Like the Jews who survived the Holocaust to found the State of Israel, the current generation of Palestinians is deeply scarred by the dehumanizing experience of living in squalid refugee camps, and this is bound to affect the nature of their own state.

How, then, can we break this abusive cycle? I have no easy solutions, but I do believe that we can learn a lot by applying recent discoveries about the dynamics within dysfunctional families to the present situation. Abusers almost always turn out to be people who were themselves abused, and whose self-esteem has been severely damaged. Inside every Kahane is an angry little boy who was beaten up on the playground because he was a Jew, and inside every Palestinian "terrorist" is a child who was humiliated and dehumanized simply because he was an Arab. Both have fantasized what they would like to do to "get even," and when either one comes to power, he ends up acting exactly like his previous oppressors because that is the behavior he internalized when he was a victim.

What nonviolence training offers is a third alternative to this "fight or flight" reaction. That alternative is respectful dialogue. Instead of each side struggling to be on top controlling the other, nonviolence teaches us how to interact as equal human beings seeking to solve a mutual problem. Once real dialogue has begun, both sides are frequently amazed at how similar their feelings and experiences really are. As they begin to empathize (literally "to feel together"), a bridge of understanding can be built.

This process does not erase history. In the real world, it is impossible simply to "forgive and forget," because "forgetting" often means refusing to acknowledge somebody else's pain. The Holocaust was real and the occupation is real, and denying the horror of either will not make the current problems go away. Rather than "forgive and forget," we need to forgive and move forward, working through our mutual problems together, while keeping the histories of both peoples intact. Only through openly confronting our psychological wounds can we begin to heal them and change our behavior toward each other.

Mahatma Gandhi's word for nonviolence, satyagraha, *has often been mistranslated as "passive resistance," but it literally means "holding to the truth." There is nothing passive about true nonviolence. Anyone can hide behind a gun or a bomb and feel brave, but it takes a great deal more courage to hold to the truth under all circumstances. Sometimes that means actively confronting one's own inner "demons," while responding to an enemy with understanding and patience. A true practitioner of* satyagraha *is a warrior in every sense of the word, using truth, faith and love as the weapons for waging peace. This is not an easy path, but I do believe it can offer both Jews and Palestinians a way out of the madness that is destroying the souls of both our peoples.*

The Truth About Terrorism Is Contained in Encyclopedia Entries

By Isaac Melton

Growing up in a Houston, Texas, neighborhood with a large Jewish population, I have been on the fringe of Jewish society since I was seven years old. In my high school (San Jacinto), many classes were reduced in size by two-thirds or more on Jewish holidays.

One summer I went to Scout camp with the troup from the nearby temple. I spent a lot of my free time talking with a lovely old Jewish patriarch named Mr. Mittelman from "the old country." He increased my insight into traditional Jewish religion and told me moving tales of the Nazi persecution he had survived. I continue to have the deepest respect for and interest in traditionalist Jews and their religion.

I grew up assuming that the Jews had a God-given right to the land of Israel. After all, isn't that what the Bible teaches? But in my late teen years, as an Anglo-Catholic ("high church Episcopalian"), I learned the traditional Orthodox Catholic teaching that the Church, not some modern secular political entity, is the "New Israel."

The New Testament teaches that through and in Christ, the Church is the continuation of ancient Israel. Baptised into the Body of Christ, we Christians become Children of Israel by adoption and grace. This teaching, also traditionally accepted by Roman Catholics, Anglicans and Lutherans, is roundly denied by large numbers of fundamentalist Protestants, who see the secular state of Israel as the fulfillment of Old Testament Prophecy. That view has contributed significantly to American foreign policy.

Still, until I was in my 40s, I continued to believe that there was certainly nothing wrong with the Jewish state of Israel, and I believed the Jews had every right to it. I couldn't fathom what those crazy Arabs were upset about. A bunch of fanatic tent-dwellers, I thought. I realize now that this mental image of the Palestinians was engendered by the American media. It certainly appears the media bias is pro-Israel, and favors the Palestinians only when their mistreatment is so blatant it can't be ignored.

I'm still in favor of the Jews having a homeland. The Church's belief that She is Herself Israel, renewed in Christ, does not imply we would deny the Jews their rights as a people. And Israel is an accomplished fact: let it stand. But now that I know in detail the story of this modern Jewish state, I'm very disheartened by the way the Israelis have accomplished their purpose.

My change in thinking was the result of a dinner party conversation in 1983 with an elderly Palestinian immigrant who attended the same church I did. Aziz, a fun-to-be-with roly-poly Orthodox Christian, now departed this life, remarked he had once met Yasser Arafat and thought of him as a great leader. He even showed me a picture of himself and Arafat together. I was horrified.

"But he is such an evil terrorist," said I.

"No more so than Menachem Begin," replied Aziz.

"Begin!?" I cried. "But he is such a spiritual man. I remember how when he met with President Carter at Camp David he prayed in Hebrew on television. I was very moved by that. How can you call that beautiful old man a terrorist?" I asked, while thinking to myself, these Arabs sure are fanatics.

"It's a matter of history," he replied. "Go to the library and look it up."

So I did.

Looking It Up

I started with the encyclopedias, first the *Encyclopedia Britannica*. Looking up "Begin, Menachem," I learned that Menachem Begin "joined the militant Irgun Zvai Leumi, and was a commander of that group from 1943 to 1948." (*Encyclopedia Britannica*, Volume 2, page 47.)

What exactly was the Irgun Zvai Leumi? So I looked that up. The Irgun was "an extreme nationalist group...whose policies called for the use of force, if necessary, to establish a Jewish state on both sides of the Jordan. Irgun committed acts of terrorism and assassination against the British...and it was also violently anti-Arab..." *(Encyclopedia Brittanica*, Volume 6, page 382.)

According to *Colliers Encyclopedia* (Volume 3, page 782), "Another such group was the Stern Group, or Stern Gang, headed by Yitzhak Shamir." In Volume 13, page 343, *Colliers* speaks of "the terrorist groups, the Irgun Zvai Leumi and the Stern Group."

In the *Encyclopedia Americana*, contributor J.C. Hurewitz of Columbia University tells us "the Irgunists claimed that their acts of terrorism against the Arabs and British largely forced Britain's decision to end its mandate in Palestine." (Volume 15, page 438.) These terrorist acts included the murder of the British representative, Lord Moyne, in Cairo in November, 1944, and the murder of Count Folke Bernadotte, the U.N.-appointed mediator, on Sept. 17, 1948.

The *Americana* tells us, "Shamir was believed to have played a prominent part in planning the murders of a British minister and a U.N. diplomat." (Volume 24, page 665.)

In the *Britannica Year Book* for 1948, page 577, under the entry "Palestine" I read, "Meanwhile the [Jewish] terrorist attacks in Palestine continued, taking almost every conceivable form. Attacks on airfields and radar stations, armories and military posts, the wrecking of railway lines...and bank holdups all bore witness to organizaton on a larger, dangerous and ingenious scale, and were by general admission made possible chiefly by the active or passive support which the terrorists received from the great majority of the Jewish population [in Palestine]."

Returning to the *Britannica* (Volume 6, page 382), I learned that "On July 22, 1946, the Irgun blew up a wing of the King David Hotel in Jerusalem, killing 91 soldiers and civilians...On April 9, 1948 [remember Menachem Begin was at the time leader of the Irgun], a group of Irgun commandos raided the Arab village of Dayr Yasin [also spelled Deir Yassin] killing all 254 of its inhabitants." That massacre occurred some 60 years after Wounded Knee, about which we all know. But how many Americans know about the massacre at Deir Yassin and its direct contribution to the conflict in the Middle East today? How many Americans realize that "this highly publicized act terrorized the Arab villagers, who began a mass exodus from Palestine"? *(Encyclopedia Britannica*, Volume 22, page 143.)

Twenty minutes of study and I realized Aziz's remark that Begin was a terrorist was hardly a symptom of Palestinian fanaticism. And not only Begin, but Yitzhak Shamir, his friend and successor in the Israeli government. I had to dig to get this information, but there it was. Why hadn't I ever read about this in the papers? Heard it on TV or the radio?

With my tail between my legs, the next Sunday after Liturgy I apologized to Aziz for not believing him. He laughed and said Americans usually react the way I did. Now he told me more, about how his family moved to Ramallah (now in the occupied West Bank) in the 13th century (!) from Syria. They owned a sizable piece of property upon which they had established a lovely orange grove which the Israelis confiscated shortly after moving into the area in 1967. He told me how after the massacre at Deir Yassin and the consequent Palestinian exodus, the Israelis simply took title to the real estate of the fleeing Palestinians as "abandoned property." When Palestinians tried to return home, they found they had nothing left to their names.

Ramallah, along with Bethlehem, Nazareth, and a number of other Palestinian towns, have long been predominantly Christian. Aziz told me that some 25 percent of the Palestinians are Christians, of whom half are Orthodox. I have read that figure in several other places. But you get the impression from the media that all Arabs are Muslims. Have you ever seen a documentary or even a news story focusing on the Christian Palestinians?

He told me that the Zionist slogan "A people without a land for a land without people," was sheer nonsense, for a very large population of Palestinian Arabs had lived there for more than a thousand years. Arab fury at Israel is based not on some sort of wild hysteria: it is the anguish of people who have been systematically and ruthlessly dispossessed from their homeland and personal property.

The Zionist movement began sponsoring Jewish settlement in Palestine early in this century. At first the Arabs and the Jews got along well. But more and more Jews began to move in before World War II, and the idea spread among the Arabs that the Jews were planning to take over Palestine completely for themselves. The rapid influx at the end of World War II increased Palestinian Arab fears. To take over completely was in fact precisely the plan, and still is. The actions of Begin and Shamir, now recognized as great statesmen and, unlike Arafat, welcome in the United States, have made that clear.

So of course the Palestinians were and are upset! You would be too! The irony of all this is that the Zionists claim all of Palestine on the grounds God gave it to them 3,000 years ago, but the majority of Israeli Jews are "not religious." Probably most of them are agnostics or even atheists. So it's as if they are saying, "There is no God, but He gave us this land, and we intend to take it all."

In any conflict it takes "two to tango," and there are of course two sides to this issue. Arabs have certainly committed their atrocities, starting before World War II. The Arabs have made their mistakes, and in several cases have failed to take responsibility. Both sides have refused compromises, and at this date, compromise they must, or we'll all be destroyed in a new holocaust. Also, I hate "Jew bashing," and I'm at pains that this admittedly forthright criticism of the state of Israel not be construed as that.

But it seems "Arab bashing" is quite okay in this country, and we only faintly hear the Arab side of the story. It's okay to caricature Arabs unkindly, but no one would dare so abuse the Jews. We all remember how Leon Klinghoffer was thrown into the sea in his wheelchair by Arab terrorists. But how many remember that Alex Odeh, a spokesman for the Arab viewpoint, was also murdered that same week by Jewish terrorists in Los Angeles! Alex also had loved ones; his murder was as tragic as Klinghoffer's.

Up until the nearly four-year-old intifada, the media-created impression was that the Jews are always the good guys, and the Arabs the bad guys. Media coverage of the intifada, however, has brought home to Americans how brutal the Israeli military very often can be. I sometimes wonder if it has sunk into the brains and hearts of the American public that most of the Palestinians killed by the Israeli troops have been teenage boys. Two I have read about were shot in the head for writing slogans on the wall! Can you imagine the outcry if American soldiers were shooting down rock-throwing Black or Hispanic youthful protesters or gunning down young boys writing anti-government slogans on a wall! Ironically, American Jews would be the first to protest, and justly so!

Raising Jewish Voices

I have no negative agenda for the Jews. I do indeed wish them well. But in the name of integrity and decency, let's have more prominent Jewish voices raised, confessing the Israeli part in the Middle East mess. The whining of some columnists, "We're always innocent victims, first it was Hitler, and now it's the Arabs" is being consciously used to manipulate public policy, and that is disgusting. The Jews were innocent in Nazi Germany. But the Israelis are hardly innocent of great offenses.

I see some Jewish leaders setting themselves up for backlash, and I wish they'd take heed. The perception is growing that powerful Jewish interests wish to control our politicians' votes on, and media coverage of, Israeli questions. I don't know if that's the truth: but it would help dispel that perception if vocal and courageous Jewish leaders would encourage both dissemination of media information about Israel's dark side and public debate on Israeli issues. We certainly know plenty about the Arab dark side!

We're told by Israel that its policy is none of our business, but we American taxpayers are asked to foot Israeli bills. Israel now wants an extra $10 billion, and I'll be very surprised if that gets debated in public. What a subtle form of taxation without representation! Why shouldn't we publicly debate this like any other multi-billion-dollar issue?

The Arab world can only become filled with rage when virtually every person in the street knows full well the U.S. has tolerated Israel's continued incursions into foreign territory and other violations of international law, but has attacked Iraq, ostensibly for its violations of international law. For the life of me I don't know how any of the liberal Jews I knew in the days of the civil rights struggle and the anti-war movement in the '60s and '70s can stomach these double standards. Today some have become Jewish jingoists saying, "My Israel, right or wrong."

The war in the Gulf was certainly not simply a long-term result of the way the Zionist movement has proceeded in the past 50 or 60 years. The Palestinian-Israeli conflict is not the only serious issue afflicting the Arabs. But only if you are blind to or ignorant of history can you fail to recognize the destabilizing effect Israel's policies have had on the Middle East. In response, demogogues like Saddam Hussein will continue to emerge unless wrongs are redressed and apologies offered.

I believe that if the Zionists from the beginning had been willing to share Palestine with the native Arabs, without wanting to take over completely, there would have been no major strife. Contrary to popular opinion, at several times in history the Jews and the Muslims have gotten along very well. The Jews rose to great heights in Islamic Spain. When, after the Reconquista, Isabella and Ferdinand expelled the Jews, the Muslim Sultan of Turkey sent ships to bring them to his domain! A Sephardic rabbi in Atlanta once told me the sultan wrote Isabella thanking her for sending him her crown jewels.

I believe if Israel today will quit its ruthless expansionism and begin to respect the God-given civil rights of the Palestinians, the strife will be reduced to the point where there is no physical violence. I would like to see more American Jews who want to see Israel change its tactics speak up openly and loudly, because their voices will be heard in Israel.

Let us pray for peace in the Middle East, that justice and love will prevail. Let us pray that the Palestinian-Israeli issue will become a matter of open discussion in this country. ✦

This article was first published in Doxa *(P.O. Box 16286, Santa Fe, NM 87506), a quarterly review serving the Orthodox Church, edited by Mr. Melton.*

Eleven Months Chained to a Wall—
Time to Reach Some Conclusions

By Jerry Levin

In December, 1983, I went to Lebanon as Cable News Network's Lebanon bureau chief and correspondent determined to measure up as a reporter to one of my company's promotional slogans: "You have a right to know the score." That, of course, meant looking at causes, as well as effects, objectively and even-handedly, and telling the public, as far as humanly possible, the whole story—everyone's story.

My personal views regarding the general situation in the region did not change while I was there. They were only strengthened and enhanced by what I experienced as a willing practicing journalist and as an unwilling hostage. What I resent most about my captivity besides the fright it gave my loved ones—and me—is that it ended my assignment covering one of the toughest, and inherently most spectacular, but also one of the most often distorted stories of the decade. It was a plum, and I'm sorry to have lost the opportunity of doing my part to shed some light into the dark corners of that tragic event.

After my Syrian rescuers turned me over to my countrymen in Damascus on Feb. 15, 1985, one of the first questions I was asked by reporter colleagues was how did it feel to "be" the story, rather than to be reporting it. My answer was, "very uncomfortable."

Even then I had a sinking feeling that my life was going to be complicated in a way that the lives of the Americans who had been held hostage in Iran years before had not been. When they came home, they left no fellow citizens behind still in captivity; so they could put their ordeal (at least in that respect) behind them. But as I fled down a mountain in the dark, early on the chilly morning of Feb. 14, 1985, I knew that I was leaving behind four or five other hostages in the house from which I had just escaped.

Despite the fact that I never knew them, talked with them, or even saw them during my captivity (because I was isolated in lonely solitary confinement), I was aware of their presence. I could hear the muffled sound of their footsteps as one by one they were led blindfolded to the bathroom each morning. A few moments later I could hear their knocks on the door to be led out. Then I could hear the door being opened and them being led back to their own lonely isolation and chains.

So, as I made my way in the dark to freedom, I felt an aching bond with those unfortunate men. I was certain that my getting away was going to make it more difficult if not impossible for them to escape too. And it has turned out that way.

Once I was free, that attachment, that concern for those hostage strangers, motivated both my wife and me to discuss publicly our perceptions of the meaning of my captivity and theirs—in particular its American foreign policy context. We probably would not have felt the need to do that so strongly if we had felt more secure about the national press's interest in those perceptions, or the administration's interest in having them heard. But we did not.

The barely comprehended context of our captivity has been this: our captors made a specific demand (exchange for 17 Al Da'wa commandos imprisoned in Kuwait, convicted of blowing up the American and French embassies there); the genesis of those violent acts was in part retaliation for America's deadly and provocative entry into the Lebanese civil war. Two of the 17 prisoners in Kuwait were Lebanese.

Once in captivity, as angry as I was about it, I had to admit to myself that there was a certain grim and plausible logic for my frightening restraint at the hands of terrorists, although obviously their actions against me and their other innocent victims could not and can never be condoned. A decades-long United States policy of diplomatic dialogue and negotiation in the Middle East had been abruptly abandoned in 1983 in favor of the use of military force as a coercive tool of foreign policy.

In Lebanon it took the form of violent military intervention which set the stage for the deaths of more Americans in that part of the world than at any time since our soldiers fought in the Middle East during World War II. Also, and just as important, the stage was set for more deaths inflicted by us on inhabitants of that part of the world than at any time since World War II.

But the administration, spurred on too often by an obliging press, promoted the typically jingoistic idea that the captivity and the agony of the Americans taken hostage in Lebanon in 1984 and after had to do solely with callous, irrational acts by terrorists. Although there has been a brutal side to their captivity for which there can be no rational, moral apologetic, examination reveals another critical component for which there also was and is no rational, moral apologetic: our nation's violently dehumanizing, one-sided interference and one-sided involvement in Lebanon's already pervasively cruel and brutalizing civil war.

Back then our leaders explained that we had entered the civil war on behalf of our Middle East military proxy, Israel, in our continuing effort to help it contain or roll back Soviet influence. In Lebanon, however, Soviet influence was neither ideologically, confessionally, socially, nor economically the critical issue. But when we began to use our military forces directly to oppose the straw man of Soviet penetration in Lebanon, and innocent Lebanese and Palestinian men, women and children were killed and their property destroyed, retaliation was inevitable.

When I reached freedom, I learned to my amazement that those facts were hardly realized because they had hardly ever been a matter of public examination and discussion; and they still are not. The result was and continues to be the forestalling of debate where it needs to count most heavily—in the legislative and other domestic political arenas.

Counselors for candidates Reagan, Mondale and Ferraro picked the brains of my wife and her key counselor, Landrum Bolling, at length before the 1984 election debate on foreign policy. But the Middle East—in particular Lebanon, the hostages, or the Israeli-Palestinian issue—was never mentioned. That was inexcusable in view of the record number of American lives lost and still in peril at the time, with nothing constructive to show for the losses in terms of shortening the distance to peace.

It is not difficult to conclude why both presidential candidates shied away. The genesis of our confinement, the genesis of the deaths of the 241 Marines, the genesis of the deaths of scores of Americans in embassy bombings in Beirut and Kuwait, and equally important, the genesis of the deaths of innocent noncombatant Lebanese and Palestinians, was Israel's invasion of Lebanon.

But the candidates had a technical excuse for not voluntarily addressing this issue. The format was controlled by the panel of reporters who never brought up the subject. For them not to question the candidates on the issue was journalistically scandalous.

And in 1988, despite the Palestinian uprising, despite the well-documented horrors of Israeli collective punishment and continued confiscatory aggression, and despite the shredding of our Constitution by the Iran-contra masterminds, the situation did not change. The only candidate to bring up those subjects regularly was Jesse Jackson.

During the presidential debates in the 1988 general election, the only way the Middle East was brought up by the panels of reporters was within the context of what the candidates would do about insurgent terrorism. The reporters made it easy for the candidates to come out foursquare against free-lance terrorism while ignoring the official Israeli reign of terror that has made a mockery of Palestinian human rights.

The first six months of the Bush administration do not indicate that the president intends to act more kindly or gently toward the Palestinians than his predecessor. This continued impersonal attitude was ominously demonstrated to my wife and me by a high State Department official who said to us, "You've got to understand, in the Middle East we still must be guided by practicality, not morality."

Sadly, in the one-sided battle between Rambo and reconciliation, Rambo still gets most of the attention. I was once uninvited from the "Today" show after the producer who asked me to participate was overridden by her boss who, she said, told her, "We can't use him. He's been criticizing the president."

Amazingly, while I was still in captivity, my wife's even-handed, reconciliation-oriented public statements at home and in Syria, where she lobbied tirelessly at the highest levels on my behalf, gained her an enmity in pro-Israeli quarters that actually erupted bitterly on the very day she learned I was free. While we were in separate airplanes wing-ing our way toward a reunion on the airport tarmac at Frankfurt, West Germany, a spokesman for the Israeli cause in the United States was telling a producer for Cable News Network, my employer, that Sis Levin was a Syrian spy.

Since then we have been subjected to other forms of character assassination. I have been accused of having the Stockholm syndrome, being un-American, unpatriotic, and—last and not least—a self-hating Jew. (I wonder: Since I have been critical of government actions, does that make me a self-hating American? Or does the little bit of tattling I've done here about the press make me a self-hating journalist?)

The sad fact is that while there has been some balance in the general American press (and it has grown during the uprising), the motivation has been, in my opinion, very often self-interested tokenism to protect circulation or viewership, and not necessarily something that can be counted on over the long haul.

Despite these problems, my wife and I have learned since we began our do-it-your-self enlightenment campaign four years ago that there are plenty of good-hearted people in our nation who can be motivated toward making their voices count. But we also have encountered tens of thousands of other decent people with decent convictions who are still by and large an untapped resource. In their isolation, when they do speak out or write they are often then intimidated to the point of silence by a form of neo-McCarthyism that equates sympathy for Palestinian suffering and support for Palestinian aspirations with anti-Semitism.

Finding a way to support these people of good heart and good will is essential. Because they have not been reached, they are a potential powerhouse that is still unorganized and uncoordinated.

In a democracy where persuasion is mandatory, quality of argument when the quantity of advocates is limited is not a guarantee of national acquiescence. In my opinion, it will take nothing less than massive education leading to massive political action at the grassroots level to make the critical and irrevocable dent in the issue of Palestinian rights that is needed.

It will also take nothing less than an energetic professional effort at the top working full time to inspire that kind of grassroots action and also to persuade the legislative and executive branches of government to be maximally responsive. What is needed is a kind of AIPAC but without intimidation, dirty tricks, or character assassination.

Only through such efforts will there ever be the quantity of voices needed to give weight to the cause a steadfast few have been trying to keep alive in the United States for so many years. There is no other way. And it is the quintessential American way. ✦

Jerry Levin was the first of the so-called forgotten American hostages in Lebanon. Kidnapped on March 7, 1984, he spent 11 months chained to a wall in solitary confinement in Lebanon's Bekaa valley until he was able to slip through a window one night and find his way to a Syrian army patrol. Since January, 1991, he has served as direc-

tor of news and information services for World Vision, an international relief and development organization based in Monrovia, California.

POSTSCRIPT: *As to the piece I wrote in 1989, I am not surprised to observe how much of it still holds. It's with sadness I contemplate how little the lessons of Lebanon were learned by our leadership and how successful they remain in selling their out-of-step policies to the American people.*

For Me, Discovering the Middle East Was Discovering Myself

By Laika Dajani

My father is a Palestinian from Jerusalem. My mother is an American from San Francisco. I was born in Beirut but have lived in Saudi Arabia, Paris, Amman, London and Washington, DC. I am a product of the Palestinian diaspora. The Middle East is my heritage, and thus an indisputable part of my being, but it is also my passionate interest; one that has gradually developed and matured, as I have, over the years.

My awareness of the Middle East is present in vivid flashbacks of people, places, comments and emotions. My first such conscious recollection dates back to when I was five years old and living in Jeddah, Saudi Arabia. I was in the kitchen with my mother on a warm, moonlit night. I stood on tiptoe to look out into our garden and saw our Sudanese nanny kneeling on a small rug. She bent forward and lightly touched the rug with her forehead. I asked my mother, "What is she doing?"

"Praying," my mother said. "Don't stare, and come away from the window." I silently obeyed. My mother then explained to me the five tenets of Islam, belief in the one God, prayer, fasting, pilgrimage, and charity.

Another memory, more long-term than the first, is my struggle with the Arabic language. Every Saturday, from the time we were 8 until we were 11 years old, my twin sister, Lena, and I underwent Arabic lessons. We grasped the alphabet quickly, but memorization of simple Qur'anic texts proved more challenging. It was an uphill struggle, and one that I have yet to complete to my satisfaction.

My adolescent years were spent primarily in British schools. I recall various hurtful remarks: "If your father is an Arab, does he wear a teacloth on his head?" "Those Arabs are taking over the bleedin' country." At the time, I knew that such comments were racist and I felt angry and uncomfortable. Although, as yet, I did not feel my own identity to be that of an Arab, I felt that my father had been insulted.

In 1982, when I was 15, I transferred to the American School in London. That year was significant to me for two reasons. One was the Israeli invasion of Lebanon. The other was the beginning of my emotional attachment to the plight of the Palestinians and the

Arab world as an entity. I vividly recall the televised images of Israeli tanks and the sounds of Israeli jets racing across the Beirut skyline. I remember the horror and sadness on my parents' faces as they watched the destruction of a city they had loved.

Soon after the invasion, I asked my parents for advice on a book explaining, in a relatively simple format, the history of the Palestinian diaspora. I had grown up hearing stories of the flight of my father's family from Jerusalem in 1948, but had never fully absorbed the historical background. In three days I read *O, Jerusalem* and my emotional interest rapidly expanded into an academic one.

In my senior year in high school, I took a course on international relations and wrote my final paper on U.S. aid to Israel. I was shocked to discover that the U.S. had given far more financial support to tiny Israel than to any other country, even big countries with huge problems like India or Egypt, or countries maintaining armies or major bases at U.S. disposal, like Turkey, Pakistan or the Philippines.

In the spring of 1985 I was accepted at Georgetown University for the coming fall. I deferred my acceptance for one year, however, and in August I went with my mother and sister to join my father for a year in Amman, Jordan. I had visited Amman for countless summer and spring holidays, but I had not lived in a Middle Eastern country since those very early days in Saudi Arabia.

The adjustment was difficult. I had grown up in London, and did not speak or understand Arabic, even though I could read it. I was envious of my fellow high school graduates, who were off at Brown, Georgetown, and other universities. Although my sister and I were happily enveloped by my father's extensive family, there were problems that made us feel out of place.

Our main frustration was transport. Neither of us had a British driving license, so we had to rely on our parents to take us back and forth to the University of Jordan, where we were studying Arabic, and to the houses of our friends for tea and conversation. After two months, we started a 35-day driving course. We had to chaperone each other, as our driving instructor was male. The driving test was conducted in a small village about half an hour outside Amman. Because there were forms to fill out, scribes were seated at makeshift tables to provide their services for the illiterate.

First came the "road signs" test, normally a written procedure. As our Arabic was far from adequate, my sister and I were sent to the back of the room with the "illiterate" crowd. After everyone else had finished, we were ceremoniously summoned to the front of the room. A rotund official pointed a stubby finger at about 20 miscellaneous signs. We responded in simple English and passed. The practical driving test was more challenging. Screeching sounds accompanied by the squawking of frightened chickens testified to my less than adequate driving skills. Much to my distress, I failed my test, but my sister passed, thus paving the way for automobile adventures.

Once we had our freedom of movement, we began to settle in to the Amman pace of life. There were many excursions to the desert palaces, the Dead Sea, and to the north of Jordan. Our Arabic improved, and we were able to communicate effectively with taxi drivers and waiters.

I also was able to cross the Jordan River and visit the occupied West Bank and Gaza Strip. My first visit there was one of the most emotionally draining experiences of my life. I simply was not prepared for my first personal encounter with the Israeli military occupation.

I was "strip-searched" at Allenby Bridge, along with other foreign passport holders of Arab descent. Our Arab taxi was stopped at night checkpoints on the road up to Jerusalem from Jericho. I saw the angry, defiant faces of young Palestinian men being interrogated by Israeli soldiers in Nablus.

But these cold, frightening memories are filed away among other, warm recollections of meeting my cousins in their homes in the Gaza Strip and being deeply moved by the faded, dusty, time-warped quality of the city of Gaza itself. I traveled to the occupied areas, as well as to Israel, five times during my one year in Amman. Each visit proved to be as enriching, and heart-wrenching, as the first.

By the time I left for Georgetown University, I was "hooked" on the Middle East. I took courses on Islam, the Ottoman Empire, and 20th Century Middle Eastern History. And I joined the Palestine Club. The next summer, in 1987, my sister and I went to the West Bank to spend a month as volunteers in a summer camp program for Palestinian refugee girls run by the YWCA. It provided a rare opportunity for children of the camps to escape from their claustrophobic environment and to indulge in such childhood pursuits as painting, singing and dancing.

Throughout that exhausting but enriching month, my Arabic was stretched to its limit as I learned about the lives of these children in the camps, their families (average size 10), their pride in being Palestinian, and how each child knew the exact village from which her family had been driven in 1948 or 1967. I learned how to dance the *debke*, how to pluck a chicken, and how to be authoritative.

I became fiercely protective and proud of my new protégés. I applauded their successes, and I chastised their carelessness. Most of all, I felt madly proud of my father, his people, and our Palestinian heritage as I simultaneously absorbed it and became a part of passing it on from generation to generation.

With a B.S. from Georgetown in international relations, I elected to pursue a master's degree in London in Middle East studies. My dissertation was focused on the political themes of identity, ideology, and nationalism in relation to the Palestinians. My studies effectively melded my emotional attachment and my academic passion for the Middle East.

Having been born looking "Western," raised in England, educated in American schools, and now married to a French national while retaining U.S. citizenship, I'm sure it comes as a surprise to people I encounter that I consider myself a Palestinian in spirit. My emotions are triggered by the Middle East, and, most especially, the Palestinians. For me, "Seeing the Light" has been an emotional discovery of my own identity, and an intellectual exploration of the rich and multilayered Middle Eastern heritage which became mine at birth. ✦

Laika Dajani received her master's degree in Middle Eastern studies from the University of London.

Rediscovering Palestine

By The Rev. Phineas Washer

My trip to the occupied West Bank and Gaza opened up a new world for me! In July 1985, under the auspices of the Palestine Human Rights Campaign, I traveled to the occupied territories with 13 academics and one other cleric. Our group investigated academic freedom on the West Bank.

That inquiry propelled me into a new world where teachers are not allowed to teach. West Bank educators were consistently harrassed and obstructed by Israeli occupation forces: teachers were detained frequently, soldiers patrolled university campuses, equipment requisitions were snarled in red tape for months, instructors' homes were raided. Professors wanted to teach; students wanted to learn. But Israeli officials made that very difficult to do.

However, I did learn something about Palestinians. Before my trip I had never heard the word "Palestinian" used except as an adjective modifying the word "terrorist." But that's not what I found when I encountered West Bankers. I met a wide cross-section of the population, including attorneys, university people, an ex-employee of the Mennonite Church, librarians, bus drivers, hotel clerks, scientists, physicians, refugees—people wanting to do their jobs, people wanting to live in peace. Brilliant people and average people. People deeply hurt and people decidedly determined. People who love their homes, their land, their families. Palestinians—people like everyone else, like you and me.

We met an attorney from Law in the Service of Man, the West Bank affiliate of the International Commission of Jurists. Our group of 15 gathered in a small meeting room to hear his story. As coolly and detached as a professional could be under such circumstances, he told of the frustrations and harassments he encounters every day in dealing with the Israeli military courts.

Struggling to work through the courts to redress the grievances of his people, he reported how slowly justice moved, how over and over again every legitimate effort of his was blocked. The military authorities dug up Israeli laws, Jordanian laws, British Mandate laws, Ottoman laws—whenever a law was needed to stifle his inquiries, the military authorities found such a law.

"Since the legal system moves so slowly, will you ever resort to violence to further your cause?" one of our members asked him. The lawyer thought a moment, and when he spoke his voice had a quiet, determined resolution that suggested he had asked himself this question many times.

"No, I will never resort to violence," he said.

I remember meeting a professor from An-Najah University in Nablus. There must be some way, he said, to break the impasse that keeps apart the two societies, Palestinian and Jewish. Looking for that break, he brought together a handful of students from his university and a similar number from Tel Aviv University for a "let's get acquainted and get to know each other as human beings" meeting. This was a pilgrimage for peace, but an Israeli military official told the professor that these meetings would have to stop. "I don't want my people to get confused," said the official.

Neither shall I forget the Palestinian brother who spent a morning showing us the Jewish settlements surrounding Arab East Jerusalem, a perspective not offered your average tourist. The settlements looked like fortresses, and their groupings suggested that their purpose was to isolate, seal off, and intimidate the Palestinians under Israeli occupation in Jerusalem's Old City.

In the United States, I think we are overdue for a more realistic picture of the Palestinians and what they are up against. When I hear the word "Palestinian" I no longer see a terrorist. Instead, I have images of warm, caring human beings who love their land and their families, and who wish to live in peace.

Previously I had only known the Holy Land through Biblical studies, slide shows, reports of others, and books. What new worlds of understanding have opened up to me in the study of Scripture as a result of riding over the terrain, observing the shepherds, visiting the holy places. The Good Samaritan did hike down from Jerusalem to Jericho, like the story says. Standing in the Carmel mountain range, I realized why fiery Elijah must have attracted so much attention. He ministered in lands and on mountainsides as dramatic as his personality.

Another new world I had not anticipated is a new world of friends, friends made in the Holy Land as well as friends here in my city of Houston who are interested in the Palestinian issue. Friends with roots and ties to the land I visited. Friends long interested in the cause of freedom, justice and human rights.

As a result of my trip and since my trip, many new worlds have opened up to me. Eat your heart out, Christopher Columbus, you're not the only one who discovered a new world! ✦

In 1987, the Reverend Phineas Washer was minister of the John Knox Presbyterian Church in Houston, Texas.

Giving Something Up, But Gaining So Much More

By Janet McMahon

My enlightenment began in 1985 when I quit smoking. Not that I was a pro-Israeli smoker, especially following the invasion of Lebanon. I had some strong opinions: for example, if Israel chose to act on the basis of morality, I might be willing to treat it as a moral entity; however, it was acting like any other political state (particularly like the U.S. in Vietnam, I thought), and I intended to oppose its actions as I had opposed my own country's. And I refused to be considered an anti-Semite for doing so.

For me the second point was and is particularly important, because I would not be who I am today if I hadn't moved to a largely Jewish community in seventh grade. I reached political maturity there, and became active in the civil rights and anti-war movements because my friends and teachers were aware and involved. But it was difficult to resolve the contradictions posed by the Arab-Israeli conflict, and I often felt confused. For me, "seeing the light" has been more analogous to emerging from Plato's cave than to switching on a light bulb.

When I stopped smoking on March 18, 1985, I decided to use the money I had spent on cigarettes to sponsor a child through an international children's organization. I requested a girl, wherever the need was greatest. In response, I received a picture of and information about Rania N., a seven-year-old Shi'i Muslim living in the Israeli buffer zone in southern Lebanon. It became even more difficult to read the frequent newspaper accounts of Israeli raids there.

Soon afterward, I came across *The Vanished Imam* by Fouad Ajami. Since the subtitle referred to the "Shia of Lebanon," and since the author is one himself, I decided to read his book. (I wouldn't have read a book on the subject by Henry Kissinger, for example.) I was amazed to read Ajami's description of the Lebanese Shi'i as "historically quiescent." I had assumed they were all "terrorists." I am grateful that I realized relatively early on that I knew abysmally little about the people and history of the Arab world, but I am still appalled by how little I knew then, and how much there is to know.

I continued to experience shocks of ignorance, for want of a better phrase. However,

I must confess that I was pleased with my progress when I recently read in Hannah Arendt's *Eichmann in Jerusalem* that Eichmann was a Zionist. Five years ago I would have shouted, "What?" Last month I muttered, "It figures."

I have seen the light in a more literal sense as well, having lived in Cairo for a year as a student at the American University there. In Egypt, I experienced the many wonderful characteristics of the Arab people, their warmth, graciousness and deep human concern which is such a basic element in human relations there. Before I went to the Middle East, I didn't think twice when I heard the term "Arab terrorist"; now I find it completely unacceptable and misleading. I also quickly recognize the half-truths and untruths which appear in the daily media of this country, and I am outraged.

What I continue to find disconcerting is the almost accidental nature of my enlightenment: Suppose I had ended up sponsoring a child from Nepal? One's ignorance is only reinforced because there is so much written about the Middle East: a well-read and informed person can easily believe she knows what the background and issues are, an assumption one would not so readily make about Africa, for example.

In addition to its ultimate value as the popular expression of the Palestinian people, the intifada has had the added benefit of causing Americans to question their assumptions about the history and nature of the Zionist movement and of their automatic support for Israel. This is a crucial first step on the road to enlightenment.

Of course, the Israeli lobby is still formidable and the media continue to project racist images of Arabs. But I believe there has been a breakthrough, however small. My hope is that the resulting shocks of ignorance Americans will experience as they learn more about the Middle East will occur in ever decreasing degrees of magnitude.

In the meantime, I think of Rania. ✦

Janet McMahon is managing editor of the Washington Report on Middle East Affairs.

POSTSCRIPT: *Rania and her family moved, and I now sponsor another Lebanese girl, who lives in Sidon. But the dangers remain: in his 1996 field report, the charity's program officer in Lebanon reported that five sponsored children had been killed in Israel's April, 1996, attack on the U.N. compound at Qana.*

Righting the Balance Between Truth and Falsehood

By Greg Noakes

I can pinpoint exactly my first exposure to the politics of the Middle East, and more particularly to the Israeli-Palestinian conflict. It came when I was five-and-a-half years old, during the 1972 Summer Olympics at Munich. My family was visiting my grandmother in Ruston, Louisiana at the time, and amid the ABC television coverage of Mark Spitz, Olga Korbut and weightlifter Vasily Alekseyev there were more sinister images. I remember seeing grainy pictures of men in ski masks on the balconies of the Olympic Village and thinking that their system of signaling to one another by opening and closing doors was quite ingenious. I also remember the televised aftermath of the bungled West German operation to rescue the Israeli athletes held by the Black September commandos.

These first grim images of Middle Eastern conflict were reinforced the following year with the October 1973 war between Egypt and Israel. Again it is a specific television image that I recall, in this case CBS news footage of Egyptian soldiers celebrating after penetrating into what I now realize was Sinai. At the age of six I was confused about which were "the good guys" in this war, and asked a friend's mother for clarification. "The Israelis," she answered. "They're more like us." This conviction was only reinforced in the following months, when the Arabs began to hold up "our oil."

By 1975 and the age of eight my impression of the Middle East as a brutal and dangerous place was fixed. I held the firm conviction that there were three places in the world where I did not want to live: Cambodia, Belfast and Beirut. The TV often flashed pictures of the effect of the Lebanese civil war on the capital and its people, and I was thankful that I wasn't there.

Still, my interest in and exposure to the Middle East were marginal. Cairo and Casablanca were a long way from Fort Worth, Texas, where I grew up. Lawrence of Arabia and Sindbad the Sailor represented a whole culture for me.

This perception changed quickly and radically in 1985, during my second year as an undergraduate student at the University of Virginia. Unlike many who develop a personal fascination with the Middle East as a result of some great political crisis, humanitarian catastrophe or personal contact, my sea-change came through more prosaic means—academic lectures and textbooks. Even as an architecture major, I had to take a certain number of social science and foreign language classes. Partially on a whim, and partially to learn about an area of the world of which I was wholly ignorant, I selected "Islamic History to 1258" and "Elementary Arabic 101" as my required courses. It was a decision that changed everything for me.

I quickly found the intricacy and beauty of Arabic and the vicissitudes of Middle East history far more interesting than Mies van der Rohe and the physics of designing basements. My old notion of the Arab world as a hotbed of violence, intrigue and fanaticism was replaced by a new appreciation of the history and cultures of the region.

I realized what a disservice was performed by sensationalist media coverage of the Mideast, interested only in the latest bomb blast or bloodbath and not in the complex issues underlying the political, social and economic problems of the region. It's not a bad rule of thumb when dealing with the Middle East to assume that anything facile is false, and I quickly came to the conclusion that real understanding came only through time and effort, not sound bites and snap judgments.

By the end of my third semester at Virginia, I decided to focus on the Middle East and transferred from the architecture school. In 1988 I graduated with a B.A. in history and a minor in Arabic, then went on to do a master's degree in Middle Eastern Studies at the University of Texas, working principally on North Africa.

The Middle East came to dominate more than my academic career. As part of my classwork I had read about Islam and its teachings and found it appealing, its ethics not far from my upbringing as a Protestant Christian and its theology resolving some lingering questions. Over several years I dug deeper, reading and studying on my own, learning about the faith and the global culture it had spawned.

It was difficult at first to know which books were accurate, and which laced with bias. Centuries of tension between Islam and the West have colored nearly everything written about the faith. Yet works like *Islam and the Destiny of Man* by the European Muslim Charles LeGai Eaton and Marshall Hodgson's difficult but detailed *Venture of Islam* volumes enticed me further into the religion and its traditions. By my first year in grad school in Austin I decided to make my profession of faith—"There is no god but God and Muhammad is His Prophet"—and became a Muslim. My understanding of Islam as a living faith, applicable not just in the mosque but throughout daily life, has profoundly affected me.

A Deepening Involvement

My involvement in the region deepened with my arrival at the *Washington Report on Middle East Affairs*, first as the advertising director and later as news editor. While my main interest still lies in the countries of North Africa (where I now have a personal stake, having married an Algerian woman in 1991), working at the magazine has brought me into contact with individuals on the staff and outside the organization who feel just as passionately about Palestine, Bosnia, Iraq, Somalia, Kashmir and other lands and peoples. I agree with the views of some, disagree with others, yet have learned something from all of them. The give-and-take of editorial decisions, the breadth of the area and the range of topics the *Washington Report* covers, and the need to report facts and opinions fairly and accurately has not only deepened my understanding of the region, but also forced me to rethink some of my own ideas—always a worthwhile exercise.

One of the ideas I have mulled over most is the importance of clear, factual and accessible information when dealing with the Middle East. The mainstream American news media failed me as a youngster, and it has shown only slow improvement in its coverage of the Islamic world in the two decades since that time. Few Americans have the time or inclination to dig deep into the enormous body of writing on the Middle East or Islam in search of a few nuggets of truth. Even fewer have access to the engaging and inspiring professors I enjoyed in school.

Stereotypes die hard. Public opinion on the Middle East changes only in the wake of accurate and useful information—the kind that can be acted upon in the classroom, newsroom, courtroom, picket line or voting booth. The outlets for such information are few, but they appear to be growing in both number and quality. I'm fortunate to be in a position to contribute to one of the oldest, largest and most influential of those outlets.

It is perhaps not too unrealistic to think that what once was an audacious challenge to "conventional wisdom" on the Middle East will not only inform the mainstream—a process already well underway—but will *become* the mainstream. As Muslims know from the Qur'an, "In this way does God set forth the parable of truth and falsehood: for, as far as the scum is concerned, it passes away as all dross; but that which is of benefit to man abides on earth." ✦

Greg Noakes is a former news editor of the Washington Report on Middle East Affairs.

Teaching About Palestinians: A Lesson About America

By Daniel McGowan

It started around 1985, when colleges and universities were overwhelmingly demanding that their pension funds no longer invest in South Africa. As a conservative professor of economics at Hobart and William Smith Colleges in Geneva, New York, I disagreed with such prohibitions and political obstructions to the free flow of capital.

I began publicly to ask questions: "If apartheid is evil, why is it bad for South Africans and acceptable for Israelis? Why is the expropriation of land for the exclusive use of whites condemned, but the expropriation of land for the exclusive use of Jews condoned? If Krugerrands are to be banned, why not diamonds? Does cutting them in Israel remove the Black blood on them? If Israel, Taiwan, France, Germany, Britain, or any other ally continues to send arms or military advisers to South Africa, should U.S. military aid to that country be withheld? In order to make economic sanctioning more effective against South Africa, should the U.S. further subsidize Israel so that it can purchase elsewhere the coal, uranium and other minerals that it now imports from South Africa?"

Such uncomfortable questions for comfortable members of the college community were largely answered by silence. The one exception was Richard Rosenbaum, the flamboyant vice chairman of the board of trustees of Hobart and William Smith and later a gubernatorial candidate for the state of New York.

In a letter to the *Chronicle of Higher Education,* he expressed "grave concern…that a professor might be teaching students distorted and, in some cases, totally false information." He vowed to take me "on a mission" to Israel "in the certain knowledge that anyone with a shred of an open mind would come back a friend of Israel." But, alas, Mr. Rosenbaum could not get Executive Director Malcolm Hoenlein of the Conference of Presidents of Major American Jewish Organizations to pay for the trip. So he reneged on his offer by relaying a parting insult from "a wise man" with whom he shared my correspondence. This unnamed person allegedly said, "Why take him to Israel? He's obviously a bigot, and that experience will make him think he's an informed bigot."

But if Rosenbaum and friends found my questions on the efficacy of divestment and the comparisons with Israel to be offensive, others, like Walter Williams, John M. Olin Distinguished Professor of Economics at George Mason University, found raising them to be courageous. Invariably, my supporters would first ask if I had tenure. When informed that I did, they would encourage me to use it and freely express opinions and beliefs which, although politically incorrect, were well-founded or irrefutable.

The South African divestment confrontation caused me to begin to study Israel and to use it in pedagogical examples. When lecturing on international trade, for instance, I would point to the fact that the Israeli diamond-cutting industry provided a living for some 20,000 people in South Africa and accounted for over a fifth of the value of the country's viable foreign trade (1990). Nevertheless, while a U.S. ban on the sale of Krugerrands was considered a politically acceptable way to fight apartheid, to ban the sale of diamonds was not.

Stimulating Discussions

When studying labor markets, I often stimulated discussion by illustrating disequilibria caused by ethnic or religious discrimination. For example, I would point out that when workers from Gaza come to Israel they work largely with no benefits and protection in a country with a very strong labor union orientation, at least for Jews. So it is no surprise that as Palestinians they are confined to jobs in agriculture, menial construction, and sanitation.

I wanted to study Islam. So I went to the religion department at Hobart and William Smith Colleges. The department had five full-time faculty and offered 39 courses, 10 on Judaism and the Holocaust. But there was no course on Islam. I was astounded! Not a single course was offered on this major religion to which roughly 20 percent of the world's population adheres. I compared it to an economics department which offers no courses on macroeconomic theory or a math department with no courses in calculus. In response to my queries, the religion department said that Islam was very complicated and that there was no one qualified to teach such a course.

One member defended the department's shortcoming, saying the colleges had very few Muslim students, as though that mattered. The colleges have no students who are art historians, yet they teach art history. They have no Russian students, yet they teach Russian.

The idea of identifying students by religion raised new questions in my mind. In searching for answers I first consulted a standard source of data for economists, the *Statistical Abstracts of the United States*. I wanted to find out how many Muslims there were in the United States.

It seemed like a simple question. Sixty religious bodies were listed and I read that the U.S. had 58 million Catholics, 6 million Jews, 4 million Presbyterians, 900,000 Jehovah's Witnesses, 99,000 Mennonites, etc. But apparently it had no Muslims. I was shocked. What about all the Americans who have come from the Arab world? What about those from Pakistan, Afghanistan, Iran, Bangladesh and the Philippines? What about the Black Muslims? Why are their numbers not recorded? I wrote to the Department of Commerce and the editors assured me that the failure to present such data was not due to any political motive or lack of ability on their part. The Department claimed that most estimates place the number of Muslims at around 300,000. Other sources set the number at around 7 million, but, in any case, no number was furnished and printed in the *Statistical Abstracts*.

One of the truly unique features of Hobart and William Smith Colleges is that the faculty is encouraged to teach new courses, especially those which cross disciplines, involve women's studies, and lead to travel or terms abroad. I proposed such a course, called "Palestine and the Palestinian People: Political, Social and Economic Issues," to begin in the winter semester of 1990. The course was to be a senior forum and would be taught by three professors: a political scientist, an anthropologist and an economist. Because the course precisely met the stated goals of the Colleges' curriculum, it was approved by the committee on academic affairs, in spite of some Zionist reservations and insistence that at least one of the professors be Jewish. The latter demand was met by adding a second political scientist who was Jewish, although not a Zionist.

In order to gain knowledge of the Palestinians, I went to meetings of the American-Arab Anti-Discrimination Committee (ADC) in the spring of 1989. There I found a wealth of books, films, and potential speakers for the forum I planned to lead nine months later. It was also there that I first learned of ADC's Eyewitness Israel Program which made it possible for small groups of Americans to visit Palestine at their own expense, and experience at first hand the brutality of the occupation. I immediately applied for the program, but was rejected because I did not fit the stereotypical profile. Instead of being a doctor, sociologist, labor union leader, clergyman, or an organizer for human rights, I was a conservative, an economist, and a life-time member of the National Rifle Association. Those were not considered auspicious credentials. Nevertheless, I continued to call and write to ADC, pleading with them to let me go. When another participant dropped out at the last minute, I was ready with passport and money to pay my own way.

While in Palestine, I lived in Jabalya, the largest of the refugee camps in Gaza. I visited hospitals and cottage industries and spoke with doctors, social workers, lawyers, and leaders of the intifada. I photographed Israeli patrols shooting live and rubber bullets at children who routinely attacked them with stones, I went to Hebron, Jerusalem, Ramallah, and Jenin. I tried to visit the large West Bank settlement of Kiryat Arba, near Hebron, but permission was denied. I offered to retain the services of Israeli human rights lawyer Lea Tsemel to take me to the Ketziot prison camp in Israel, but she was unable to provide me access.

I made many contacts among the Palestinians and some among the Israelis. In all it was a very energizing trip and one which made me eager to read and learn more about Palestine in preparation for the new course.

It is a gross understatement to say that teaching a course on the Palestinians at a liberal arts institution is challenging, especially where 20 percent of the student body, key people in the administration, and key people on the board of trustees are Jewish. In 28 years of college teaching it was the only time that I was summoned to the provost's office and, in the second week of the term, told that there were grave concerns (a now familiar warning) about the course and that it might "need to be cancelled" unless it was immediately given "more balance," meaning, of course, a more pro-Israeli spin. I pointed out that the course was already "balanced," and that for the administration to cancel the course for such a spurious reason would most certainly damage the college's reputation when the argument was aired in the *Chronicle of Higher Education* or in the local press.

Constant Challenges

But it was not just criticism by some Zionist administrators that made teaching or saying anything positive about the Palestinians difficult. It was a sense of constantly being on guard and of having to back up any statement with a Jewish source. If you wanted to talk about Palestinian refugees, you first had to refute the Zionist propaganda that there were no Arabs living in Palestine when the Jews returned; many students came with the well-worn doctrine that it was a "land without people for people without land."

You had to get by the propaganda in Golda Meir's claim that there is no such thing as a Palestinian—they are all just Arabs. You had to break the image that the Arabs were Nazis; that Palestinians are inherently anti-Semitic (which is a bit oxymoronic, since Palestinians are Semites); that today's settlers are peace-loving, devoutly religious pioneers; that all Palestinians are terrorists, and that Jews practice the "purity of arms" and never use terrorism.

If you wanted to speak about Israeli concentration camps, such as Ketziot, you first had to distinguish a concentration camp from an extermination camp, like Auschwitz, and your numbers of prisoners had to come from the *Jerusalem Post* or some other non-Arab source. You had to correct the impression that the Six-Day War was started by the Palestinians; you had to clarify that a "pre-emptive strike" is when *our* side initiates war and a "sneak attack" is when the *other* side fires first. You had to show that to describe the attack on the USS *Liberty* is not to bring up a gratuitous anti-Semitic footnote, but to recount a piece of U.S. history which has been flushed down the memory hole, where unpleasant things are put to be deliberately forgotten.

The most frustrating part of teaching this course, however, was that in order even to begin to lecture about Palestinians, you inevitably were forced to speak about the Holocaust, to which the Palestinians did not contribute, which was a genocide committed by Christians, and which had nothing to do with Muslims. In spite of Zionist tales of "Hitler meets the Mufti," the Palestinians no more collaborated with the Third Reich than did the Zionists themselves. Yet if guilt for the Holocaust cannot be laid on the Palestinians, its horror serves as the final apology for injustices committed by Israelis against Palestinians. (The apology goes something like this: "Yes, what the Zionists have done, and continue to do, to the Palestinians is not right, but you really can't blame them after all Hitler did to the Jews." It is the ultimate excuse which covers not only Zionist behavior immediately after World War II, but every year and every generation since then.)

The course was intended to address the issue of Palestinians and yet it was forced first to review the darkest chapter in Jewish history, pointing out that far greater numbers of Jews have been victims than have Palestinians. The fact is that if every Palestinian in the West Bank and Gaza were executed tomorrow, the number of victims would not equal half of the number of Jews executed in World War II. But why does a description of the political, social, and economic characteristics of one people in the Middle East have to be prefaced and twisted to fit the history of another in Europe? Many courses are given on Jews with no mention of Palestinians; no courses are given on Palestinians without extensive discussion of Jews and Zionism.

In spite of pressure, more subtle than overt, it is a tribute to Hobart and William Smith Colleges that such a course on the Palestinians was allowed to be taught at all. Yes, I was forced "to balance" the course. "Days of Rage" was shown for the *quid pro quo* of "Exodus"; *The Gun and the Olive Branch* was read for the *quid pro quo* of *The Israel-Arab Reader*; Mubarak Awad was invited for the *quid pro quo* of Philipa Strum. But I was allowed to buy "Palestinian" books for the library, although there was no special budget as there is for Judaic Studies. I was allowed, and indeed encouraged, by the president of the Colleges, to present a "balancing" speaker when then-Likud party leader Binyamin Netanyahu visited the campus. Jerusalem-born Professor Edward Said of Columbia University was chosen and he presented a wonderful lecture (which the Colleges were allowed to tape) for roughly a third of the amount charged by Netanyahu (who refused to allow the use of a tape made during his lecture). I also was encouraged to invite Palestinian human rights activist Hanan Ashrawi to "balance" a presentation by Elie Wiesel, who has defended the causes of Soviet Jews, Nicaragua's Miskito Indians, Argentina's "disappeared," Cambodian refugees, the Kurds, South African victims of apartheid, prisoners in the former Yugoslavia, and most other oppressed people with the glaring exception of Palestinian victims of Zionism, who have been treated consistently to a deafening dose of Wieselian silence.

Teaching a course on Palestinians sparked interest all across the college community. After an Israeli woman artist and close friend of the provost held an art exhibit, I secured support for an exhibit by the Palestinian artist Kamal Boullata. The art department helped with the exhibit; seven pieces of Boullata's work were purchased by people in the local community; and his moving film, "Stranger at Home," was shown with hardly a dry eye in the audience.

It was trendy at the time for Hobart and William Smith professors to use vanity license plates to stimulate interest in their disciplines. A geology professor's plate read "DEVONIAN"; a science professor's read "BOTANY." My plate on an old Peugeot read "INTIFADA." People who didn't know intifada from enchilada began to recognize the word and to understand that it meant the shaking off of occupation and control not only by the Israelis, but by the Egyptians, the Jordanians, the Syrians, and by others who, while providing refuge, sometimes also have oppressed Palestinians. Although some people expressed fear of riding in a car with "INTIFADA" license plates, I drove the car for four years, including trips to New York City, with no incident other than a few finger gestures.

Parked in front of the Colleges on Main Street, the license plate was said to have dissuaded some potential students and some potential donors, but at no time was there any pressure to remove it. To the contrary, the plate become a symbol of someone who was willing to stand up for the human rights of a people others have been taught to despise at worst and to ignore at best. It caused me to be invited to present lectures to local community groups and to colleges throughout the upstate New York area.

I believe, however, that it is not enough "to see the light" regarding Palestinians, their victimization, and their struggle to survive as a nation. Even as more Americans "see the light," only the Palestinians themselves can make real change happen. Crying for the world to recognize injustice and to do something is no more a solution for Palestinians than it was for Jews under the Nazis or for the Bosnians under the Serbs. The path toward achieving human rights and a national state for Palestinians has been blazed by others, including Mohandas K. Gandhi of India and Nelson Mandela of South Africa, and by Jews who have contributed directly and indirectly to the establishment of Israel. "Righteous Gentiles" can see the light, work tirelessly for the cause, and even sacrifice their own lives for it, but only the victims, in this case the Palestinians, can make the change a reality. ✦

Daniel McGowan, a professor of economics at Hobart and William Smith Colleges in Geneva, NY, is the founder and director of Deir Yassin Remembered.

Palestine: Fact and Fable

By Debbie Kuehn

Palestine has many moods. This was the first thing I noticed on my first trip to the West Bank. Western stereotypes led me to believe that every day would bring the same hot cloudlessness, but I quickly learned that there are varying degrees of heat in a land as complex and changeable as the political situation within it.

In the morning, when the countryside is awakening, you hear activity. The banging of breakfast pans. The early laughter of children. The clanking of the irrigation pump performing its important community function.

At noon, you hear nothing, but feel the heat. The cucumbers sweating on tangled vines. The flies buzzing about your head. Later, you hear the children laughing again as they come out to play in the long, cooling shadows of afternoon. By evening, you hear people talking and visiting as the sun sets behind the mosque and the emerging coolness of dusk carries with it the wonderful scents of jasmine and honeysuckle.

In spite of the peaceful look of this place, there is an undeniable tension in the landscape and in the country itself. You feel it just beneath the surface.

I went to the Middle East a few years ago to visit the family of friends I had met in the U.S. I went first to Amman, Jordan, where my friends met me and helped me secure permission to cross the Jordan River into the West Bank. My friends had to cross the river at a different checkpoint, however, because I was an American and they were Palestinian.

I passed through my checkpoint on the Allenby Bridge relatively hassle-free, although my friends had a very different experience. They spent three hours in an Israeli checkpoint interrogation room answering questions about where they were going and what they were going to do there. Even their little nieces and nephews who made the trip with us were body-searched.

In the West Bank, the contrast between life as an Israeli and life as an Arab is immediately obvious. I saw what remains of some Arab-owned land as it sits parched and unirrigated next to lush green kibbutzim owned and operated by the Israelis. The sparkling new concrete Israeli settlements spilling down the West Bank hillsides and encroaching against the ancient Arab villages made my friend's family nervous. How long would it be before their own land was seized, and they were forced to tend it for the meager wages paid by the land usurpers?

Another day we took the bus from Tel Aviv to a city close to our village. On the bus, a young Jewish boy wearing his religious skullcap asked an Arab man at the back of the bus to put out his cigarette, which he did. The boy continued to stare at the man, finally asking him for a cigarette, which the Arab refused to supply. So the boy demanded to see the man's "identity papers." The man made no move. The boy ran up to the bus driver and demanded that he take the Arab to the police station, which he did. We all ended up at the police station, at which point Israeli officials escorted the Arab off the bus with the Jewish child running close behind, shouting.

Gradually I began to understand that such irritants are a part of my friends' lives. As an American, I have been raised believing I have a birthright to freedom and democracy. The U.S. Constitution allows me to express my opinions. However, Palestinians under Israeli occupation have none of these rights.

It angered me to watch my friends constantly having to produce their orange, plastic-covered identity cards. They risk jail if they even go to the market without them. It was interesting how much those orange cards resembled the yellow Stars of David the Jews were forced to wear on their own clothing in Europe during World War II.

When I returned to the U.S., I noticed that when it came to the Middle East, the American media generally solicited and accepted the views of Israelis or pro-Israeli American officials. And of course I noted that when Alex Odeh, the Southern California regional director of the American-Arab Anti-Discrimination Committee, was given an opportunity to discuss on national television his views of the *Achille Lauro* incident, he was murdered the next morning with a bomb triggered to explode when he opened his office door.

I thought this was a perfect example of terrorism, but no paper I saw reported it this way, if they reported on the incident at all. However, my government invited Mrs. Leon Klinghoffer, widow of the elderly, crippled *Achille Lauro* murder victim, to the White House to be treated as a heroine. Had Mrs. Alex Odeh, widow of the murdered ADC regional director, been invited to the White House at the same time, it would have told our own people, and the world, that our government grieves for all of the victims of terrorism, and that it cherishes and seeks to protect all of its citizens. Unfortunately, Mrs. Odeh is still waiting for her invitation. ✦

Debbie Kuehn is president of Kuehn Creative, a marketing communications agency in Minneapolis, Minnesota.

POSTSCRIPT: *This article was written after my first trip to the West Bank in 1985. On my second trip there in 1987, the "tension in the landscape" was even more intense. On that trip, I conducted a graduate study project entitled "An Elusive Peace: The Israeli-Palestinian Conflict" to survey "average" Israelis and Palestinians on their thoughts about the conflict.*

Three findings are worth noting: 1) The Palestinians and Israelis "share" many things—same land, same desires for a country—but do not share many others—right to vote, right to myriad other things Americans and Israelis take for granted; 2) there is great dissension among the Israelis themselves on how to resolve the conflict, a huge obstacle to any serious peacemaking attempts; and 3) the Israelis I approached were much more reluctant than the Palestinians to take my survey and commit their feelings to paper.

I left in October, one month before the start of the intifada. But my host family, like every other Palestinian family in the occupied territories, was affected by the intifada. In January, 1989, one of my host family's relatives, a 20-year-old young man, was shot by plainclothes Israeli soldiers in an ambush near his village, allegedly for "promoting the intifada." Now he walks with a cane. But he was luckier than his best friend, who was shot dead beside him. I wrote an article about this incident and sent it to our local newspaper, never believing they would print it. But they did.

Finding U.S. Friends

By Seema and Aisha Ahmed

When our father told us we would be moving to Hawaii, where he would be an agricultural engineer at the East-West Center, we were sorry to leave behind our friends and cousins in Pakistan, but we were excited about living in the United States, particularly such a beautiful and glamorous state. What we didn't tell our parents, or even each other, was that we were also frightened. Since at first we kept our fears to ourselves, we will tell our stories separately.

Seema's Story

My name is Seema Ahmed and I'm a freshman at University High School in Hawaii. I'm a Muslim and at first I was a bit hesitant to tell people that, because I was afraid of what they might think of me. My new friends said that my religion didn't matter to them, but I had to find out for myself.

One of my first assignments in the English class at my new school was to write a speech on one view of a controversial subject, and then present it to the class. The subject I chose was the unfairness of the American press.

I said that it tries to create a stereotype that Muslims are terrible warmongers, and even tries to promote hostility between Americans and Muslims. To back my point I brought in two newspaper headlines. One read "Muslims kill 97 in Beirut," the other referred to a horrible act committed by terrorists from another religious group, but the terrorists' religion wasn't revealed in the headline. I then said that when Muslims kill people, the press goes out of its way to mention that point. But when non-Muslims kill people, their religion doesn't seem to matter.

As I read my speech, I was afraid of my teacher's and classmates' reactions. What if they thought my reasoning was unfair or irrational? What if I got an "F" on this presentation?

The next day I rushed to my English class. I wanted to find out my grade. It seemed like eternity before the teacher passed back my paper, but, when I received my paper it had a big "A" written on it! In addition, the teacher also said my speech was very good because I brought in the newspaper headlines which proved my point! I couldn't believe it—she agreed with me!

My experience taught me that not all Americans believe whatever they are told about Muslims, and they can be fair when judging us. Now I don't hesitate to tell people I'm a Muslim.

Aisha's Story:

I wanted badly to make new friends in my new home, but I was hesitant at first about entering the 1986 Hawaii Junior Miss competition. Although Hawaii is a state where everyone, even the original Hawaiians, represent some kind of minority, I felt that if I overreached, I might be singled out for unfavorable attention. I entered anyway, and although I didn't become Hawaii's Junior Miss, I went further than I expected.

The Kraft Hostess Awards contest, held in conjunction with the Junior Miss competition, was the "turning point" for me. Each contestant was required to create and organize a party theme, using Kraft products. I immediately thought of a theme based on the Middle East. Visions of Sindbad the Sailor, Ali Baba and Aladdin raced through my mind. By describing the setting of my party as the Sultan of Araby's tent, which he opens to weary travelers who stop overnight at his oasis while journeying across the desert, I felt I could show Americans the hospitality of Arab people. But then some hesitancy gripped me as I asked myself, "How will the judges react to a positive portrayal of Arabs?"

But then determination replaced my hesitancy. The only way one could change the stereotyping of Arabs was to expose Americans to these positive aspects of Arab culture.

I discussed this with my parents and my younger sister. They wholeheartedly supported my idea and it gradually became a family affair. As each day passed, my ideas became clearer, and my determination grew stronger. When that fateful day arrived, I submitted my entry, entitled "The Sultan's Feast," with pure confidence.

As I reflect on this, I realize how glad I am that I went ahead with my idea, giving Americans a positive projection of Arab culture, rather than being cowed by the aura of anti-Arab stereotyping the U.S. media generally projects. I made new friends and, equally important, increased my respect for myself and for others. I learned that Americans are very objective people who are eager to learn of other cultures and values. I know now that the ball is in our court. We must take the initiative and present the unknown aspects of the Middle East with pride. When we do, we will find Americans to be eager learners—and friends.

P.S. I won the award!

Seema Ahmed is a student at the University of Puget Sound, in Tacoma, WA, where she is studying politics and government, and French. In 1990, she was selected "Hawaii's Young Woman of the Year" (formerly the Junior Miss Program), and was first runner-up in the national "America's Young Woman of the Year" contest.

Aisha Ahmed received her BA in English from the University of Puget Sound in Tacoma, WA, and is a reporter and photographer for the Madison Daily Leader *in Madi-*

son, South Dakota.

POSTCRIPT BY AISHA: *In the years since I wrote my article for the* Washington Report on Middle East Affairs, *I have noticed a slight increase in the Christian American's willingness to learn more about the Arab/Muslim culture. More and more Americans realize that, in order for there to be peace in the Middle East, an understanding and acceptance of the Arab peoples' way of life must exist.*

It is true that not everyone's perception of Arabs/Muslims as warmongers has changed, but I think that is partly because the leaders of the Arab nations have not realized the power and importance of unity among their own people, and partly because stereotyping continues in our media. Thus, there is an urgent need on the one hand for Arab leaders to inculcate a greater sense of tolerance for others' viewpoints among their own people; and, on the other hand, for mainstream Americans to acquire an objective understanding of developments that continually occur in the Middle East. For the latter, the Washington Report *provides an excellent source; similarly, grassroots organizations such as Americans for Impartiality in the Middle East are building up an awakening among mainstream Americans that is so vitally needed to help bring about change.*

Being There Is Being No Longer Able to Explain

By Parker L. Payson

In seventh grade American history class we were given a pop quiz. The assignment was to draw the fifty states and label major cities, rivers and mountains. I was the only one in the class who made no mistakes. I prided myself on my understanding of geography; I also knew all the European countries and their capitals.

Yet if I had been tested on the Middle East, I would have failed miserably. What would Egypt, an Arab country, be doing in Africa? Was Palestine the same as Israel or part of Lebanon? My geographical ignorance made me incapable of understanding any of the news generated from the region.

As I got older and more interested in current affairs, I developed a simplistic understanding of the Middle East: Israel was a country settled by Jewish immigrants who were reclaiming the land that they were driven from in Biblical times. All Arabs were modern-day Philistines, anarchists aiming to overthrow Israel. Arab belligerence toward Jews stemmed from the days of Abraham, when his illegitimate son, Ishmael, was ousted from the family in favor of his half-brother, Isaac.

Because I understood the Middle East in this framework, it was not important to draw distinctions between George Habash and Anwar Sadat, Muammar Qaddafi and King Fahd. They were all terrorists who blew up buses, hijacked airplanes and killed hostages. They were a menace to the "civilized" world, bringing bloodshed to the Olympics and forcing a worldwide recession by raising oil prices. If any Muslim was pro-American it was not evident during the Iran hostage crises in 1979.

I carried these views with me to college. During the spring of my freshman year, I signed up for a class in Middle Eastern studies, primarily because I did not want to take any early morning classes.

Imagine my shock when I learned that Arab nations were not supportive of the Iranian anti-American protests, and that Palestinians fought other Arabs in a Jordanian civil war. These events were inexplicable. My ignorance led me to pursue more Middle Eastern studies, and I graduated with a degree in Middle Eastern history.

In the summer of 1986, I went to Jordan to study with a group of 15 other American students. My experience there put a human face on the suffering caused by the Israeli occupation of Palestine.

In Jordan, we toured refugee camps and met with families who had been living in camps since 1948. Old mothers showed us pictures of their children who died fighting in the occupied territories. We heard stories of grandfathers, on their deathbeds, who encouraged their children to remain in the refugee camps until their people were allowed to return to their homes. At a camp meeting, elders showed their resolve by protesting a Jordanian decision to upgrade camp sewage facilities. They argued that any increase in comfort might promote complacency in the Palestinian struggle to return home.

As I grew more aware of the mediating role that America needed to play in the region, I began to understand Arab frustration toward American policy. The Reagan administration was reluctant to pursue any diplomatic efforts to solve the Arab-Israeli conflict after the failure of a U.S.-backed peace plan in 1983; Congress had just denied arm sales to both Jordan and Saudi Arabia, and we had recently bombed Tripoli.

It was a very scary time for Americans to be in the Middle East. Palestinian sentiment toward the U.S. was nearing an all-time low. Out of caution, I often disguised my nationality, and when traveling alone, I limited my meetings with Palestinians to exchanging pleasantries.

One day, I made an exception and accepted an invitation from a Palestinian man to come to his house for tea. I met his family, stayed for dinner, and ended up talking late into the night. He was very interested in my life in America, and so I showed him pictures of my family and friends. He asked me if I was looking forward to returning home; I told him that I was. "That is all I want, too," he said. Then he handed me an old photograph of his family farm which has now been developed into an Israeli housing project. When he admitted that he would probably die before he could return to the land where he was raised, his eyes swelled with tears. I swallowed hard. He then grasped my arm and asked, "Why is America against us?" Unfortunately, I could not begin to explain. ✦

Parker L. Payson is a former news and elections editor of the Washington Report on Middle East Affairs.

From Television Images to Personal Involvement in a Never-Ending Struggle

By Katherine Hughes-Fraitekh

My first clear memory of interest in anything Middle Eastern was during my sophomore year in high school in Albuquerque, New Mexico. It was 1978, and I remember the intensity of my emotions as I saw on television the White House ceremony marking completion of the Camp David negotiations. As I watched my president, Jimmy Carter, a man I greatly respected, presiding over the historic Anwar Sadat-Menachem Begin handshake, tears rolled down my cheeks and I felt proud to be an American.

I'm not sure why this event affected me so deeply. I grew up in middle America, the descendent of Scotch-English-Irish and German ancestors, in a family that never traveled overseas. The only Arab American I'd ever known was a friend whose father's family had emigrated from Lebanon years earlier. Little did I know then that 10 years later I would be personally involved in the continuing search for peace in the Middle East, attending meetings with Secretary of State James Baker and the Palestinian peace delegation.

At the University of Texas at Austin I majored in government with a specialty in international affairs. I chose to do my year-long honor's thesis on the effects of rapid modernization on traditional Islamic populations.

To convince my skeptical advisers that I could handle the project, I read more than 100 books on the Middle East in one semester. One author argued that Middle Eastern modernization, spurred by oil revenues, was proceeding 10 times faster than had industrial development in the West. Therefore, political, social, economic and psychological upheavals were inevitable. This intensive immersion began to reverse the denigrating generalizations about the region I had acquired from the mainstream U.S. media over the years.

After receiving my degree, I headed to Washington, DC, hoping to land a job in international affairs. I found that although there were more international jobs available than in Albuquerque, NM, or Austin, TX, there also were many more qualified applicants. So my Middle Eastern education in this period was confined largely to conversations with an Israeli and a Syrian, neither of whom ever met the other. I would listen curiously to one's position on a Middle East issue over coffee or at work, and then present it as if it were my own in conversation with the other. Over many months, I was surprised to discern that I was in closer agreement with the "radical" Syrian position, which seemed more rational to me, than that of my friend from "allied" Israel.

A three-month Eurail trip in 1987 gave me my first glimpse of an Islamic country. When I traveled by overnight train from Thessaloniki, Greece to Istanbul, Turkey, a lone and somewhat anxious female, a young conductor on the train became my self-appointed guardian, locking my train compartment door so that I could sleep without fear and checking on me periodically throughout the night.

He spoke not a word of English, nor I a word of Turkish, but he led me to safe and affordable lodgings upon the train's 5 a.m. arrival in vast and confusing Istanbul. During my week's stay he introduced me to his beloved and historic hometown, picking me up early in the morning for a day of exploration and then dropping me at my pension when darkness came. This was my first of many encounters in the Middle East with its fabled code of honor and hospitality.

Back in Washington, DC, I enrolled in a joint International Development and Middle East Studies graduate program at The American University and Georgetown University. When the intifada erupted in Gaza in December, 1987, I joined students in front of the Israeli Embassy and the State Department, protesting the Palestinian civilian casualties.

Strangely, until this time, I had known only peripherally about this single most fundamental Middle Eastern issue. When, during one of the first protests in which I was participating, the chant "PLO, yes! Israel, no!" went up, I felt very uncomfortable and wondered if the FBI was keeping files on those of us in the demonstration.

It took me many more months of reading and discussions with Palestinians and their American supporters to supplant the media-induced demonization of the PLO with its reality—that of a national movement and quasi-government for a dispossessed people which includes, in addition to revolutionary militants, educators organizing schools, doctors building hospitals, and social workers seeking to ease people's pain and poverty. At last I was able to explain to other uninformed Americans, including my parents, that the PLO members were neither angels nor devils, but the Palestinian people's chosen political representatives.

Through personal acquaintance with several Palestinians whom I admired greatly, including one who had survived the Sabra and Shatila massacres and another whose father was a founding member of the PLO and head of its education department, I began to comprehend the tragic consequences of the 1947 U.N. Partition Resolution, the subsequent wars, occupations, displacements and violence. I decided that if I were to make any significant contribution to solving the problems, I needed to experience them at first-hand.

Witnessing the Intifada

So I traveled to Jordan, Israel, and the occupied Palestinian territories in the early days of the intifada as a member of a fact-finding delegation sent to witness and document human rights abuses. My parents were frightened, yet supportive, making me promise again and again not to do anything impulsive. Their intuition flashed through my mind when, toward the end of my trip, I watched helplessly in Gaza as heavily armed Israeli troops chased and threatened groups of Palestinian children, some of them already wearing casts on arms methodically broken during previous roundups. I thanked God then that I carried no weapon, because the desire to use one against those brutes might have been uncontrollable.

During my stay in the region, Israeli stories I heard sounded increasingly hollow, condescending and arrogant, while the usually understated Palestinian accounts had the ring of naked truth. I experienced simultaneous adrenaline-charged fear and exhilaration when I came under fire for the first time in Bethlehem. Within weeks I felt like a veteran, having been shot at by soldiers during that first market clash, at a funeral in Beit Sahour, and in daily protests in the Gazan refugee camps of Jabalya and Shati. Each time that I and other civilians were targeted, I felt a compulsion to stand up and shout: "My taxes are paying your salaries, I order you to lay down your guns."

Between such fantasies, however, I began to see the problem that I had studied in the abstract with blinding clarity. I realized that my country's official human rights reports had been omitting evidence of offenses by our Israeli allies for years, and that the U.S. media and government had insidiously planted in American minds the argument that state terrorism is somehow acceptable, while acts of terror by individuals whose countries are being stolen from them are not.

I saw with my own eyes the falsity of claims that Israelis were killing Palestinians in self-defense. And I realized that the Palestinians, not the Israelis, were the underdogs, struggling bravely for their national existence against inexorable Israeli pressure, backed by unconditional and seemingly inexhaustible American military and economic aid. These startling insights led me to question all of the other "truths" I had been spoon-fed through the years, but which I could no longer count on as certainties.

I returned transformed and ready to "spread the word." But although concerned organizations were spending large amounts subsidizing delegation tours like my own, there was no efficient institutional structure developed to utilize "returnees" like myself, willing and able to act as educational resources. Frustrated, I finally found someone to sponsor development of a slide show production and then presented it at university, church and civic functions, wrote newspaper articles, and took part in formal debates. At one of those university lectures I met my husband-to-be, a Palestinian journalist from Nablus, who through the years has taught me many valuable academic facts as well as an extremely personal side of what it means to be Palestinian.

Other stereotypes were erased through my close friendship with a Kuwaiti woman during my last year of graduate school. I learned that at least some conservative, religious, Arab Muslim families raise daughters to be independent and totally support their rights, choices and career aspirations; that religious Arab women can possess views and values very similar to my own; and that these same women can be at least as independent, forceful and open as any of their American counterparts.

During travels the next summer, I stayed with the family of a Damascene friend. There, in a reputedly closed and unfriendly society, I was surprised to encounter the same warmth toward me as a person and fascination with American universities, cities and lifestyles I had found among the Palestinians. I realized that Americans have no natural enemies among the Arabs; rather, it is largely our government's unconditional support for Israel that baffles and angers them.

After returning from Syria and completing my master's degree, I started a professional job with a nonprofit organization in Washington, DC that sent American students, educators and members of Congress on visits to Arab countries and young journalists for apprenticeships on English-language newspapers in the Middle East. This was during the period of Saddam Hussain's invasion of Kuwait and the U.S.-led war on Iraq. Troubling as this period was for a deeply divided Arab and Muslim world, and for the clear U.S. double standard toward the Kuwaiti and Israeli occupations which it highlighted, it led me to the most exciting job of my life.

I was approached after the war by the director of the Palestine Affairs Center in Washington to work with the Palestinian delegation on preliminary talks to re-start the peace process, and I gladly accepted. After several months of building trust, I attended meetings between Hanan Ashrawi, Feisal Husseini and U.S. State Department and National Security Council representatives.

Fascinating Interactions

It was fascinating to see the interaction between the participants. Secretary of State James Baker's sincerity and knowledge of the matter impressed me as the serious issues later put on the table in Madrid were discussed, and each side's positions clarified. I also gained great respect for Dr. Ashrawi's intelligence and command of the English language during the negotiations and as we worked on press releases and reports together.

By the time of the formal Madrid Conference in late 1991 and the negotiations that followed, however, I no longer was personally involved. I had become the mother of a son and accompanied my husband to Atlanta, GA, where he enrolled in graduate school at the Georgia Institute of Technology.

There was a strong feeling of *déjà vu* for me two years later on Sept. 13, 1993 as I watched on television the signing ceremony between two historic enemies in the Middle East, Yitzhak Rabin and Yasser Arafat, officiated over by a southern Democratic American president. I watched the handshakes with tears of hope once again, but this time I had no illusions that I was viewing the final step toward real peace in the area, nor was I overly proud of my country's involvement.

In the summer of 1994, after my husband completed his studies, we took our two-year-old son to visit my husband's family in Nablus and to decide about working with development issues in the newly autonomous Palestinian areas. It was my first return to the occupied territories since my 1988 delegation trip, and my husband's first visit to his homeland since 1988 as well. Neither of us was prepared for what we found.

An Unrecognizable City

Nablus was almost unrecognizable. Six long years without municipal administration had destroyed the city's infrastructure and, as in other West Bank towns, there was no enforcement of traffic, health, zoning, or trash disposal regulations. Unemployment stood between 50 and 75 percent, and bright students who had missed three years of school due to Israeli closures were unable to pass their high school exit exams and continue on to college. Women, relatively liberated before and during the early stages of the intifada, were losing ground rapidly as fundamentalist Islamic movements exploited the situation to gain support.

Respect for any kind of authority, including parental and societal, had dissolved. We witnessed small bands of teenage zealots using the threat of violence to close down businesses, enforce strikes, and punish dissenters, all in defiance of the exhortations of Yasser Arafat's new Palestinian National Authority and the proclamations of the new municipality.

The solidarity and communal trust which I recalled from the beginning of the intifada had been eroded by years of Israeli infiltration and repression. Massive immigration to cities by rural Palestinians displaced by Israeli settlers had broken up traditional neighborhoods and added to the distrust.

Soldiers still patrolled the streets, often putting the city under curfew. One day we watched from a nearby roof as they used anti-tank missiles to blow up an entire apartment building with three activists inside.

Palestinians, so hopeful after the initial Madrid Conference, have seen little, if any, improvement in their daily lives since the signing of the secretive Oslo and Cairo accords. They survive by relying on deep reservoirs of internal strength and family support, but worry that all of the sacrifice, pain and deaths since the outbreak of the intifada will lead only to a limited autonomy.

As we returned, discouraged, to the United States, my mind kept turning back to my tears of joy in 1978 and 1993 as I watched the historic handshakes. Now my naiveté was gone and I realized that the hardest work to attain an independent, democratic Palestinian state still lay ahead. Nevertheless, each renewed contact with the steadfastness and determination of the Palestinian people living under occupation serves to energize and motivate me to continue to do my small part in the struggle. ✦

Katherine Hughes-Fraitekh is currently living in New Mexico and working on a book about her experiences.

Stunned by Middle East Violence, Shocked to Discover Its Causes

By Robert Hurd

My first contact with the Middle East, probably shared with most Americans my age, came with the Iranian hostage crisis in 1979. I can remember pictures of the U.S. Embassy staff blindfolded by their captors on the nightly news, which always ended or began with an announcement of the number of days the hostages had been held captive. I remember the embarrassment that came with the failure of the American rescue mission, and how *Time* magazine made the Ayatollah Khomeini its "Man of the Year," with a huge, sinister portrait of his face emblazoned upon the cover. Finally, Ronald Reagan became president, the hostages came home, and the crisis was over. However, this painful episode left me with the image of the Middle East as a region characterized by brutality and violence, whose inhabitants seemed bent on destroying the West as well as themselves.

A New Trouble Spot

A few years later, Lebanon was the new trouble spot in the region. The suicide bombing of the U.S. Marine barracks in 1983 reinforced the violent images that I had of the Middle East. Every time the news media reported on the region something horrible had happened, whether it was a car bomb in Beirut or an Israeli bombing run on a Palestinian refugee camp. I cannot recall any stories that reported positively on events occurring in an Arab or Muslim country.

During my last year of high school my best friend was a student whose family had lived in Beirut in the late 1970s. During lunch period he would often talk politics with a Jewish friend of ours, and they often spoke about groups and people of whom I had never heard, such as the Phalange, the Druze, the Gemayels and the Franjiehs.

Subsequently, I did a research paper for a government class on the Lebanese conflict. I was amazed at the number of factions involved in the political system. With the exception of the Kurds, it seemed as if every Middle East conflict was present in Lebanon, Arab versus Israeli, Sunni versus Shi'a, Christian versus Muslim, and so on. On top of this were the internal rivalries within each group and the attempts of outside governments to shape the Lebanese conflict according to their own desires. I began to follow Lebanon and the surrounding area in the news, trying to determine the motives of the different players involved in the dispute.

After high school I attended the University of Virginia, and in the first semester of my first year I preregistered for a class in Islam. The notion of studying Islam was more appealing than a history course on the Middle East. The teacher of the course was a guest lecturer replacing the regular professor, who was away on sabbatical. Although the visiting professor seemed pompous and unduly academic, his lectures were interesting and delivered with a great deal of authority. I took two more Islam classes from him the following semester.

At this time, the University of Virginia began to offer a major in Middle East studies, combining courses from the government, history, religion, and Oriental language departments. Friends had spoken highly of many of the professors whose courses were included in the major, and I chose to start taking Arabic and history classes in order to sample these courses for myself. I declared the Middle East studies major in the spring of my second year.

As I continued my education, the earlier notions I had about the Middle East were dispelled. I came to understand that the people of the region were people with legitimate grievances who were responding to their problems with the few methods left open to them. I saw the strain that colonialism and rapid modernization had placed on Middle Eastern societies, and I became aware of the problems of legitimacy facing every government in the Middle East.

It also became clear to me that many of the region's troubles were either exacerbated or caused by policies of Western governments. Whether it was supporting a repressive dictatorial regime at the expense of the country's population or intervening in a civil war, the involvement of the United States in the region continually caused more problems than it solved.

I became more and more politicized over the plight of the Palestinian people and the existence of the state of Israel. I recalled hearing about Israeli efforts to destroy the records of the state of Palestine hidden in refugee camps in Lebanon. I read daily about the abuses by the Israeli army during the intifada. After studying the history of the Arab-Israeli conflict, I could not help adopting the idea that support for Israel was a means of allowing Western governments to assuage their guilt about the Holocaust at the expense of the Palestinian people, and that misconceptions about the Arabs, Islam, and the entire Middle East prevented the West from seeing the error of its ways.

Studying in Jordan

I was able to hear some of the Palestinians' frustration at first hand when I was studying Arabic at Yarmouk University in Irbid, Jordan, during the summer of 1990. One afternoon when I was walking home from the university, two middle-aged Palestinians invited me to sit down and have tea with them. One of the two men spoke good English, and we began to discuss politics. Both men were unimpressed that I had studied the Middle East and was familiar with the Arab-Israeli conflict. They wanted to know why America was against them and had done nothing to support their cause. One of them said the only thing the U.S. had ever done for them was to send them wheat, and that came courtesy of the United Nations. I was embarrassed that I could not answer their questions, but could only meekly nod in response to statements about the injustice of the situation.

During the course of this conversation I was not very surprised to hear some very inaccurate and untrue statements about the Jewish people. I realized both men probably knew very little about Jewish history, and had probably never met a Jewish person. I fear there may be too much bad blood between the Arabs and Israelis to advocate a plan of peace through understanding. I do not think, however, that it is too late for the West to alter its own views and "see the light."

I believe the role America has played in modern Middle Eastern history obligates our country to help solve the region's troubles, and that the Arab-Israeli conflict is the largest barrier to regional stability. I also feel that education and the removal of stereotypes is an essential first step toward the achievement of this goal. I cannot help but blame the American public for being so misinformed about a region to which it has so many historical and religious ties. I remember how so many of my parents' friends asked if it was safe to go to Jordan before I left the United States. I guess the correct response would have been, "Yes, but no thanks to us." ✦

Robert Hurd is a former book club manager for the American Educational Trust.

A Spiritual Awakening

By Sayres S. Rudy

There's nothing more innocuous than a curious Unitarian, I suppose, and that's what I am and always will be. I was raised in Scarsdale, NY, by brilliant parents whose backgrounds are Jewish. I grew up in a Jewish atmosphere, was comfortable with Jewish intensity and views, and grew to have a great admiration for the Jewish people.

At Davidson College, when I changed my major from psychology to American foreign policy and Middle East studies, I understood one thing clearly. Studying the thoughts of Jews and Muslims would help me clarify the problems of the Middle East and America's involvement in them, more than would anything gained from my Unitarian bewilderment at the intensity of Jewish and Muslim devotion. Therefore, I studied, read, wrote and began to argue and disagree with people. It was challenging, and it was fun. But until I met Bilal El-Amine, it was passionless.

A Permanent Change

Bilal changed me forever, by being someone I could never have imagined, by thinking in ways I had never thought, by being a Lebanese Shi'a with more love, humor, and gentleness in him than I had ever seen in anyone before.

During long walks at Davidson, he told me how the sonic booms of the Israeli jets—made in America—used to shatter the windows in his small, south Lebanese village of Dir Kifa. He told me about carrying the smaller schoolchildren into the oldest stone buildings to take cover from air raids. He told me about a group of Israeli soldiers who had surrounded the entrance to a cave and fired into it for days before realizing it was empty. Amazingly, Bilal could still laugh at some of the stories he told me about Lebanon.

When we turned to larger issues, however, Bilal and I took opposing positions. I regularly persuaded him that the Jews needed a homeland and their own government. He persuaded me that, if the Jews needed a homeland, so did the Palestinians. American and Arab, we always ended up looking at each other with amusement as the joy of understanding dissolved the frustration of disagreement. We were both using the same argument: If one group had a right to a homeland, the other group did too. We both had come to see clearly that a person cannot logically defend a homeland for only the Palestinians or only the Jews.

In that agreement, we both achieved compassion. When I gained that compassion—for the Palestinians as well as the Jews—I knew I had to go to the Middle East. I applied for an international research fellowship with the Thomas Watson Foundation and, after winning it, began studying Arabic. I was nervous when I left the States, but I knew that people were kind in the Levant, and that it was time to meet more of the people about whom I had spent so much time reading and thinking.

In a sense, I had "seen the light" before I left for Jordan, Syria, Egypt, Israel, and the occupied territories. I had heard horror stories of Jewish and Arab victimization and discrimination. I knew what I would find and I was not surprised when I found it.

But there is a difference between knowing things and feeling things. Before I landed in Amman, I had not empathized with the victims, I had merely understood their claims. In the subsequent months, my intellectual compassion deepened into a spiritual connection, which I call love.

Perhaps this occurred while I visited the Bakaa refugee camp—77,000 Palestinians on one square mile of Jordanian land—when a smiling student greeted me from her classroom at the camp with a soft "Ahlan," meaning "welcome." Maybe I began to love rather than just observe when some sightseeing Syrian soldiers at the citadel at Aleppo were elated to talk to an American. Or it could have been during a conversation with an Israeli political science student who said that when he visited the West Bank, he realized it was religious fanaticism and bigotry that were the true threats to Israel's security. I felt the truth among Jews in Jerusalem during a Purim celebration, among Muslims at the celebration of the Prophet Muhammad's ascent from Jerusalem to heaven, and among participants in a joint Palestinian-Israeli parade for peace, when thousands of Jews and Arabs demonstrated, laughed, and danced together.

I understood, before I left for the Middle East, that there would be no peace there until the Jews, Muslims and Christians were free to celebrate their heritage, free to work, and free to prosper. Now, having lived in the Middle East, I know that the vast majority of people there want nothing more than such freedom, for themselves and for others. ✦

Sayres S. Rudy was a 1986-87 recipient of the Thomas J. Watson Fellowship for international research.

From Mathematics to Islamic Culture

By Tidge Holmberg

I attended a core-curriculum liberal arts college and it was there that I discovered Islamic culture. Not that it was represented in the books: there was not a single Arabic or Muslim author in the entire program. It first became obvious to me that something was missing in the mathematics classes.

We read Euclid, Apollonius, Ptolemy, and then Descartes, Newton, Copernicus. The cultural continuity was clear: the ancient Greeks and the modern Western Europeans. The intervening centuries, however, were silent. There was a brief mention that the Arabs had "stored" Ptolemy during those centuries, but even this incredible understatement was given grudgingly.

Descartes Presents Difficulties

I began to have difficulties with this interpretation when we read Descartes. I was amazed at the revolution he had wrought in mathemathics: his combination of algebra and geometry created the world anew. But where were the roots of this revolution? There were elements in Descartes that were decidedly un-Greek. His use of numbers, his understanding of quantity, his preoccupation with analysis over synthesis: did they just pop into his mind? Where did Algebra come from? Where did Descartes' "algorithmic" method come from?

All, all came from the Middle East. Mohammed Ibn-Musa Al-Khowarizmi (from whose name comes "algorithm"), an Arabic mathematician who died around 850 AD, wrote the *Al-jabr wa'l muqabalah,* from which Europe learned "al-jabr" (algebra), the numerical science for discovering unknowns.

I learned all of this on my own, but it was an uphill battle. My biases were insidious and subtle, often sending me tumbling down when I thought I was on firm ground. My thoughts had developed along the lines of "Yes, Arabic philosophers and mathematicians contributed much to the great march of progress. No one can argue with that. However, they never really discovered anything new and none of their works, although used to great benefit, were essential to what followed in the same sense that the Greek works were essential."

I did not realize that my second thought ("the Arabs never really discovered anything; they weren't essential") destroyed any meaning that could be attributed to the first ("the Arabs contributed much"). But that is the nature of contemporary prejudice. We all give lip service to open-minded ideals and to an even-handed grasp of past and present "facts." Our words help us feel that we have outgrown racism and parochial prejudice. The ugly reality breaks out in the particularities, in the twist of a phrase, in the use of the word "essential."

Every summer, I read non-curriculum books in order to glimpse all the history I was missing. I saw the light in terms of mathematics, but the light soon flooded everything else. Everywhere I turned, I found areas where Arabs had made essential contributions; physics, medicine, philosophy, theology, art, architecture, poetry, and prose. Science, rationality, beauty: these things did indeed exist outside of Europe.

A Painful Soul-Searching

But why did these realizations come as such a shock? I was an open-minded liberal, generous to all cultures and civilizations, and I "knew" of the Arabic/Islamic contribution to the history of mankind. Why were the facts so surprising? These questions required the kind of soul-searching that is particularly painful to anyone who believes he or she is not a bigot.

I began to realize that in my soul I held two totally different images of Arabs. One was the Islamic scholar working and writing upon diagrams and scrolls upon a vast desk; or the astronomer in a Caliph's court, staring into the night sky and tracing the patterns therein; or the physician, prodding and poking a sick patient in order to understand illness.

The other image was the mad Muslim spinning the steering wheel of a passenger bus, killing everyone aboard, or an Islamic extremist refusing women their own political and social existence. My first image was from the distant past. It was easy enough to accept, because I never really lived with it. I lived with the second image, as most Americans do.

Every time I truly felt, every time I truly saw (instead of merely agreeing that it existed) the ingenuity or the beauty in the accomplishment of an Arab, I ran into this second image. The stereotype of the barbaric, brutal Arab obstructed any vision of the truth or significance of their accomplishments. And this obstructed vision was continually reinforced by television and newspapers. Every Arab mentioned was a terrorist. Every Muslim pictured was an unreasoning fanatic. The Middle East was a whirlpool of angry factions and insanity, inside of which Israel, America's friend, had created an island of relative calm and rationality.

I began to realize that I was using this stereotype to rationalize actions that were otherwise unsupportable. Watching the riots in Soweto, I felt compassion for a disenfranchised people, frustrated at the loss of their homeland. Watching a riot on the West Bank, I felt fear of an unreasonable mob of fanatics, bent on destroying the Israeli state, the only representative of civilization.

As I climbed out of my valley of ignorance, led at first by mathematics and then by the abhorrence of prejudice, America also began to peer out of her cave, at first tentatively questioning the Israeli invasion of Lebanon and siege of Beirut, and then heartily denouncing the horrors of the massacre of Palestinian men, women, and children at the Sabra and Shatila refugee camps.

In recent years, the U.S. media image of Palestinians, at least, has improved, but not enough. The Middle East is a totally alien land to most Americans. As such, it elicits wonder, bewilderment, and fear. Now, when I express interest in visiting the Middle East to my friends, they immediately ask, "Why?" It is not at all the conversational "why" that would follow a declaration of interest in visiting Greece, Rome, or Russia. It is asked in a tone not of interest or envy, but of shock, more as if I had expressed a strong desire to be tarred and feathered.

In these times, the average American desperately needs to be educated about the Middle East. With the invasion of Kuwait, many Americans seemed to see the Middle East as an arena of backwardness and evil that is better destroyed or put under American supervision. Once again, American ignorance had led America to a foolish and patronizing attitude.

A respect and fascination for mathematics led me, finally, to discern a racist sentiment, ugly and enduring, in my soul. My lack of knowledge about the Middle East and its cultures remains vast. But with each new fact learned, each corner turned, my thirst increases and my pace doubles. I won't be fooled again. Neither, I hope, will my fellow Americans. ✦

Tidge Holmberg is a former business manager of the American Educational Trust.

Alone Among My Peers at My Yeshiva University High School Reunion

By Ronald Bleier

In the spring of 1990, I was one of some 40 men and a handful of spouses who attended the 30th reunion of the 75-man graduation class of Yeshiva University High School of Brooklyn. In the congratulatory atmosphere of renewed camaraderie that suffused those few hours on a blustery Sunday afternoon in April, not a word of politics was spoken. Nevertheless, I found myself feeling deeply isolated because, from the many references to Israel by my former classmates, I suspected I was alone among my peers in my support for self-determination and justice for the Palestinian people.

At Crown Heights Yeshiva, my elementary school in Brooklyn, we were all, as a matter of course, indoctrinated in Zionist ideology. As was usual among such yeshivas in those days, we all received pale blue and white Jewish National Fund solicitation boxes to raise funds for Israel. I remember vividly the day one of my fourth grade classmates, a tough little guy named Martin, broke into tears because our rabbi insisted that he take a new coin box and turn in the already heavy old one before Martin had filled it to the top.

Also, I recall being confused by the assertion by one of my rabbis that Israel was not an expansionary state, and had no designs on the territory of the surrounding Arab countries. Until then I had no idea that anyone had charged Israel with aggression against its neighbors, or how Israel could change its borders. At the same time, I was surprised to see for the first time how tiny Israel seemed on a map, and pained at the way the Jordanian-controlled West Bank jutted into Israeli territory, taking away so much of "our land."

I didn't question my belief in Zionism for almost a decade after my yeshiva training. After I graduated from Brooklyn College in 1964, I joined the Peace Corps and served for two years as an English teacher in Iran. I came to know individual Iranians as well as I knew my friends and family back home. No longer could I dismiss Iranians and others as faceless Third World people irrelevant to me and my concerns.

My Peace Corps experience, however, did not immediately alter my Zionist views. During the 1967 war I recall my joy and exultation at what I considered a wonderful victory for Israel and for the Jewish people. I was spending an academic year at Reading

University, not far from London, when, shortly after the war, in a blaze of enthusiasm and naiveté which still mortifies me, I approached two Egyptian students and asked them if they didn't agree that the Israeli victory established the basis for a lasting peace in the Middle East. "Never," they responded with the greatest passion. "We will never give up. We will continue to fight."

A few weeks later I had perhaps my first political discussion about Israel with someone with strong anti-Zionist views. Lunching with a lecturer in the English Department, I was shocked to hear that she felt the Israeli victory was a disaster for Middle East peace. She went on to explain that in her view the very establishment of the Jewish state was profoundly unjust. I disagreed with her very strongly. I couldn't understand how a progressive person could attack the state of Israel on principle.

Nevertheless, the views of my British interlocutor may have set the stage for the cognitive dissonance I experienced following the 1967 war. During the 1969-70 "war of attrition" I was amazed and dismayed to read in *The New York Times* that Israeli planes were dropping bombs 10 miles outside of Cairo! The *Times* printed a map with Cairo at the center of a bull's eye. The circles around the area showed how close to the city center the bombs were falling. As I read of the destruction of schools and factories and the loss of life, I found my pro-Israeli views stretched to the limit.

Nevertheless, as a committed Zionist, I put doubts about Israeli policy as far from the center of my consciousness as I could until the June, 1977, elections in Israel approached. I remember asking a friend at the time: "Is it possible that Menachem Begin will actually become prime minister?"

I regarded Begin with the kind of fear and loathing that I felt for Richard Nixon and Ronald Reagan. I was particularly distressed when, in the aftermath of Begin's Likud victory, the powerful American Jewish community didn't rise up in protest against the redoubling of Israeli settlement and land annexation policies. Menachem Begin helped me to understand, perhaps for the first time, that there was a government in Israel that was not interested in a peaceful solution to the conflict with the Arabs.

At the time I attributed Menachem Begin's belligerent attitude to his annexationist, greater Israel world view. So I was surprised to read an op-ed article in the *Times* which argued that even if the Labor Party were to take back power in the upcoming 1981 elections, there would be no significant change in the basic policy of an indefinite Israeli military occupation of Palestinian territory. I began to understand that there was no fundamental difference between the Likud and the Labor parties because the policies of both were rooted in the huge injustice done to the Palestinians when Israel was established.

By 1982, like many concerned Israelis and Americans, I could see war coming again. The absence of a legitimate *casus belli* did not hinder the Begin government's defense minister, Ariel Sharon, from invading an essentially defenseless Lebanon.

The media spotlight that illuminated the terrible cost in lost and devastated Palestinian and Lebanese lives helped me to focus on the effects of Israeli policy toward the Palestinian refugees. In my yeshivas, the Palestinian refugees were never humanized as people with legitimate rights to self-determination. As a result, I had only the vaguest notions of who they were and how they got to be where they were.

From time to time as I was growing up, I would hear references to Palestinian doctors, diplomats or lawyers. I couldn't understand how they managed to become members of the professional classes. I had imagined them as poor and miserable denizens of awful refugee camps, out of whose ranks came the terrorists who stubbornly refused to allow the people of Israel to live in peace.

Media reports that 20,000 Palestinians and Lebanese died and that many more thousands were made refugees by Israel's war in Lebanon led me to reconsider the original Palestinian refugees of 1948. I realized that some of the Palestinians so recently uprooted must be the same people the Israeli military had forced out of their homes and lands in northern Palestine in 1948. That was the first time I recognized the phenomenon of refugees repeatedly expelled from their homes by the Israelis. I began to realize that, just as there were many thousands of Palestinian refugees in Lebanon, so there were hundreds of thousands of Palestinian refugees in Jordan, Syria and the Gaza Strip who were forced out in 1948 and 1967. And, contrary to my previous notion that the Arab countries had stabbed the Palestinians in the back, I realized it was neighboring Arab countries which were forced to expend limited resources on the Palestinian refugees ever since Israel expelled them.

The issue of Palestinian refugees resonated with me because I myself was a refugee. I was born in November, 1942, on a little island called Lopud, not far from Dubrovnik, where my parents had fled from the Nazi invasion of Yugoslavia. My brother was born 15 months later on Vis, another island in the area. We came to the U.S. in August, 1944, as part of a token group of about 1,000 mostly Jewish refugees that President Franklin Roosevelt agreed to intern until the war ended.

In 1987, when I read Simha Flapan's *The Birth of Israel: Myths and Realities*, I was so shocked and disbelieving that it took me a second reading to come to terms with what he wrote at the outset: that the 1948 war was as needless and unnecessary for the "security" of Israel as was the Israeli invasion of Lebanon in 1982. Flapan argues that the Arabs were unprepared for war and would have accommodated the new Jewish state if only the Israelis had been willing to reach an agreement on territory and the Palestinian refugees.

I learned that, according to this so-called revisionist view, the 1948 war was not defensive, but a war to gain more territory than the U.N. had allotted for the Jewish state and to "cleanse" the area of Palestinian Arabs. I learned that even before the May 15 invasion by Arab armies, Jewish forces had succeeded in expelling some 300,000 Palestinians from their homes, but another 400,000 Palestinians remained in areas the Jews coveted. Since the Jewish population of Palestine in 1948 was only about 600,000, the Ben-Gurion leadership required war in order to rid the new Jewish state of most of its Arab population.

I finally understood that by demonizing the Palestinians, we were essentially blaming the victims of expulsion and land acquisition policies followed ever since 1948 by Ben-Gurion's and every successive Israeli regime. Such policies demanded endless belligerence and war, and explain why Israel's leaders have built a nuclear arsenal. The Israelis understood from the beginning that they must have the military power to prevail against the Palestinians who wanted their territory back, and all others in the world who want justice in the Middle East.

I returned home from my class reunion convinced that I would find no understanding there for my support of Palestinian rights. I understood that many of my former classmates supported the state of Israel, and blinded themselves to the horrors committed in its name, because they, too, were seared by the Holocaust that traumatized their parents' generation. But couldn't they see that by politically and financially supporting persecution and oppression, they were perpetuating precisely that which they professed to abhor?

At my reunion there was no opportunity to talk politics. If there had been, I doubt that I would have found others ready to question with me why there should be an exclusively Jewish state in Palestine, rather than a sharing of the land by all of its people. Perhaps this article will be my way of challenging my classmates, and others, to take a similar journey. I would invite them to join me on a path that substitutes friendship and peace for the arrogance of power and the yoke of oppression. ✦

Ronald Bleier (rbleier@igc.org) teaches high school in New York City and edits the Demographic Environmental and Security Issues Project (DESIP), an on-line information service.

VII. FROM THE INTIFADA TO THE OSLO ACCORDS 1987-1997

AMERICAN PUBLIC OPINION had been shocked by the televised images of the Israeli invasion of Lebanon. On Dec. 9, 1987, Palestinians in the Gaza Strip—with children in the forefront—spontaneously rose up to protest the continuing Israeli occupation. The intifada, or "shaking off," quickly spread to the West Bank as well. Again Americans watched on television as Israeli soldiers, under orders from then-Defense Minister Yitzhak Rabin, used live ammunition and systematically broke the bones of Palestinian children, who threw stones at Israeli troops. Despite the killing and wounding of their children and the imprisonment and torture of their older family members, Palestinians vowed to continue their struggle. The attention of the world was diverted, however, by Iraqi President Saddam Hussain's invasion of Kuwait in August of 1990. The U.S. and Saudi Arabia assembled an international coalition to launch a successful air and ground war to liberate Kuwait. President George Bush then used the leverage that victory provided to initiate a peace process between the Israelis and Palestinians. Secretary of State James Baker brought together the Likud government of Yitzhak Shamir and Israeli-approved Palestinian representatives at the Madrid peace conference in October, 1990. After little progress was made in the ensuing negotiations, the world was surprised by the announcement that Israel's successor Labor government headed by Yitzhak Rabin and the PLO, in secret negotiations in Oslo, had reached an agreement on "principles for peace." U.S. President Bill Clinton hosted the signing of the historic agreement by PLO leader Yasser Arafat and Israeli Prime Minister Yitzhak Rabin on the south lawn of the White House Sept. 13, 1993. A follow-up agreement, called "Oslo II" was also signed at the White House by Arafat and Rabin in 1995.

Protesting the Injustices
I Preferred Not to See

By David R. Willcox

Born less than eight months before the bombing of Pearl Harbor, and only four years old when World War II ended, I have few firsthand memories of that war, and none of the horrors of the Holocaust in Europe. Nor did I have any knowledge whatsoever about what subsequently happened in the British Mandate of Palestine. I was dependent upon our statesmen, historians, religious figures, and the media to educate me over the years.

I was a typical white, Anglo-Saxon, Protestant, American boy and, in retrospect, I fear that, as a teenager, I carried more than my share of prejudice, fear and bigotry in my head. These negatives encompassed Jews, although I had never really known any Jews on a personal level. When, eventually, I learned about the horrors of the European Holocaust, and the evils visited on the Jewish people throughout history, I was heartsick with guilt because of my personal prejudices. From that point onward, I looked upon the Jewish people with many of the same old prejudices in my head, but with tremendous sorrow and pity in my heart.

God has a wonderful way of getting your attention from time to time. When I was 20, I learned that the parents of a woman with whom I had fallen in love had come to the United States as German Jewish refugees from Hitler. Though my love truly was hopeless, in the time we dated her wonderful parents came to represent to me every decent, human ideal I could imagine.

As the years passed, I began taking an increasing interest in current affairs. The conflicting earlier feelings in my head and in my heart undoubtedly intensified my reactions to news from the Middle East. By then, the media were full of information about the state of Israel's perpetual struggle against the bloodthirsty Arab states encircling it. Because I was informed that these Arabs were bent on the total destruction of Israel and her people, I drew the obvious inference that the Arabs suffered a terminal case of what we called "anti-Semitism." This was the big picture, painted with a broad brush, and it didn't occur to me to ask myself why or how any of this could be so. I heard and saw only what my mind wished to hear and see.

Entering the 1970s and my 30s, I "witnessed," through the various mainstream media, Israel's many battles for survival. I was very supportive of the Israelis throughout this period, although I was shocked when I "witnessed," again through the media, the Israeli attack on the USS *Liberty* in 1967 in which 34 Americans were killed. I assumed that it was just a case of mistaken identity which occurred because the American ship happened to wander into the wrong place at the wrong time. (War is hell.)

In the 1970s and 1980s I also "witnessed," through the various mainstream media, much activity on the part of Arabs, particularly the "Palestinian terrorists." These bloody, random actions seemed senseless and purposeless. It did not occur to me to wonder why these people did these horrific things. I was increasingly aware, however, that something must be missing in my mental picture of Middle Eastern history.

The few times I was able to discuss the subject of Israel/Palestine with someone I thought might be knowledgeable on the subject, however, I was misled. If I feel guilt now, it is over my willingness to believe what so clearly was illogical. I was told that the situation had been going on since the beginning of time, and that the adversaries had "always" been mortal enemies. I also was told that the situation was so complex that there was no way to sort it out, and that peace could "never" be attained in the region. If I feel anger now, it is when I hear "experts" still spouting these same, tired, and completely erroneous statements.

Then came the Israeli "incursion" into Lebanon. When the mainstream media could only explain that what looked like simple aggression was, instead, "complex," my confusion became frustration. Who were the perpetrators and who were the victims of the slaughter at Sabra and Shatila? How many died there, and how many were old men and women, and young mothers and children? Then, who bombed the U.S. Marine barracks, killing 241 Americans in seconds, and why? These events were totally incomprehensible to me. The more I saw, heard and read, however, the more I was certain something was wrong. The information in our American media did not address the questions in my heart. I now realize that my difficulty can be expressed by the computer term "GIGO." It was simply a matter of "Garbage In Garbage Out."

Such was the state of my Middle East knowledge on Dec. 24, 1987. Having been away from Washington, DC for some 25 years, I decided to go to the National Cathedral that evening for Christmas Eve worship services. I did, and, as in times past, I was suffused with the joyous awe that only such an occasion can arouse. Not wanting to dissipate the feeling of fulfillment in a jostling throng, I slipped out just before the end of the service.

As I hurried down a path leading to the street, I was greeted by a young man with "Mediterranean" features wearing a scarf wrapped around his head and face. (In my inexcusable ignorance, I was unfamiliar with the Arab *keffiyeh*, and simply assumed he was showing his "individuality" by dressing oddly.) The young man, in a shy, accented voice, asked me if he could give me some information on the Palestinian people, and their struggle for freedom from Israeli occupation. I shall be eternally thankful that, still aglow with the mysteries of my religion, I did not simply avert my eyes and proceed down the path. Instead I took the little brochure and thanked him. For once I was in the "right place at the right time." I made a mental note to read that brochure after I got home. Already I had a strong suspicion that I wouldn't be reading the "usual" stuff.

The next morning, over a cup of coffee, I read the brochure. As I did, I wished I could run back up the path and thank the young man a hundred times over. In one fell swoop I discovered the "other" view on the troublesome Israeli/Palestinian issue. I had long ago concluded that something was lacking in my understanding of the subject—something that would make seemingly random, inexplicable rage and violence comprehensible. And now, eureka! Here was the mysterious missing element.

There was, in point of fact, another Semitic people who belonged to the Holy Land; a people who were struggling, unrecognized and reviled, for their freedom and independence from a foreign government seemingly bent on doing everything in its power to eradicate all physical traces, even the historic memory, of their existence.

I had been distressed and ashamed, many years earlier, when I discovered the truth about what my British/American, colonist/settler ancestors had done to the indigenous people of what we now know as America. I had been distressed and ashamed all over again when I recognized in the European Holocaust the unspeakable consequences of the same kinds of prejudices I had so casually absorbed as a child. Now, for a third time, I recognized the same tragic too-often-told story.

Why would the government of a people who had suffered so much for so long visit such pain and destruction on their Palestinian brothers and sisters? These Palestinians had had nothing whatsoever to do with the pain and suffering inflicted on the Jewish people over so many ages and in so many places.

I prayed to God for answers, or directions. In barely an instant, I felt God speaking to my heart. I realized at that moment that God had been speaking to me for a very, very long time, but that I hadn't been hearing very well.

From that day onward, however, I have felt it my duty to contribute whatever I can to the freedom and independence of the Palestinian people. I've spent a lot of time at it, and sometimes, in moments of irresolution, I've found myself wondering how much longer that might take. The answer I've always found in my heart is that the task will continue until the job is done to God's satisfaction. Meanwhile, I know that I must continue so long as I have blood, sweat or tears left to contribute.

I felt suffused with a special energy as I left the Christmas Eve service five years ago. Today, I feel equally confident of finding the means and the wherewithal to continue making my contribution, while following the guidance I find in my heart.

The "task" is the most challenging I've ever undertaken. When my message reaches another heart, as the young man's message reached mine, I'm not there to see it. I am there, however, when angry remarks are made by those who cannot understand that the message I bear is one of compassion for the Palestinians, not hatred for the Jews.

I find it takes a special kind of courage to be ridiculed or reviled, day after day, by strangers for putting Christianity into practice. These five years have given me insights into my religion that I could not have obtained in any other way.

In writing these words now, I have two wishes. I hope that young man who stood alone in the cold on a night most people were spending with family and friends will learn that his efforts, and the sacrifices of many like him all over America, were not in vain. God used him to touch my heart. My second hope, of course, is to touch other hearts with this personal testimonial.

I cannot undo the misdeeds of my ancestors or co-religionists in their time. But I can atone for them by extending a helping hand to those who need it in my time.

Whether or not you are tuned in to God, he is talking to you this very minute. Please listen. If you can't hear God's directions for personal action, then, at the very least, carry Palestine in your heart. It is her people who need your help, in this place, and in our time. ✦

David R. Willcox is an employee of the Washington, DC Suburban Sanitary Commission. Shortly after writing this article at the request of the Washington Report, *he was attacked and severely injured while carrying a sheathed Palestinian flag in downtown Washington by members of the Jewish Defense Organization, an extremist group implicated in previous beatings, shootings and bombings in various parts of the United States.*

POSTSCRIPT: *About a month after my "Seeing the Light" article was published, and the subsequent brutal attack on me—with steel pipes—by the Jewish Defense Organization (Kahane Khai), I ceased my public demonstrations and media work (radio and television appearances). You may call it fear, but my neurologist and psychiatrist calls it post-traumatic stress disorder.*

I am still working at the same old day job with the seventh largest water and sewer utility in the country. Upon retirement it is my intent to physically relocate to the Middle East—hopefully and prayerfully an independent Palestinian state. Spiritually, I have been living in Palestine for several years now. Should my physical being be extinguished or die of natural causes prior to the Spring of '03, it is and shall remain my most fervent wish that my cremated ashes will be taken to the Wadi Qilt just up the road from Jericho, overlooking St. George's, and there spread to the four winds.

I am trying to screw up my courage to get back into public demonstrations, and radio and television again. I feel my voice is desperately needed at this critical time in the ongoing struggle (does it EVER end?) of the Palestinian people.

Playwright in Palestine

By Peter Frisch

A s the artistic director of an established theater devoted to new writing and contemporary thought, I am constantly approached with wacky schemes. For example, I have considered hundreds of plays for production, including "Six Women with Brain Death," "Dancing the Hora in Rubber Shorts," and "Our Lady of the Tortilla."

In its own way, the notion of traveling to Jerusalem, the West Bank, and the Gaza Strip to gather information for a theater piece on the Palestinian situation seemed pretty remote and, well, rather wacky. Though I had dramatized primary material before, the mere fact of Jewish parentage hardly qualified me as an expert on Middle East affairs. Yet, here were several non-profit organizations ready to support composer Roy Barber and me on our mission of research and discovery.

Needless to say, I had no idea that I would be so moved and transformed by the people, the land, and the constant presence of mind-boggling injustice to be seen in every corner of every Arab village and refugee camp. As an English teacher residing in Jebalya said to me: "There are no rooms in this camp that have been untouched by tragedy."

The very first evening in Jerusalem, Roy and I walked through the deserted Old City, and I began to understand the unique pluralism at the very heart of this land. Christians, Jews and Muslims live together in this tiny walled-in labyrinth. The tradition of peaceful co-existence is long and deep. I was beginning to see the light.

The next morning two events completed my personal transformation. When we emerged from the air-conditioned mini-van into the sweltering dirt, stone, and concrete composition of Jelazoun camp, hundreds of children surrounded us, chanting "Power to the PLO" and thrusting their little-fingered "V" signs at us as they led us toward the camp center. The myth of "alternative moderate Arab leadership," as perpetrated by the Likud Party and repeated in the press worldwide, was shattered instantly by these children and their total identification with their political organization.

Minutes later, we sat with a family whose child had been murdered the day before by Israeli soldiers. Amin, who died one day before his 14th birthday, had come to the verbal defense of his sisters, who were being forced to remove boulders from a road. Unarmed, of course, the boy was shot through the eye. Amin was then flown by helicopter to an Israeli hospital and kept alive on life support systems while officials approached his parents for permission to remove the vital organs. (Israeli officials know Muslim tradition prohibits the removal of body parts.) The humiliation was complete with a demand for 4,600 shekels (about $3,000) in exchange for the return of the dead boy's body. It is impossible for a family in a refugee camp to conceive of this amount of money, let alone raise it.

And so, less than 24 hours after arriving in the Middle East, I had the basic story for our theater piece and found myself utterly devoted to the Palestinian people and Palestinian peace.

A Pattern of Usurpation

Israel and the occupied territories are rife with violence, irony, and absurdity. I will mention only a few of the images and narratives which continue to vibrate restlessly in my mind:

• During the past two years, 28 Jewish families have appropriated housing in the Muslim quarter of the Old City. The settlements form a perfect ring around the Dome of the Rock, the most significant mosque in Palestine, and the third holiest for Muslims all over the world. Hard-liner Ariel Sharon has new quarters overlooking the Dome.

• The military administration seized control of the 26 artesian wells around Jericho, and is selling the water back to Palestinian farmers at three to four times the basic cost. The director of the region's marketing cooperative told us that this extortion is primarily responsible for the drop in this year's crop output to 20 percent of normal agricultural production.

• The Palestinian fishing community is under siege—boats which roamed Mediterranean waters freely for centuries are now restricted to a six-mile limit by Israeli authorities. The few remaining families of fishermen fight starvation as they attempt to make political sense of their Kafkaesque foe.

• Soldiers used TNT and bulldozers to level 14 homes in the Arab village of Beita after a Jewish girl and two Arab boys were killed in wild shooting by a Jewish settler near the village. Authorities later admitted that villagers were not responsible for the death of the Israeli teenager, the ostensible "reason" for the wanton destruction.

• Also in Beita, troops dispersed Israeli peaceniks and uprooted 100 olive trees that had just been planted there. As the army tossed the saplings onto the road, the peace group began chanting, "Shoot the trees!"

• The prominent Israeli Peace Now group discourages Palestinians from participating in their programs and activities.

• We photographed the hole in the screen and the new pane of glass where only a few days before an American-made canister of tear gas was shot by soldiers into the obstetrics ward of Ramallah Hospital.

• Several witnesses talked of the "accidental" electrocutions that take place when Israeli soldiers force children to remove illegal Palestinian flags from overhead power lines.

• Israeli law owes much of its diabolical character to the days of the British Mandate. The fabled administrative detention statute allows police to arrest Palestinians for a six-month period without charge. We spoke with the erudite chairman of the board of Hebron University who had just returned from Ansar III prison in the Negev Desert. He told us of the subhuman conditions and treatment all prisoners are subjected to. About 2,300 Palestinians are now being held under administrative detention.

• Over 1,400 laws have been imposed by the military administration on the occupied territories since 1967. These laws amend, replace, or reinforce the repressive statutes already in force from the British Mandate.

We spoke with many Israeli settlers and government officials who continually invoked Abraham, the Holocaust, and general security as the justification for all actions taken in the West Bank and Gaza Strip. Palestinians are reduced to demographic problems, dehumanized in order to permit the continuation of deportation, harassment, repression and slaughter.

It is said that the greatest abuses are committed by the abused who have never healed. It makes sense. But I left the Middle East convinced that the resilience, flexibility, and determination of the Palestinian people will bring honor and ultimate victory to their cause. The intifada has created a unified and spirited people as age, gender, and class differences melt away. The PLO is now supporting Palestinian artists and coordinating non-violent activities, including the general strikes.

Despite the horrors, the Arabs of Palestine have entered into a promising chapter of their history. As Amin's mother told me only three days after her son's death: "If they insist, let the Israelis prepare graves for each of my children. We can no longer accept life without freedom." ✦

Peter Frisch, the former artistic director of the New Playwrights Theater in Washington, DC, is currently working in California.

Attaching Names and Faces to Statistics

By Susan M. Akram

Numbers alone don't tell the tale, but they give an indication of the pervasiveness of Israel's violations of the human rights of Palestinians in Israeli-occupied territories: After one year of the intifada more than 280 Palestinians in the West Bank and Gaza have been killed; several thousand Palestinians have been beaten by Israeli soldiers; more than 5,000 Palestinians are imprisoned, of whom 1,700 are under administrative detention; more than 150 Palestinian homes have been demolished by Israeli authorities; and 60 Palestinians have been ordered deported during the first year alone (1,500 since 1967).

I knew that Israel was systematically violating Palestinian human rights before we paid our own way and the American-Arab Anti-Discrimination Committee (ADC) made arrangements for us to spend three weeks with Palestinian families and experience life under Israeli occupation. My purpose was to document the violations because I knew that U.S. laws, such as Sections 502B and 116 of the Foreign Assistance Act of 1961, prohibit U.S. military and economic aid "to any country the government of which engages in a pattern of gross violations of internationally recognized human rights."

The delegation did not travel or stay together. We each spent time with many different Palestinian families throughout the West Bank and Gaza. So we were able to see and experience the atrocities that reporters, other delegations, and human rights observers have only glimpsed. American TV, newspaper, and radio coverage had in no way prepared me for what I saw.

Sixteen-Year-Old "Terrorists"

Instead of meeting Palestinian "terrorists," I met Laila, a 16-year-old girl who had just had surgery to remove an eye. She lost her eye when Israeli forces invaded her refugee camp to break up a demonstration. Laila ran out to get some of the little children out of the way, when a soldier a few feet from her lobbed a metal tear gas canister at her face.

I met Miriam, whose brother and cousin were both shot and killed within 40 days of each other. Miriam's cousin was running away from Israeli troops dispersing a demonstration when he was cornered by a soldier and shot in the head by a dum-dum bullet. Eyewitnesses saw the soldier put the gun up against the young man's forehead. (Dum-dum bullets spread on impact. His head was blown apart.)

Miriam's brother was killed as he was trying to pull a woman who had been demonstrating away from the grasp of an Israeli soldier. Another soldier shot Miriam's brother in the back and, as he spun around, again and again in the chest. Miriam told me her brother's body was held hostage by the Israel Defense Forces (IDF) until the family agreed to have only a small funeral. Military Commander Gen. Amram Mitzna himself told the family they could have the body only if they agreed not to participate in further protests. The day before I left the occupied territories, I learned that Miriam's uncle was among the 27 Palestinians most recently given deportation orders.

I met the owners of three homes that had been bulldozed to the ground in Jelazoun refugee camp the day before. Israeli soldiers came to the camp close to midnight. They gave the families 15 minutes to clear out their belongings before their homes were torn down. One house belonged to a 60-year-old woman. The military had been looking for her son. They couldn't find him, so they destroyed her house. A tent of the United Nations Relief and Works Agency had been erected on the rubble of one of the homes. The family came out to meet us; eight little children emerged from that tent. Their father was already imprisoned before the demolition order was issued. Under occupation law, a family is not allowed to rebuild on land where a house has been demolished.

Life Under Siege

I learned what it was like to live "under siege." I spent time in Amari, Beach, Jelazoun, and Nuseirat refugee camps, getting a taste of how to order one's life when each day may bring a new horror: curfew; house-to-house army searches followed by savage beatings; tear gas; cutoffs of electricity, water, food, and medical supplies; and army or settler raids with indiscriminate use of live ammunition. I recall nights in Gaza waking up to the sounds of screaming and shooting, and finding out that an area was besieged by troops dragging people from their homes and brutally beating them. I was never able to stay more than one or two nights in any one home because of the constant fear of the families with whom I stayed. The presence of an American was an added risk to their lives.

I spent a night at the home of Musa, a trade unionist recently released from prison whose family had moved six times in the last couple of years. He had been under town arrest and had been severely tortured during two periods of imprisonment for his union activities, although he was never formally charged with any crime. I began, like Musa and his wife, to listen carefully when a car turned down the street, to stop talking when we heard voices near the flat, and to watch when unfamiliar cars parked near the building. The last day I saw Musa he told me they would soon be moving again because police were carrying his picture and had questioned a friend about Musa's whereabouts.

Geneva Convention Violations

Deportations from occupied lands, collective punishment, demolition of homes, and imprisonment outside one's own territory are all violations of the Fourth Geneva Convention of 1949. Israel routinely engages in all of these illegal actions. Not only has the U.S. failed to condemn the violations of human rights as the Foreign Assistance Act and other laws require, but it continues to fund such violations. The Reagan administration and prior administrations have, from time to time, given Israel a slap on the wrist for continuing to build settlements in the occupied territories, for demolishing Palestinian homes, for the massive use of administrative detention and for the use of excessive force in attempting to crush the intifada. But renewal of Israel's annual grant of $1.8 billion in military and $1.2 billion in economic aid for fiscal year 1989 means the U.S. government is ignoring the language of its own Foreign Assistance Act and funding Israel's travesties.

The day settlers came to Gaza City accompanied by police and started firing live ammunition into the neighborhood, my companion and I ran out to take pictures. But we quickly dropped the idea when settlers aimed their guns at us. As we ran into an alley, one of the settlers threw a U.S.-made tear gas canister toward us. Later, doctors told us of army raids on hospitals when soldiers forcibly removed wounded Palestinians from their beds, threw tear gas inside hospital wards, and actually followed demonstrators inside a hospital in Gaza and proceeded to open fire. The arms and ammunition used were purchased with grants from U.S. taxpayers and the Foreign Assistance Act, but they certainly were not being used for defensive purposes as required by U.S. law. ✦

Susan Akram is an attorney and director of the Political Asylum/Immigration Representation (PAIR) Project in Boston, MA. She serves on the board of directors of the Boston chapter of ADC, and on the steering committee of the Coalition for Palestinian Rights.

The Middle East and Our "Received Wisdom"

By Laura Cooley

At least one good thing may have come out of the 1990-91 crisis in the Gulf. Americans are suddenly talking about the Middle East. At long last we are seeing Arabs and Arab nations as individuals and countries with political, ethnic, religious and cultural differences. No longer can the "Arab world" be seen as a monolithic bloc. Saddam Hussein may have been denied his "air time" with President George Bush and former British Prime Minister Margaret Thatcher, but some of the contradictions in U.S. policy toward countries in the region have become apparent to even the most casual observer.

Changing one's "received wisdom" about anything is, however, a long, arduous process. Several years ago I probably could not have told you what a Kurd is, would not have dared venture an opinion on the Israeli-Palestinian conflict, and might have confused Qatar with some new computer game. The Middle East was a muddle, or so I thought, and this excused my own muddled response to it. And anyway, I reasoned, as a Western woman having humanistic inclinations, I "knew" that the situation for Arab and Iranian women was reprehensible. The forced seclusion of women and, in some places, deliberate mutilation of their bodies did not pass my human rights checklist. I was thus content, at least for a while, to live with my simplistic understanding of the Middle East.

False Impressions

During the past decade I have discovered that many of my impressions of the Middle East and its people were inaccurate, stereotypical, and downright false. I had grown up near Washington, DC, and in college I majored in international relations. Yet it took me a long time to realize how years of misguided messages in film and in the media had warped my view of "the Arab," and how that ignorance continued throughout a predominantly Eurocentric "liberal arts" education which never called upon me to question these assumptions.

There were no courses offered on Middle Eastern civilization, with the possible exception of art history. We did not read literature from that part of the world. When the Middle East was discussed, it was usually in political science classes within the context of concepts like "terrorism." Happily, since that time, the curriculum at Vassar College has become more inclusive of the Middle East, as it has at most liberal arts colleges and universities in the U.S.

After graduating from college, I decided to live in a non-Western, predominantly Muslim culture. A Princeton-in-Asia fellowship took me to Indonesia, where I learned that Islam takes many forms, even, or perhaps especially, in this archipelago nation of over 13,000 islands, having the largest Muslim population of any single country. I learned the value of Javanese tolerance, and the practice of *rukun*—a philosophy of mutual co-operation and harmony practiced in Java.

In Indonesia, I lived under the constraints of a military regime whose control was not always obvious, but was sufficiently threatening to stifle any political discussion. The overcrowded villages of Central Java prepared me well for the poverty and densely populated refugee camps of Gaza, which I was to visit years later. The crucial difference, however, was that one group, the people of Gaza, was "stateless" and living under foreign occupation.

After two years in Indonesia, I returned to Washington, DC, to work at the Woodrow Wilson International Center for Scholars. I became involved in a project on the psychological motivations for political violence. After a year of wallowing in terrorism literature, I attended graduate school in London, where I met many people from the Middle East, among them Kurds, Iraqis, and Palestinians living in permanent exile.

Almost two years later, after the intifada erupted and I was living once again in Washington, the lack of American response to human rights violations in the occupied territories seemed inexplicable to me. How could Americans watch film footage of Israeli soldiers deliberately breaking Palestinians' bones and not be outraged that our tax dollars were supporting these crimes?

I went to the West Bank on a human rights delegation in 1988 and met Palestinian women, men and children with nerves of steel. Through the experience of visiting Palestinian homes and villages, textbook abstractions of the "revolutionary spirit" which I had carefully collected over my years as a student of politics at Vassar, in Paris and London came to life in the people I was meeting. These Palestinians had decided "enough is enough," and were intent on preserving their dignity and their state, regardless of the cost to themselves.

Sitting in a Nablus apartment in May, 1988, I found myself in sympathy with a Palestinian woman who tried desperately to prevent her curious 14-year-old daughter from exposing herself to gunfire by leaning over the balcony to watch Israeli soldiers below. Minutes later, the same soldiers tried with an axe to break down the door to the complex we were staying in. I was terrified, both for myself and for the Palestinians hosting me. Upon returning to the U.S., I gave slide shows to various groups about the human rights violations in the occupied territories. For this I was called "pro-Arab" and "naive."

A Dearth of Information

I believe that the dearth of information, and the abundance of misinformation, about the Middle East in the United States is a tragedy. I consider myself fortunate that the many stereotypes and false impressions I acquired from American media and academic sources have crumbled through my first-hand exposure to the Middle East.

In the last two years, I have been tear-gassed and shot at by Israeli soldiers, and I have been cursed by Palestinian men on the streets of Jerusalem. I have discovered that there is nothing terribly romantic about living under occupation ("Casablanca" notwithstanding) and that when searchlights shine in the windows of your home every few minutes and army jeeps rumble past at all hours of the night, you lose sleep. Ask the people of Nablus.

At home I have been subjected to personal criticism for my involvement in efforts to balance U.S. Middle Eastern policy. I continue to see the ambiguities in U.S. actions, and am increasingly discomforted by pat solutions to complex situations. As an American who has lived and worked abroad, the ethnocentric approach often adopted by U.S. policymakers never ceases to astound me. How is it that, with all our so-called "experts" on the Middle East, the common level of knowledge about this part of the world is so inadequate? I hope that our "received wisdom" about the Middle East can become more balanced and respectful of its rich history and cultural traditions. ✦

Laura Cooley is a social scientist from Washington, DC.

Unhealthy Occupation

By John T. Duelge, M.D.

As a physician who deals with statistics which represent individual human beings, I am frightened by the matter-of-fact attitude in America to the steadily rising toll of dead and wounded in the Israeli-occupied territories. I have just returned from two weeks in Jordan, Israel, and the West Bank and Gaza. Although it was my first trip to the region, I admit that my reading about the history of the conflict had made me skeptical of both Israeli and American positions even before I left Wausau, Wisconsin.

I arrived in Amman on March 12, and renewed my friendship with Dr. Hani Jumean, whom I had met in medical training 10 years ago. Dr. Jumean, a Jordanian, immunized me from that time on against stereotyping. He is as good a physician and human being as I have known. His wife, a Palestinian physician, is equally dedicated and compassionate.

In Amman, I visited two Palestinian refugee camps, where I met some of the hundreds of thousands of Palestinian refugees who were violently driven from their homes by the Israelis in 1947-1948, and again in 1967. Those who live in the camps have chosen to stay together so they can return to their homes in Palestine. I learned that Palestinians, whether living under Israeli occupation or outside, support the PLO, both to fight for their freedom and to negotiate the peace.

After crossing into the occupied territories, I visited the Arab Development Project near Jericho. Here I saw for myself the many ways that the Israeli occupation tries to break the spirit and the resistance of the Palestinians who choose to stay in their homes and stand up for their human rights. Both the project and its school had been closed for months.

I went to the village of Ein Karem, but I met no Palestinians there. It is just one of the villages whose Arab inhabitants were driven out by Israeli brutality, or even massacres. More than 300 Palestinian towns and villages have been obliterated forever. Ein Karem's homes were left standing, inhabited now by Israeli settlers.

I met Gideon Spiro, a former Israeli soldier who is now a peace activist. A soldier can be acclaimed a hero for killing. A man of peace like Gideon Spiro can save thousands of lives and get no credit. Such is the fate of soldiers in the battle for Palestinian-Israeli reconciliation.

At Tantur I met Landrum Bolling, a distinguished American devoted to solving the dispute, and heard of torture, indiscriminate arrest, and collective punishment. Also, I learned about the cohesion and determination of the Palestinian people in their struggle for freedom and democracy.

One of the high points was meeting Mubarak Awad, a Jerusalem-born U.S. citizen who was director of the Palestinian Center for Non-Violence until his deportation.

He believes that through mass nonviolent protests the Palestinians can beat Israeli occupation after violence has failed. Israeli authorities, he believes, have come to depend so much on violence that nonviolent confrontation scares them. Mr. Awad speaks of a strategy that could take years, but will finally succeed. Emotional acts of revenge, however personally gratifying to those who are abused and oppressed, Awad says, are giving way to long-term goals and strategies. Mr. Awad, like the other Palestinians I met, supported the people's choice of the PLO to represent them.

Israel's Arabs

The Palestinians within Israel's June 5, 1967 boundaries seemed in concert with the Palestinians on the West Bank and Gaza. Anglican Canon Riah Abu Asal spoke of the discrimination against Palestinians in Nazareth and the rest of Israel. Although they have much to lose, these Israeli Arabs are supporting the Palestinians.

It was as a physician visiting the Makassed Hospital, one of seven Palestinian hospitals in the West Bank, that the true meaning of "military occupation" came home to me. This hospital alone admitted 171 patients with gunshot wounds in three months. More than 700 other severely beaten patients were treated.

Of a total of 900 severely injured young people treated, half will be permanently disabled. More than 40 of those were permanently paralyzed. Palestinians, one-third of them children, suffering not only shattered bones, but shattered lives and dreams, filled hospital rooms and corridors. Rubber bullets inflict blindness and broken bones. Tear gas causes convulsions, amnesia, miscarriages, and in the very young and old, death from breathing complications.

These grievously wounded Palestinians and their dead compatriots are fellow human beings who should not become just statistics. If it is our American money that buys the rifles, the bullets, and the tear gas that shatters human flesh, lungs, and bones. We must demand media access to the oppressed and accountability of the oppressors. Let us insist that this brutal and pointless occupation be halted before more innocents die. ✦

Dr. John T. Duelge, a specialist in oncology and hematology, now practices in New Mexico. He is national medical director from New Mexico of the American Cancer Society, and vice-chairman of Medicine and chairman of the Cancer Committee at San Juan Regional Medical Center. In 1988, he ran as an independent candidate for the U.S. Congress against incumbent Representative David Obey, from Wausau, Wisconsin. His platform included support for a Palestinian state.

Yes, Israelis Shoot at Children and at Americans Who Get in the Way

By Deirdre L. Boyd

One sunny day in the spring of 1989, two jeeps carrying Israeli soldiers cornered some Palestinian boys and me, an American, on a dead-end dirt road in Gaza and opened fire on us without any provocation whatsoever. Then they dragged one little boy away and drove off in a cloud of dust.

Since then, whenever I have told my story, people have reacted by asking incredulously: "They didn't really shoot at you, did they?" Yes, they really did.

An Israeli reservist studying in the U.S. came up to me after I told my story at a B'nai B'rith teach-in, sponsored by an unusually progressive Hillel chapter, on "Considering the Possibility of a Two-State Solution to the Israeli-Palestinian Conflict."

I asked him, as an Israeli soldier who had served in the occupied territories, if he could tell me why they shot at us when they could clearly see that I was a foreigner just talking to some children outside their homes. He took me through the whole incident blow by blow in order to make sense of it. I told him that there was no demonstration, the boys weren't waving "subversive" Palestinian flags, and I was merely taking a photo of them.

"Oh, you were taking photographs of them! That explains it. The army doesn't like people taking photographs of the locals [i.e. Palestinians]."

Using Bullets to Hide Crimes

Israel doesn't want any exposure of its crimes against humanity—even if it entails shooting at tourists and journalists. But here is my story and the photo I took that precipitated the attack and left one little boy to an unknown fate.

My visit to Gaza was on the last day of my most recent trip to Israel and occupied Palestine. Traveling in a white and blue UNRWA van to avoid both Israeli bullets and Palestinian stones, we had already visited an UNRWA Refugee Feeding Center, where Palestinian school children in blue uniforms waited in line for their daily ration of pita bread, a dollop of hommous, and an orange. They gave us excited "V" signs before taking their orange and single piece of pita bread home to share with their families.

The Gaza Strip looked like one big refugee camp. Only 5 by 25 miles in area, and one of the most densely populated areas in the world, it is home to more than 445,000 registered refugees, the result of Israel's first orchestrated "population transfer" of Palestinians in 1948-49.

We drove over a dirt track to the outskirts of a camp town. The U.N. van parked at the top of a dead-end road, and the other passengers filed into a walled compound. I dallied outside, distracted by a russet rooster that was pecking among the wildflowers in front of a big stand of pale green prickly pear cactuses called "*subar*" in Arabic. As I adjusted my camera lens, the coy rooster darted right through the high wall of cactuses into the yard behind.

A group of boys in bare feet and sweatsuits appeared out of nowhere. As they milled around, curious and friendly under the sunny blue sky, I chatted in my broken Arabic, first with the brash ones, then with the shy ones.

"How do you do?" a bell-like voice called out from around the side of the cactuses. There were two girls in long brightly embroidered dresses leaning over the fence, their faces framed in the sheer white headscarves that Palestinian women have worn since the time of Mary and her son, Jesus of Nazareth. One was surprisingly beautiful, like a flower blooming in the desert. "What is your name?" she asked in her schoolgirl English.

Then the owner of the rooster, a stalwart mother with a wide canny face, peered through the prickly pears and called out in Arabic, "Where are you from?" I went back to talk with her and the boys. Then the boys posed for a picture in front of the *subar*.

"The Jews! The Jews!" someone cried out. Startled, we froze as a jeepful of Israeli soldiers came barreling along the dirt track that encircled the walled compound.

I turned my head just in time to see another jeepful of soldiers lurch to a stop at the top of the road next to our U.N. van. A pincer movement. Maniacal shouts came from the jeep and the crack-crack of shots. The soldiers were shooting at us.

As one soldier leapt down from the jeep and ran at us, rifle in hand, the Palestinian woman opened the compound gate for me. As I darted inside I could see, but she could not, that a little boy in a bright green shirt was running behind me, the soldier in hot pursuit. Slam! The gate was shut and barred against the soldiers. The little boy had nowhere to go. Crack, another shot.

Outside the walls, I don't know what happened. It was all over so fast. Someone saw the soldier drag the boy away. Was he shot? I don't know. Someone saw his silhouette sitting upright in the jeep—so he was still alive at that point. I still don't know which little boy he was or what happened to him. Is he alive? Is he in jail? Or is he lying in a ditch somewhere?

Women and children ran out wailing and shouting at the soldiers in the other jeep. The mother of the missing little boy started to run after the jeep which held her son. It spun around, then passed her in a cloud of dust.

[People later told me that this sort of thing happens every day. There are no constraints.

And now most of the media and tourists have been frightened off by such tactics.]

As one of the women in our tour group talked over the compound wall to the women and children, a toddler tossed a stone in the direction of the soldiers. The jeep returned and a soldier lobbed a percussion grenade right into the group of women and children talking to the American. It exploded against the wall.

A stout woman in the group shouted at the American: "See? Tell! Tell!" Another woman ran along the wall shrieking at us Americans inside the safety of the compound:

"It's because of you! Because of you! Your money pays for this. Your money!"

"It's Because of You!"

She was right. Without its annual $3 billion in direct U.S. government grants, Israel could not sustain the occupation. Israel receives more U.S. aid per capita than any nation in the world and the aid has just been increased by another $666.1 million. It can only appear that the U.S. is rewarding Israel for its mounting human rights violations. One out of every 30 Palestinians in the occupied territories (50,000) have been imprisoned without charge since the intifada began two years ago. Hundreds have been killed. Half of the dead are under 10 years old. Tens of thousands are maimed for life: broken bones and spines, missing eyes and limbs.

If you include such indirect aid as trade breaks for Israeli goods which compete with U.S. goods, the loss of U.S. military sales to friendly Arab states because of the Israeli lobby, tax breaks for charitable contributions which go to build illegal settlements in the occupied territories, the purchase of Israeli bonds by leading U.S. unions and state governments, etc., then the total cost of U.S. support for Israel now reaches $21 billion per year and is rising. It struck me that day how those soldiers didn't think twice about shooting at an American. Or about tossing a percussion grenade to stop an American dialogue with the Palestinians.

There were many burning memories from that trip: two houses being demolished by a big gnawing crane, all the furniture in the yards, women crying. The dairy outside the besieged city of Nablus, which had been "under curfew" for 13 days running. The cows' udders bursting with milk, while the army prevented milk and food from entering the city. At Al-Makassad Hospital, the eyes of the young paraplegics and the old man who had been pushed off a wall by soldiers and left in a ditch until his daughter chanced to find him.

I'm haunted by the cries of those Palestinian mothers in Gaza: "See? Tell! Tell! It's because of you! Because of you! Your money pays for this. Your money!" And, most of all, I wonder what happened to the little boy. ✦

Deirdre L. Boyd, a free-lance artist and writer living in the Washington, DC area, has an M.A. in Middle East studies from the American University in Cairo and has traveled extensively in the region.

Thus I Became a Mideast Addict

By Paul Findley

To this day people ask how and why I became entangled in Arab-Israeli politics. Sometimes I scratch my head and wonder the same thing. It was an unintended, accidental, unnatural attachment, and occasionally—as at this moment—I sit back, stare through the bay window by my desk in this small Midwestern city, and ponder the amazing extent to which my life is dominated by events in the far away Middle East.

Beyond the computer on which I type these words is a tall case where I keep books autographed by the authors and another filled with unautographed books. Nearby, six four-drawer filing cabinets—four of them in the basement—are full of correspondence. Almost all these books and letters relate directly to Mideast politics. One drawer in frequent use is reserved for current correspondence with people who live abroad, mostly in Israel or Arab states.

Seven years ago, I helped found the Council for the National Interest, a Washington-based organization that advocates policies that serve the U.S. national interest in the Mideast. I serve as chairman of the council and frequently consult by telephone and fax with Gene Bird, the retired foreign service officer who serves as president.

Since leaving Congress I have written two books, both on the Arab-Israeli conflict, and have discussed the subject in dozens of university lectures and in more than one hundred appearances on television and radio programs. I have written more than 300 articles for publication, over 90 percent of them on the Mideast.

I rationalize new endeavors, along with the others, in the name of Mideast peace. If all religious communities come to understand and appreciate each other and work toward common goals, I am convinced that a just peace will emerge. If they keep demonizing each other, violence is inevitable.

When did I get hooked? It came in mid-life. When appointed to the Foreign Affairs Committee in the House of Representatives in 1969, I would have been hard put to name more than three or four states in the Middle East. I represented a mixed agricultural-small industry constituency and spent most of my time on farm-related issues.

The involvement would never have occurred I believe, if I had not been a member of Congress. Nor did it happen overnight or from a single personal experience.

In my earlier role as a country newspaper editor, I had met and admired Lyle Hayden, who headed the Near East Foundation. Hayden's earlier private-sector work to improve the life of people in Iran and Iraq had earned him the unofficial title of "America's Shirt-sleeve Ambassador." It was the title of a *Reader's Digest* article about his work.

After my election to Congress, he and his Lebanon-born wife urged me to keep an open mind about Mideast policy and cautioned against responding only to Israel's demands and interests. We continued our discussions when he retired to a farm in my congressional district. His calm, unemotional arguments were persuasive.

So were the observations of Jacksonville, Illinois, businessman George Ziegler, and his wife Elizabeth, a college professor who annually invited me to lecture to her classes. World War II had taken both of them to assignments in the Mideast. Like the Haydens, they warned against the rising influence of Israel's U.S. lobby. These constituents triggered my concern about America's pro-Israel bias. For the most part, I kept these doubts to myself, but not in fear of consequences. In fact, in my innocence, unaware of how deeply Israeli interests had penetrated U.S. institutions, I assumed I could question policy anywhere without getting into trouble. I had worked hard to keep political fences mended back home.

When first assigned to the Committee on Europe and the Mideast, I had never heard of Israel's principal U.S. lobby, the American Israel Public Affairs Committee (AIPAC). My public involvement with Mideast politics deepened as the result of a constituent problem, called casework in the bureaucratic lingo of members of Congress. It had only an indirect connection with the Arab-Israeli conflict.

It began in 1973 when a letter arrived from a woman who wrote neighborhood news for a weekly newspaper I once edited. She pleaded for help in securing the release of her son, who had been charged with espionage and sentenced to five years' solitary imprisonment in Aden, then the capital of the People's Democratic Republic of Yemen, a country since united with the Yemen Arab Republic. My quest for his release was severely handicapped, because the U.S. government had no diplomatic representation in Aden.

First Trip to the Middle East

A year later, despite my efforts, her son was still locked up, and I concluded that if I did not go personally to plead for his release, he would probably die in prison. I headed for Aden in March 1974—my first trip to the Middle East—a journey that thrust me into the middle of the Arab-Israeli conflict.

En route, I stopped at Beirut and visited Palestinian refugee camps that would soon be the site of dreadful massacres at the hands of "Christian" militia. Then, before continuing my rescue mission, I rode overland to Damascus where, to my surprise, I was welcomed to an hour-long discussion with Syria's president, Hafez Al-Assad. At Aden, I had a series of interviews with officials.

This agenda provided my first glimpse of the Arab world. I found Arabs warm and likeable even when they bristled with indignation over U.S. policies. For the first time they emerged as human beings from false stereotypes, and I found their grievances against my government fully justified.

Clearly eager for friendly relations with the U.S. government, the president of the People's Democratic Republic of Yemen granted my request and let me take my constituent to a joyous homecoming in America's Midwest.

Back in Washington, word of my experiences got around, and soon my congressional office became a stopping place for people going to and from the Middle East. It was unusual, almost without precedent, for a member of Congress to visit Arab countries and express publicly an interest in their problems.

I began to speak out, arguing that failure to talk directly to Arab government officials and the political leadership of the Palestinians handicapped our national interests, especially our search for a just peace there. One step led to others—personal meetings with PLO leader Yasser Arafat, debates with leading congressional spokesmen for Israel, initiatives at State Department request for release of other U.S. citizens imprisoned in the Mideast, then election-day showdowns with opponents heavily financed by Israel's supporters. The last election campaign took me out of public office but into private endeavors for Mideast justice—books, lectures, articles, travel etc.

The Middle East is an incurable personal addiction and, to my knowledge, there is no therapy that will loosen this obsession. I may bear it until the Grim Reaper arrives. ❖

Former Congressman Paul Findley (R-IL) is chairman of the Council for the National Interest and the author of They Dare to Speak Out: People and Institutions Confront Israel's Lobby *and* Deliberate Deceptions: Facing the Facts About the U.S.-Israeli Relationship, *both of which are available from the AET Book Club.*

Middle Eastern Leaders Fear Lobby Control of U.S. Congress

By John B. Anderson

Four senators, led by Connie Mack (R-FL) introduced legislation in 1990 to cut off any further dialogue with the Palestine Liberation Organization (PLO). One of the constituent elements of the PLO is the Palestine Liberation Front (PLF). It is headed by Abul Abbas, who that spring had launched an abortive attack on beaches near Tel Aviv with heavily armed small boats. The senators' grounds are the failure of PLO Chairman Arafat to rid the executive committee of Abbas. Although disavowing any advance knowledge or complicity in the terror tactics of the head of the PLF, Arafat says only the Palestine National Council, the 400-member parliament-in-exile of the proclaimed state of Palestine, has authority to remove Abbas. Abul Abbas is clearly a violent leader of a maverick faction which does not accept the disavowal of terrorism by the umbrella organization, the PLO.

Was This The Time?

Was this the time to break off U.S.-PLO talks of a year-and-a-half duration? Should we have abandoned any further effort to engage the PLO in talks which could lead to Palestinians and Israelis sitting down to settle their dispute, which in more than four decades has resulted in five wars? Just two months before the invasion of Kuwait, I returned from two-and-one-half weeks in the Middle East. As a member of a Peace Mission for a Just Solution in the Middle East, sponsored by PAX World Foundation, I had the opportunity to visit Jordan, Syria and Egypt, before going on to Israel and the Israeli-occupied territories of the West Bank and Gaza.

From King Hussein of Jordan, President Hafez Al-Assad of Syria and the foreign minister of Egypt we listened to extended criticisms of U.S. foreign policy. For me, they shed a great deal of light on why so many Palestinians are critical of U.S. intervention in the current Gulf crisis, and why Saudi Arabia and other friendly Arab states are so concerned about accepting the U.S. military assistance they feel they need to defend their countries against possible Iraqi aggression.

Interestingly enough, Middle East leaders were more critical, or so it seemed to me, of the U.S. Congress than of either the president or his secretary of state. They are convinced that members of Congress are both ill-informed about what is happening in the Middle East and anti-Arab in their views. My former colleagues would not find it very flattering to discover that they are universally regarded as totally under the control of lobby groups which see only one side of the Arab-Israeli dispute.

A Matter of Survival

Mayor Elias Freij of Bethlehem complained: "For us, peace in the occupied territories is a matter of survival. All our universities have been closed, some even before the intifada, which began 30 months ago. More than 40,000 of our high school graduates have been deprived of any opportunity for higher education.

"Between midnight and 3 a.m., the Shin Bet [the secret service of the occupying Israeli military authorities] drag our young men out of their houses. Some are simply beaten. Others are detained, often without charge or trial for many months."

He concluded, "We want a demilitarized state of our own, and then eventually a Benelux arrangement or economic union with both Israel and Jordan. I would like to see my grandchildren and those of Shamir playing football together without fear."

Mayor Freij, who has been mayor of Bethlehem for 25 years, is a moderate. He offered a total disclaimer of the use of force and violence, but he warned that events on the West Bank and in Gaza were becoming more explosive with each passing day. I was reminded of what our ambassador in Jordan had told us a few days earlier. We were in a region where if events were not moving in the direction of peace, they would almost inevitably be moving toward war.

Visits to a refugee camp and a hospital in Gaza provided powerful evidence that the intifada will not be suppressed with rubber bullets, tear gas, curfews and other forms of collective punishment. A girl with a severe head injury, and a young man with a bullet in his knee both assured me they intended to continue the struggle. The cry for independence and freedom is a passionate one.

Talks with Moshe Arens, foreign minister in the last government of Israel, and just named defense minister of Shamir's newly formed rightist government, were highly revealing about likely future Israeli positions. Shamir himself had refused to see us even after several requests were made.

The government of Israel does have legitimate security concerns. Certainly a two-state solution, with an independent state of Palestine existing alongside Israel, would require iron-clad international guarantees. However, the thinking of the new government utterly precludes any arrangement which would provide for a state of Palestine. In Arens' words, "It already exists. It lies in the state of Jordan." Not only does King Hussein reject this proposition, but so does every single Arab leader with whom I met.

The winds of change which toppled regimes and brought democracy to Central and

Eastern Europe have not produced similar results in the Middle East. But make no mistake about it, those winds are reaching gale force. Yehoshafat Harkabi, former chief of Israeli military intelligence, has written *Israel's Fateful Hour,* in which he argues persuasively that it is precisely because of security reasons that negotiations leading to an independent Palestinian state must proceed. The present policy of not negotiating is a dead end. He then cites a former longtime U.S. ambassador to Israel, Samuel Lewis, for the proposition that in the realm of foreign policy a mistake by a great power is merely an episode. However, for a small state of 4 million people like Israel, a mistake is a tragedy.

Those of us who have long cherished and admired an independent state of Israel want to see tragedy averted. That is precisely why a policy based on a continued refusal to negotiate is wrong. It would be wrong for either the U.S. or Israel to assume that stance. ✦

John B. Anderson, a Republican member of the House of Representatives from Illinois for many years, was an independent candidate for president of the United States in 1980. He joined the board of directors of the Council for the National Interest on Sept. 8, 1990.

POSTSCRIPT: *The Gulf crisis served to point up the urgency of a speedy resumption of U.S. efforts to be the facilitator of serious Arab-Israeli talks about the fate of 1.7 million Palestinians in the occupied territories. The fourth point of the president's list of U.S. objectives in defusing and settling the situation created by Saddam Hussain's occupation of Kuwait has always been stated as achieving peace and stability in the entire region of the Middle East. That simply cannot be achieved without a resolution to the festering problem of human rights and dignity being trampled under foot in the continued occupation after almost a quarter of a century by Israel of territory which it simply claims by right of conquest. The principle of self-determination is as sacred to the people in the West Bank, Gaza and East Jerusalem as it is to the people of Kuwait. We cannot support the latter and ignore the former. The latest barbarity of deportations and the rising tide within Israel itself for a policy of expulsion can only exacerbate the human suffering and misery of which the world has already seen too much. If the confrontation with Iraq was not fundamentally about oil, but about human rights, self-determination, and a refusal to recognize aggression, we must demonstrate our willingness to stand behind the fundamental justice involved in facilitating the achievement of Palestinian statehood with appropriate international guarantees for both Israel and that yet-to-be-created autonomous state. Anything less will defeat the president's own stated purpose, or one of the most important reasons for the U.S. presence in the Gulf.*

Saudis "Trust in God But Keep a Rock by Their Side"

By Deborah B. Akers

In late July of 1990, I was aroused early from my sleep in our home in Jiddah, Saudi Arabia, by cries from our Pakistani driver. "Yella, Yella," he said. "Come quickly, there is an emergency." I dashed to the back garden. There, a fellow Pakistani had just dispatched a cobra snake. Yes, he explained with a proud smile, this was the most venomous cobra known. An ounce of venom spit into a person's eyes would surely result in instant death. It writhed a final spasm, then died inches from the children's swing set.

I was horrified. That snake, I knew, was not common to the Hijaz. Where did it come from? How did it get past our outside walls? Nonsense, reassured my Saudi friends and neighbors, there is no reason to fret. One must trust in God. But, they added with quiet smiles, a wise man keeps a rock by his side.

That August 2, our driver came again with news of another emergency. Iraq had invaded Kuwait. Confusion reigned in the local Saudi community. Throughout the summer, Saddam Hussain had been hailed as the next Nasser, a leader who would draw the Arab world together. Now, incredibly, threats began to pour over Radio Baghdad suggesting that the Kingdom could be next. Astonished and surprised, the Saudi press began condemning Hussain's action.

Piercing the Calm of Daily Life

In our home we listened to the shortwave radio throughout the day, switching between the BBC, VOA, and Radio Baghdad. It became our routine, and all of this news was hungrily ingested. Accounts of horror from Kuwait were sandwiched between threats from Baghdad. Throughout the ensuing weeks, entire populaces of Dhahran, Riyadh and Jeddah experienced periods of fear that pierced the calm of daily life.

There was the immediate threat of a missile attack. Saddam made it very clear that missiles now located in Kuwait were aimed at each important center in the Kingdom. For those in Dhahran, on the Gulf, or in Riyadh, the capital, the border was uncomfortably close. For us in Jeddah, along the Red Sea coast, Kuwait seemed farther away. But

Saddam dispelled any sense of safety we might have felt. His Scud missiles, he announced, now had an extended range which made it possible to penetrate the farthest reaches of the Kingdom. From that day forward it was hard to rest well at night, trying to distinguish the roar of an airliner overhead from something that could be much worse.

Preparing for chemical attack became necessary. The Saudi government circulated leaflets with instructions concerning the proper procedures for protecting oneself and one's family in case of an attack. The bad news was, if caught outdoors, there was absolutely nothing that could be done.

Indoors, there was a chance. If an attack occurred, we were instructed to turn off the air conditioning, turn on the shower and remain in the bathroom, for approximately four to five hours—all the while breathing through wet towels.

I admired the Saudis' ability to find calm through "trust in God." I, too, trusted in God, but in what must be an American cultural trait, I could not help continuing to fret. Among the expatriates, there was plenty of gallows humor. There were also the frantic midnight calls from America and elsewhere from worried family members. Sobbing grandmothers and concerned friends all advised those among the expatriate community to leave. Were the Saudis underreacting, or was their attitude similar to "let's not worry the women"? Were our friends and family in the U.S. overreacting? There was not much time to ponder the issue.

Next, there were waves of refugees from Kuwait pouring into the Kingdom. Each night the television interviewed both men and women of all nationalities who had fled Kuwait. Every one of them had suffered from the ordeal. With them they brought tales of horror and something else—anger. An anger which was contagious.

The Saudis were shocked at the atrocities reported. At this point it was clear that Saddam was a madman. In a war one expects looting and death. But the personal outrages which were committed were not to be expected from the soldiers of a Muslim country. Women and men whom I had known for years broke their traditional Saudi reserve and polite manners. They cursed Saddam for his atrocities. Saddam was beyond mad, he was the embodiment of Satan himself.

Preparations For War

The Saudis psychologically prepared themselves for war. Staple goods were stockpiled. Savvy Saudi women had purchased pounds of rice, tea, canned goods, and kerosene. Safeway supermarket managers in Jiddah said business had never been so good.

Weddings were postponed and vacations canceled. Saudis abroad were undecided whether to return. Our lives went on hold. We hoped it would be possible to resume more normal lives once enough international troops had arrived. Every day we all listened to the radio, awaiting such a word.

On a visit to a friend's house, her father drew us together to listen to Radio Baghdad. For some inexplicable reason there was no commentary, only the chanting of the Qur'an.

This was done, he said knowingly, only when a leader dies or if the Iraqis are beginning to launch an assault. We sat there, hoping for the former and dreading the latter. We were on this type of emotional rollercoaster throughout the month of August.

By October, there were enough troops on hand for both Saudis and expatriates to relax somewhat. I noticed, however, that life had not really returned to normal. Expatriates I knew had calmed their rattled nerves by resuming such habits as smoking. The Saudis, on the other hand, maintained a calm which I greatly admire. Now we hope that a diplomatic solution will be found and Desert Shield, the rock at our side, will not be needed after all. ❖

Deborah B. Akers is an American-born Ph.D. student in anthropology at Ohio State University. Her husband is a Saudi national and her permanent residence is in Jeddah.

I See My Two Beloved Countries on the Verge Of a Horrifying War

By Sali Qaragholi

Before August of 1990, I never had a problem disclosing my birthplace. But since the invasion of Kuwait, I rather hesitate in admitting I was born in Iraq. It seems to me that the media have portrayed the situation in such a way that people get the impression of Iraqis as bloodthirsty people seeking to gain from a smaller country's misfortune. It is a fact that most see Saddam Hussain in this fashion, and isn't a leader, after all, viewed as both a product and a reflection of his society and culture?

My purpose is to give the Iraqi point of view—something one doesn't really see on CNN; and if it is presented on television, then it is portrayed in such a way that it only results in aggravating the already negative American sentiment.

I am privileged, in a sense, for I've been on both sides of the fence. I've lived in the United States most of my life and have come to regard it as my home. In fact, my family and I still recall with gratitude how warmly we were received in the U.S. and how people here made us feel a part of their community—not like unwelcome foreigners.

A Warm Welcome From America

We always recall with particular emotion the day I came home to tell my parents what my teacher had said to me at school that day. She had taken me aside to ask what my father did for a living. I had replied that he did not work, for at the time he had not yet found a job. She then proceeded to offer me free meals at school. I thanked her and said I would tell my parents.

When they heard about the goodwill of my teacher, they were both very touched. I still recall the tears that sprang to my mother's eyes, at the kindness with which the American people were treating us. And yet my father replied, "Tell your teacher, thank you very much, but that won't be necessary."

When I asked him why, he responded: "Sali, if we take this meal, it would mean that we would be depriving another, truly needy child." I did not take the meal, but we have never forgotten this incident.

This kindness of the American people, in fact, is one of the many reasons we love this country and feel such warmth for it. At the same time, I cannot forget where I am from, for it has played an integral role in shaping the individual I am today. I am grateful to both of my homelands. Both have taught me. Both have cared for me. I am the child of both.

In this sense, I am privileged. But I am unfortunate, as well. For I see and feel what many cannot. I see my two beloved countries on the verge of war. I see both of my peoples ready to lash out at each other when, in truth, they are the most natural of allies.

The interest of the United States would be well served by good relations with Iraq, for it possesses vast reserves of oil that the U.S. needs. Conversely, the U.S. has the largest reserves in the entire free world of creativity, technology, and its vast wealth of education. Iraq could teach the U.S. to understand the Arab mentality and thus help it to improve its relations in the Middle East. The U.S., on the other hand, can instruct Iraq on the advantages of democracy, freedom of the press, and freedom of speech. Both countries are in dire need of what the other possesses—if they act upon it they could complement each other.

Observing From the Inside

Having offered my two-cents' worth on the political advantages of friendship, allow me to proceed directly to the heart of the Middle East, breaking through Arab stereotypes and observing the people from the inside.

The people of Iraq, as is typical in that part of the world, live in a very moralistic society. Things there are pictured in black and white. There is right and there is wrong. There is also a tremendous feeling of injustice—injustice inflicted upon them by Western governments.

Instead of furthering Iraq's interests in return for Iraqi oil, they feel that Britain depleted the country of its resources, and split the Arab world into spheres of influence—the very old technique of divide-and-conquer. Arabs have felt the pain of this transgression for generations, and cannot bring themselves to forgive the West. Indeed, no apology has been offered.

As a society, the Iraqis are a very warm, hospitable people. With one another, they behave as family. Everyone is either "Uncle" or "Aunt" whether the individual is actually your aunt or uncle, whether you've known the particular individual for years, or whether he or she is a total stranger.

I clearly recall an incident when I was last in Baghdad in 1985. My aunt, cousins and I were in the car driving to the house of a friend whom we had never before visited. We got lost along the way. My aunt stopped the car, and my cousin popped her head out to ask a woman walking on the street for directions. I remember her saying, "Aunt, do you know how to get to such and such a road?" And then, once having been given the directions, "Thank you very much, Aunt."

Although I grew up in Baghdad until I was seven, I had forgotten that part of life there is this tremendous warmth and family-like relationship with everyone around you. I added that to my mental catalogue of the similarities and the differences between my two cultures, the American and Iraqi: Both peoples are warm and friendly, and yet there are differences in the way the two peoples express these qualities.

Although Iraq is a Second or Third World country (depending on your particular conception of these terms), there are a lot of advantages to life there. Crime is insignificant compared to that in the U.S., and rape is almost unthinkable. A person feels safe there. By contrast, as a city dweller, I can't remember the last time I felt totally safe and secure in the U.S.

As well, life in some major respects is easier in Iraq for the average individual than it is in the U.S. Although Iraq is not a rich country, it provides its people with free hospitals and free universities, so that the poor have access to good education and medical care, and are not shut out by virture of enormous health insurance costs.

Thus, although most Iraqis live at a much lower standard of living than their American counterparts (at about a lower-middle-class level), they simultaneously have securities denied the poor in the U.S.

Further, if a son, for example, is not financially independent when he marries, it is common for him to live at home until he has saved enough money to make it on his own. In the U.S., such familial support is not always taken for granted.

An interesting fact of which few Americans are aware is that anyone in Iraq who has a complaint can take it straight to a government-appointed committee. The committee listens to the individual's problem or problems and tries to resolve them. If it cannot, the Iraqi individual can even meet with the president if he or she feels the need to have a personal interview in which to voice the grievance.

On the negative side, ambition among Iraqis is lacking compared to Americans. After a bloody eight-year war with Iran, the Iraqi people were worn out, exhausted and severely depressed. Every family had lost at least one person in the war. Iraqis could hardly believe that the war was over, that they could finally live in peace and begin to rebuild shattered lives. Then, only two years later—BAM!—they have to begin all over again, preparing for another possible war.

People in Iraq are not happy to have their young sons dying again. So much destruction has already occurred. There has been so much death and bloodshed. They don't want war, but at the same time they are not being given a chance to be heard or to find a way out. The only offer they've received is, get out and then we'll talk. They want to know, before they move, what they will be talking about and whether anything will really be done about their grievances.

A Double Standard

They see before them a double standard, enacted by the West solely for them. They might respect a U.N. resolution had all other U.N. resolutions been supported so insistently and with such fervor. But, unfortunately, this has not been the case, particularly in the Middle East.

Obviously, I've given only one point of view in this matter. It is my purpose to do so because the American public is already aware of the points of view of the Kuwaitis, of other members of the international community, and certainly of their own government.

It is true that politics can be ugly and inhumane. We must focus, however, on the lives at stake. Thousands should not have to be sacrificed for yet another conflict between political leaders.

We Iraqis are people with families, children, hopes and dreams of our own. We do not want our country and our homes and our loved ones burned to ashes. We want peace.

We Americans are people with aspirations, lives to fulfill, children and families to love and nurture. We do not want our sons killed in a foreign land. We want peace.

My question, therefore, is a cry from the heart, a scream of anguish and pain. How can two peoples so inherently good, so warm, so desirous of peace, be on the verge of such a harrowing, horrifying war? ✦

Sali Qaragholi, an undergraduate student at Cornell University at the time of the Gulf war, worked after graduation as a political analyst at the Jordan Information Bureau in Washington, D.C. She is currently a first-year student at the University of Virginia School of Law, where she hopes to specialize in international law.

From the Gulf War to Palestine— The Evolution of an Advocate

By Katherine M. Metres

For my 16th birthday, my best friend gave me a black-and-white houndstooth scarf. My Lebanese-American father said to me, teasingly, "That's a Palestinian scarf." Feeling as if I'd been accused of colluding with terrorists, I denied it with annoyance.

That was just six years ago. Today, being Arab American and a passionate supporter of Palestinian rights are the most meaningful aspects of my life. But it wasn't until college that I was conscious of being Arab American at all, much less pro-Palestinian.

The Gulf war was a pivotal coming-of-age experience for me. I was a first-year student at the University of Michigan, a school I had chosen in part for its tradition of student activism.

That fall, I attended a presentation by the campus chapter of the American-Arab Anti-Discrimination Committee (ADC) on "Arab Americans, the Gulf Crisis, and Internment." The speaker described the hardships of Japanese Americans interned during World War II, and charged that the U.S. government had contingency plans to do it again to Arab or Iranian Americans in the event of war in the Middle East.

By January, the campus was near hysteria over the prospect of the coming war. Reservists were being called up, and my father was an officer in the Naval Reserve. I also had a brother of draftable age. When they told us how many body bags were being sent to Saudi Arabia, everyone around me began to anticipate another Vietnam. Learning that innocent Arab Americans were being interrogated by the F.B.I. and that others were the victims of anti-Arab hate crimes, I thanked God my family didn't have an obviously Arabic surname.

The teach-ins my college friends and I attended taught us about a region of which we had known nothing. We also learned that the U.S. government was willing to "kick butt" to punish an Arab occupier, but had supported the Israeli occupation of Arab lands for decades.

When the Gulf war was over, I transferred my passion for human rights and my awakened interest in the Arab world into a summer internship with Amnesty International on

Capitol Hill. As a government relations intern on Europe, the Middle East and North Africa, it was my responsibility to handle inquiries on human rights conditions in specific cases and countries, as well as to bring human rights concerns to the attention of U.S. and foreign embassy officials. It was in this context that I heard former Arab League Ambassador Clovis Maksoud describe the denial of national rights—"collective human rights" as he called them—to the Palestinian people under occupation and in the diaspora.

I returned from Washington eager to prepare for a career in foreign relations. I concerned myself with learning about the root causes of human rights abuses and of armed aggression so that I could understand and someday help prevent or resolve international conflicts before my country again resorted to the destructive methods chosen by the Bush administration.

A Lot to Think About

That fall, spurred on by nothing more noble than the requirements of a scholarship, I became a member of my campus ADC chapter. The first activity I attended was a lecture by Dr. Haidar Abdel-Shafi, then the head of the Palestinian negotiating team. His viewpoint impressed me and gave me a lot to think about as I went home for the summer.

In addition, the head of the ADC chapter had given me a gift subscription to the *Washington Report on Middle East Affairs*. As I perused the pages month by month, a whole new world opened up to me. Slowly, I began to see the reality of the Israeli-Palestinian conflict. In place of the media image of Palestinian terrorists, I began to see a people struggling for the freedom to control their own destiny—and often being thwarted by U.S. favoritism for Israel.

The next fall, I was asked to chair the campus ADC chapter. When I accepted the job, I knew that I had no idea of what I was undertaking. Nonetheless, student members who had come directly from the Arab world wasted no time in educating me on their concerns for the Palestinians and Lebanese who were bearing the brunt of Israeli military occupation and bombing raids.

Simultaneously, I contributed to campus debate on political issues as a *Michigan Daily* editorial board member and columnist. My first column, which focused on anti-Arab racism and hate crimes spawned by the Gulf war, drew accolades from a wide sector— including the chair of the campus American Movement for Israel (AMI). Cheerfully, I pressed on—and stepped on a political land mine.

The day after presidential candidate Bill Clinton held a campaign rally on campus, I published a column asserting that his promised emphasis on human rights rang hollow as long as he ignored Israel's repressive military occupation of Arab lands. I argued that Clinton's pro-Israel rhetoric would damage the peace process. Quoting his statement that "If I ever let Israel down, God would never forgive me," I posed two questions to him: "Wouldn't it be best for Israel in the long term to resolve its conflicts equitably? And, you're running for president of which country?"

Even though my student editor told me she didn't think the column was "based in fact" and that "some people would consider this anti-Semitic," I felt very proud of that column. Still, the confrontation with the editor, who frankly told me she considered herself an Israeli, left a bad feeling in my stomach. My suspicions were confirmed when she told me a month later that my biweekly column would be canceled. Even though she was the one who had hired me, based on my writing clips, to add a "new perspective" as an Arab American, my column suddenly was "not what we're looking for."

I spent the rest of the year championing free speech on the Palestinian-Israeli dispute. Based upon the manner in which my own column had been canceled as a direct result of my criticism of the intrusion of U.S. domestic politics into the Middle East peace process, I became convinced that something was very wrong with the national debate on the issue. This awareness culminated in my speaking on the topic of "Academic Freedom: The Reality and the Ideal" as part of ADC's oratorical competition at the 1993 convention in Washington, DC. I won the first prize of $500, and I knew just how I should spend the money—for tuition at a Palestinian university.

So, in the summer of 1993, I set out to see for myself the reality of the Palestinian-Israeli confrontation. In the Paris airport en route to Tel Aviv, I met Dr. Abdel-Shafi and a priest from Beit Sahour. Dr. Abdel-Shafi told me that the negotiations were faltering because of the American draft of principles, which ruled out some concessions that the Israelis had already indicated they were willing to make! My column appeared to be coming true, and as an American I felt ashamed.

The Palestinian priest regaled me with humorous anecdotes all the way to Tel Aviv. But the atmosphere changed when I was confronted by Israeli airport security people upon arrival. Again and again they demanded to know: "Why are you going to Birzeit University? Why do you want to study Arabic?" They took my bags into a back room and returned them only after I was further interrogated by a supervisor.

Intimidated, Then Welcomed

When I finally was released I learned that the Palestinians who were to meet me had been unable to reach the airport due to the closure of the occupied territories. So my new priest-friend took charge of transporting me from the airport to the West Bank. This pattern of being intimidated and harassed by Israelis, and then comforted and welcomed by Palestinians, continued throughout my stay. Contrary to my expectations, the Palestinians never discriminated against me for my government's policies (I wouldn't have blamed them) or for my inability to speak their language. I only hope most Americans treat Arab visitors as considerately.

For seven weeks, then, I lived on the West Bank, studying Arabic and the Palestine question at Birzeit University. Living under occupation brought the problems into sharp focus and gave me visceral experience in the importance of enforcing international humanitarian law. I never got used to looking down the barrel of a gun, as a person walking along the streets of Ramallah is forced to do whenever an army convoy passes. In reality, I was safe from the soldiers because I was American. It was the Palestinians who had to fear for their safety.

During my first week in Ramallah, my roommate and I heard shots from our hostel window. The next day we found out that two young men had been killed by undercover Israeli death squads. One of the men had been "wanted." Instead of arresting and trying him, as in a truly democratic country, the Israelis had simply killed him and an unaccused companion.

Another time, I was in Ramallah window-shopping when a settler drove through the center of town. (This is forbidden by order of the Israeli authorities.) A couple of teenagers hurled rocks toward the vehicle, and then a hand came out of the vehicle window with a gun and began shooting wildly into the busy marketplace.

A few weeks later, the whole city of Ramallah was put under a military curfew of indefinite duration after an Israeli soldier was murdered. The students were warned that if we violated the curfew we could be shot on sight. Our planned excursion to the Galilee had to be postponed.

Nevertheless, eventually we visited the Galilee, the Jordan Valley and the Negev, and the university trips turned out to be the most eye-opening experiences of the summer. Viewing the sites of dozens of Palestinian villages that were destroyed in 1948 and 1949 to change the demography of the new state of Israel was heart-wrenching. I was particularly galled when we saw that the remains of al-Ghabisiyya village had been hidden from the road by a forest planted in artificial rows. One grave still marked by a handmade wooden cross seemed to beckon to the conscience of Christian visitors.

Equally disturbing was the obvious fact that even the occupied territories were being stolen from the Palestinians, piece by piece. The countryside surrounding Jerusalem supported an unbelievable number of Jewish settlements, and almost all the agricultural land in the Jordan Valley had been confiscated for the use of Israeli moshav (cooperative) and kibbutz (collective) farms.

When it was time to leave, a close friend I had made during my stay gave me an olive-tree necklace that says "Palestine" in Arabic. (Such jewelry was illegal by order of the Israeli military authority.) "I want you always to remember Palestine," he told me, "because a country is much more important than one person."

I returned to Ann Arbor, eager to share my experiences and new insights, in the same month that the Declaration of Principles was signed on the White House lawn. I wrote an opinion piece for the *Michigan Daily* entitled "Real Peace Starts With Real Palestine," in which I stated that the agreement could be helpful in providing the Palestinians a small space to organize for democracy and a better life, but that Israel was far from being in compliance with international law in terms of protection of populations under military occupation, land and water confiscation, political prisoners, and the refugees' right of return. I attacked Zionism at its roots for displacing and disenfranchising the indigenous population of Palestine. At the suggestion of a Jewish friend, I also noted that the Zionist movement in the 1940s deprioritized rescuing Jews from the Nazis in favor of building a strong state and a "Jewish national museum" in Palestine. Long discussions with this friend about the historical persecution of Jews in Europe and its similarities to Israel's treatment of the Palestinian Arabs had deepened my conviction.

A Phone Call

A couple of weeks after the article was published, I received a phone call from a man who told me that he was very interested in my article. He said that his father had been born in Palestine, and that he didn't know very much about the issue. At his request, I agreed to meet him for lunch to share what I had learned.

Afterward, I opened the campus newspaper and found an entire article by this man—who turned out to be an Israeli American—attacking things I had said in the article and during our discussion. He wrote that upon reading my article, he was curious to discover the origin of my "hate." Upon finding out I had spent the summer at Birzeit University, which he described as "a hot bed of Islamic fundamentalism," he wrote that his question had been answered.

Never mind that as a Christian and a feminist I am not sympathetic to Hamas. Never mind that I had spent hours detailing the history of how most of Palestine was overrun by Zionist forces in 1948-49, why the Palestinians refused partition, and why the PLO preferred secular democracy in all of Palestine but would settle for just the territories. Never mind that I told him the most impressive and surprising thing I found in the occupied territories was the Palestinian spirit—dedicated, positive and warm, not revanchist in the least.

Why did the *Michigan Daily* print the article without at least checking to see if I had consented to be quoted by this imposter, or whether I had been quoted accurately? The pro-Israel opinion editors admitted that they had been personally delighted to receive something "from the other side," although they already had printed an equally inaccurate, but less personal, rebuttal to my article.

A New Dimension

Meanwhile, my struggle for Palestinian rights was taking on a new dimension. Missing my Palestinian friend, Majed, I invited him to spend Christmas with me and my family in Chicago, or to come at a later date and look at U.S. graduate schools. Majed had graduated from his university and wanted to continue his sociology studies, which necessitated going abroad.

He applied to the Israelis for an exit visa, but after a month he was still getting the runaround. Therefore, he decided to use another method. As a West Bank "resident" (Palestinians born and raised in the occupied territories are not citizens of any state), he was entitled to Jordanian travel documents. His Jordanian passport was renewed and brought to him from Amman by a cousin.

Then, to apply for a visa to the United States, he had to travel to the U.S. consulate in Jerusalem. Entering occupied East Jerusalem is illegal for West Bank Palestinians under current Israeli rules, but somehow Majed avoided the heavily armed soldiers at the checkpoint. However, he was denied a U.S. visa.

When I got the news, I was shocked and angry: Why couldn't a Palestinian intending to study in the United States visit for a few weeks? Consulting with others, I found out that refusal was the norm.

On advice I received at the University of Michigan, I called area peace organizations to obtain an invitation for Majed to lecture. Finally, word arrived that the visa had been granted!

Majed packed his suitcase, said good-bye to all his friends and traveled to the Allenby Bridge to cross into Jordan to start his trip to the U.S. After he had waited four hours in line, an Israeli official told him he could not travel because his "name is in the computer." He tried again the next week, but the Israeli soldiers would not budge.

Majed was frustrated but not defeated. He went to the Palestinian human rights organization al-Haq for help. Assigning him a lawyer, al-Haq sent a letter to the Israeli authorities requesting clarification of the problem. That was at the end of January, and the letter still has not received a response.

The nature of the problem, however, became crystal clear when Majed met with an Israeli intelligence officer. The officer reminded him that he had been put into administrative detention for his activism while a member of the Birzeit student council. He had not been charged with a crime or tried, but he had been held in solitary confinement and threatened with rape if he did not provide information about Palestinian activism.

"We want to punish you because you did not give information when you were in prison," the Israeli intelligence officer said. "If you decide to give us information, we will let you travel."

Nobody should have to live under such repression. And no person of good conscience should remain silent when others are treated so inhumanely. To those who have persecuted me for questioning U.S. support for Israel's occupation and its disenfranchisement of the Palestinians, I am (strangely) grateful. The red flags they raised for me made me realize that one of the greatest tragedies of this century has been the support of the United States—the beacon of freedom?—for Zionist oppression.

Yet in the midst of this tragedy the Palestinian spirit survives, flourishes, and inspires. I wear my "Palestine" olive tree every day, and I will not forget. ✦

Katherine M. Metres graduated in 1994 from the University of Michigan, which named her one of two outstanding undergraduates and awarded her the Virginia Voss Memorial Scholarship for excellence in journalism. She received her Master of International Affairs from Columbia University in 1997, and plans a career in diplomatic service.

Tea Time in Bahrain— A U.S. Sailor's First Middle East Encounter

By W. John Vandenberg

People always ask me how I became so involved in the Middle East, and I greet these questions with open arms. A question means that they are listening for a response. I tell them that I am involved because I like a challenge. As I have found, the American public in general hasn't the faintest idea what people of the Middle East are really like, yet many are curious. Most Americans have been conditioned to accept the negative stereotypes of Arabs as terrorists, bedouins, or oil sheikhs. However, if those who know differently take the time to show others what a rich cultural heritage the Arabs possess, and how far the stereotypes are from the truth, then people will change.

In my diary, I called my first encounter with Arab culture "Bahrain Tea Time." I was a sailor assigned to a ship permanently based in Manama, the capital of Bahrain. About once a week, when I got off work, I would wander into the *souq*, sometimes with friends and other times alone. One day I was a bit hungry and saw an old man selling dates from a large square tin. "How much?" I asked. He didn't speak English, but a Bahraini gentleman from a nearby teashop overheard us, and came over to offer help. He asked how many I wanted, and when I offered him a dinar for a handful, he laughed.

"That is way too much," he said. "Why don't you just come sit with us?"

Before I knew it, everyone was speaking to me, buying me tea, dates, and *bajellah*. They were just as interested in my culture as I was in theirs. From this group of friends I learned how to count in Arabic, say hello and good-bye, and introduce myself. I also learned how much they value their families and like to laugh. As I visited my new friends each week our basic similarities became more apparent. The stereotypes, about them and the Middle East, began to fade away.

"Where are the terrorists? Where are the 40 thieves? The fanatics?" I asked myself. I wandered the streets alone late at night, safer than in almost any American city. I started to question the way I had been conditioned by the American media. Why did I so easily take it for granted that these people, who by now had voices and faces, were barbaric, or backward, or evil? I began to look for answers.

Flourishing Interest

After six months I returned to America, and my interest truly began to flourish. I tore into every book I could find about Middle Eastern history, culture and Islam. Yet when I tried to tell anyone about how I loved the Middle East, how these people had struck me as exceptionally friendly and noble, and how we could learn from their society, I was met with a blank stare. No one understood; they were all trapped inside a web of deceit stretching back to their youth. Didn't the Arabs control all of "our" oil? Were they not trying to bomb us, and our brave allies, into oblivion?

I wanted to change this pattern of misunderstanding, and realized that I needed a degree to validate my convictions. The following year I enrolled in the Middle Eastern Studies program at the University of Texas at Austin.

There my inspiration acquired a solid grounding, and I became an activist. I took all the classes: Arabic, Politics of Oil, Contemporary Arab Thought. But after I learned about the history, the politics, the land, and the people, there still was something missing.

I remember well what sparked my interest in activism and group leadership. Dr. Walid Hamarneh, a professor of Middle Eastern literature at the university, in a fit of exasperation at what appeared to be apathy, asked his class, "Why don't you make a student group? Why aren't you more active? Why don't you *do* something?" He was right, and the situation was about to change.

There was a vacuum at the University of Texas. How could one learn about Palestine or Israel short of the AP stories? Where could an average person turn for an educated discussion on the Middle East? Nowhere, until the Students' Association for Middle Eastern Studies (SAMES) was established. In the summer of 1995, five close friends (two Americans, one Egyptian, one Persian Jew, and a Palestinian) and I founded SAMES. Dr. Esther Raizen, our earliest and strongest supporter, allowed us to hold the first meeting at her home. SAMES quickly became a forum for all people interested in the Middle East to meet and talk about their views, a source for information and a vehicle for energetic people with ideas to make their mark. By all accounts, we succeeded.

SAMES enabled the many people who are curious about the Middle East to get together and do things that weren't possible before. The campus responded overwhelmingly, and everyone was amazed by how hungry people were to learn more about the region. One of our proudest moments was the sneak preview of Elizabeth Fernea's film, "The Road to Peace: Israelis and Palestinians."

The showing, held in a local theater, was free due to its co-sponsorship by the campus Hillel group and the Palestine Solidarity Committee. There were so many people wanting to see this feature, a documentary about Israelis and Palestinians slowly and individually finding ways of living together, that we had to turn away over a hundred of them or risk violating the fire code! The Middle Eastern poetry reading, in which poems were read in a Middle Eastern language (Arabic, Hebrew, Turkish and Persian) and then in English, was another event attracting more people than the room could hold. A Middle

Eastern banquet at the end of the year featured food, music, and dancing, with over 200 people in attendance.

But no matter how much one wishes to dwell on culture, one can never escape politics. I had always been disturbed by the quality of media coverage (or lack thereof) on the Middle East. Only in the wake of the Qana massacre did I see with my own eyes what happens when a newspaper attempts to provide objective coverage.

When our campus newspaper, *The Daily Texan*, printed a number of articles and editorials containing brutal facts about the April 1996 Israeli bombardment of Lebanon, there was hell to pay. The Israeli consulate called the editor to complain and threaten his job, and a Jewish student delegation had a closed-door session with him. To his credit, he kept the coverage fair and accurate, but I will never forget the unfair treatment he received simply for refusing to candy-coat an atrocity.

And that is the good news: not only do I see the light, but many in my generation do as well. We don't have the mental baggage of older liberals who can only think of those "brave Israeli pioneers, waging a good war against their barbarous neighbors."

Young journalists and editors are calling the shots as they see them, and don't pull their punches. Students on many campuses across the U.S. are beginning to come together, attempting to find solutions not through the rhetoric of their grandfathers but through their own understanding of each other.

More and more American students actually know someone who is an Arab, Arab-American, or perhaps Palestinian, and they are beginning to ask questions. Their questions may elicit responses different from many things they have heard before. They will also see the light.

Because I began my trip with a journey of discovery, I will end it with one of hope. In 1990 I was on a warship in the Arabian Gulf, near Kuwait, scared to death that we would hit a floating mine as we sailed through the darkness. Six years later the National Council on U.S.-Arab Relations provided me with an opportunity to visit Kuwait for a second time.

I stood on a marina pier one night and watched a pleasure boat cruise into the darkness. "Things have changed," I thought. Kuwaitis no longer have to fear the unseen and dangerous minefields. I hope that someday my efforts will be rewarded by more Americans who venture out into the Middle East, undaunted by the minefields of misunderstanding that I and others are trying so hard to clear. ✦

John Vandenberg received his B.A. in Middle Eastern Studies from the University of Texas-Austin in May, 1996. He is the business and public relations manager for the Washington Report on Middle East Affairs.

Re-examining the Myths by Which We Live

By John Thompson

I have never been to Palestine, and only recently have I come to know some people from that occupied nation, but since I was a little boy, I have heard many first-hand accounts of what it is like to live under an occupying power. My mother, a Dutch woman who emigrated to the U.S. as an adult, endured with her family the five-year oc-cupation of the Netherlands by the Nazis. I treasure the stories that she and my uncles and aunts have told me, because together they constitute a moving narrative about en-durance, bravery, and victory over oppression.

Some of the injustices my family endured were small, such as the commandeering of their bicycles by SS troopers; others were unforgivable. The stories they tell are sweet, however, because of Holland's eventual liberation by the Allied forces—or, as most who endured the occupation insist on putting it, by the Americans.

My favorite is the story of my uncle's return home after the country's liberation. He had gone underground and joined the resistance several years before, and no one knew whether he was alive or dead. One day, unannounced and unexpected, he appeared at the door. He was wearing the uniform of the British army, in which he had been serving to liberate his country. That night, the family celebrated his safe return by dancing the hokey pokey, which my uncle had learned from his British comrades-in-arms.

Together, these stories constitute a sort of personal myth for me. I use the term "myth" in the sense of a story illustrative of bigger principles—a vivid narrative that helps me to understand such imponderables as suffering, endurance, family, and of course, war. My myth is not literal, experienced truth. It cannot be. World War II ended 20 years before I was born. My myth is, no doubt, a romantic version of what actually transpired—but I am fortunate in that the version I cherish has proven basically consistent with the facts of history.

Because of my family's involvement in World War II, my personal myth differs some-what from the public myth held by most Americans my age, which centers around such events as Pearl Harbor, D-Day, Hiroshima and Nagasaki, and of course, the Holocaust.

This myth is formed by a melding of facts and nostalgia, of history books and *Life* magazine photos. Like my personal myth, it is not the literal truth, but it is, in the case of World War II, at least, close.

Out of this myth was born another, the myth of Israel. The myth of Israel has, I now realize, a stunningly powerful appeal in the U.S. because it strikes so many basic chords within the Western mind: it is a haven for an historically "homeless" people, a land created to right an ancient wrong. Its very existence is evidence, for those who suffer guilt at the historical treatment of the Jews, of the expiation of their sins.

The popular image of Israel resonates with religious imagery. It is a new Eden, a garden blooming in the desert. It is a place of redemption. For some Christians, the state of Israel represents nothing less than a step toward the apocalyptic culmination of history and the Second Coming of Christ.

It is a faraway place, both exotic and familiar. It is situated in the Middle East, an area as foreign and forbidding to many Americans as the surface of Mars, yet Israel's own people are mostly Westerners of European descent. They're just like us, right? They're pioneers in a hostile wilderness, manning an outpost of Western civilization. The myth of Israel pushes a hundred buttons in the Western mind.

I have long been aware of this myth, but not particularly swayed by it, perhaps because it had little personal relevance for me. I had few Jewish friends when I was growing up. The horrors of the Holocaust made less of an impression on me than those endured by my own family and adopted countrymen. (In my mind, Anne Frank has always been not the Jewish girl who wrote *The Diary*, but the Dutch girl who wrote *Het Achterhuis*.)

Similarly, my interest in Middle East events was marginal. I remember the big events: the Israeli invasion of Lebanon, the Marines killed in Beirut, the *Achille Lauro*. I belonged to that majority of Americans who, when it comes to Middle East events, throw up their hands at the complexity of the conflicts there.

"It's not my concern," I thought. "They've gotten themselves into this mess, let them get out of it. They've all got blood on their hands."

This was the perception I carried with me until I applied for a temporary position replacing an art director on maternity leave from a magazine publisher of whom I'd never heard. "Go home and read these first," said the editor, handing me some back issues. "You don't want to be working for a magazine with which you don't agree." The magazine was the *Washington Report on Middle East Affairs*. I took the issues home and read them. "Okay," I thought, "these guys have their angle. No problem." Having no strong opinions on the subject, I took the job.

I soon saw that the magazine was an honorable enterprise, and it seemed to have the facts to back up its assertions, but I assumed that a good portion of the story was being left out. Most small magazine publishers, at least in Washington, have a pet issue to tout, a personal crusade. I reasoned that, had I taken a job with AIPAC instead (an organization I learned about after starting work at the *Report*), I'd be getting the other, just as valid, side of the story. This assumption is a common one, I think, among those of us who are too confused, or too busy, or too tired, to sort out anything beyond our laundry.

Stories I Had Heard Before

What I could not dismiss, however, were the first-hand accounts of daily life under occupation in Palestine. The reports came from a part of the world I'd never seen and knew very little about, but these were stories I had heard before. My own mother had told me what it was like to be stopped in the street to show her papers to a soldier, what it was like to huddle for hours behind drawn curtains during curfews, to endure capricious harassment, searches and raids.

Reports of the same abuses being poured on the Palestinians hit home with me. I began to wonder if there was, indeed, blood on the hands of all parties in the Middle East. Whose blood was it? How and why had it been spilled?

Working on a magazine, one has to read every story in every issue, over and over again, in the process of creating it. Inevitably, the full import of what one is reading sinks in. I began to realize that the Israeli-Palestinian dispute could not be dismissed as a conflict between parties putting a different spin on the facts. When I heard Martin Peretz, editor of *The New Republic*, categorically deny on television that a huge percentage of Israel's land is reserved for ownership by Jews alone, I realized that either he was lying or we were.

So who was telling the truth about Israel's policies toward its citizens, its practices in the occupied territories, and the validity of its claim to those territories? If it was us, why were so many Americans silent? Why was the U.S. funding an illegal occupation that seemed in no way to benefit U.S. interests? Was it possible that an entire nation could be fooled about transgressions so blatant?

The answer to the latter question came with the military operation called Desert Storm. I remain undecided today about its wisdom or justice, but it taught me a great deal about how completely people believe what they choose to believe—in other words, about the power of myth.

No matter what one's stand on that war, our victory did not warrant the parades and all-around orgy of self-congratulation that followed it. The Iraqi people paid, and are still paying, an incredible price for the transgressions of their leader. All Americans, regardless of our individual stands on the purpose or necessity of the war, should have bowed our heads in grief over its terrible toll.

But we wanted, instead, to kiss strangers in Times Square, while ticker tape rained down and cheers filled the air, the way we did at the close of World War II. We wanted to revive the myth of America as selfless defender of the civilized world. That myth had credence on V-E day—but not on the day we came home from Desert Storm, an operation that was less a battle than an incredibly sudden and violent mopping-up operation, performed in accordance with a nebulous mix of moral values and self-serving goals.

I doubt that any of us can or should live without our myths. They give us strength and wisdom. But each of us has a responsibility to check his myths against reality. When I began to question the myth of Israel, it took a surprisingly small amount of probing to bring the whole structure crashing down.

I believe now that our foreign policy toward Israel is guided by a powerful myth, fueled by the work of lobbyists, by collective guilt over past events, and by all of the symbolic and religious connotations evoked by the mere name of that state. If a maturing individual has the responsibility to measure, from time to time, the myths he treasures against reality, and adjust his conduct accordingly, certainly we as a maturing nation have to measure the facts as they are revealed against the principles by which we live, and adjust our foreign policy accordingly. ✦

John Thompson is an editor living in Delaware.

An Omani Dress Pointed the Way to a Trove of Arab Cultural Treasures

By Christine Harland

When asked by my international studies professor, Melissa Prevatt, to participate in the 1991 Brevard (FL) Community College Ethnic Fashion Show, I accepted, thinking it would be a great way for me to meet new people. She suggested I model for an Arab country since my eyes and hair are dark, and Switzerland was the only other option.

On the day of the show, she gave me a black and gold dress, and white trousers with lovely red and gold embroidery at the cuffs. I emerged from the changing room dressed in an outfit from southern Oman. Melissa had spent several months there visiting former students and researching the culture. She had received the dress as a gift. She was the first American I had met who had visited an Arab country, and I was fascinated to hear about her adventures. To be frank, before she told us about it, I had never heard of Oman.

As I walked down the runway during the show, the audience on all sides stared at me intensely. I realized that, like me, they were seeing something so new to them that they were unable to digest the experience. I was suddenly aware that everything about the culture and the people that I was representing had been somehow ignored, suppressed, distorted or exaggerated into a great myth which I grew up believing.

After the show, as I walked to the changing room, several students approached to ask where I was from. When I explained I was American, they relaxed. "Where did you get your costume?" one asked.

"This isn't a costume. It's the Omani equivalent of a Western gown," I replied to the student, who seemed confused at this possibility. It seems no one had bothered to tell her about the myth either.

As my semester with Melissa continued, each class chipped away at the enormous myth I had been conditioned to believe. We listened to Arabic music one day while chewing on small pieces of frankincense which Melissa had brought back from Oman.

She explained, "Those notes that are making some of you wince are called quarter-tones. Western music doesn't use them." Like a child I listened to these new sounds, wondering why no one had played such music for me before.

Melissa burned frankincense on another day and explained that it has antiseptic properties and was burned in a house after a child was born to keep the air clean. I thought of the three Magi, the only positive image of Middle Easterners during my childhood. They had traveled from afar with gold, frankincense and myrrh to bring to Bethlehem where the baby Jesus was born in a manger.

As a Catholic, I know the story so well, but had never been told much about these wise men. I had never thought about what frankincense smelled like, or the importance of the gifts, or even associated these wise kings of the past with the Iranians or Arabs of today. Rather, the myths perpetuated by the media led me unconsciously to reject the association. Such people somehow were not worthy of my attention, and couldn't possibly be wise.

Melissa spoke about Islam, and I learned that this was not the totally alien religion I had imagined it to be from the images of waves of bowing figures that flashed on the nightly news so often when I was a child. Upon hearing that Abraham, Moses, and Jesus were regarded as prophets by Muslims, I realized the myth again had misled me. I shared beliefs with these people.

The more I discovered, the more I realized how my mind had been manipulated by this myth. My education offered no relief. The myth was supported by history classes, in which the Egyptians stopped existing with the last Pharaoh, and the wondrous birth of civilization in the Fertile Crescent was somehow dropped out of our ancient history lessons after the sixth grade.

In high school, we never talked of the 1967 war. I recall watching American Marines pulling away the rubble of their bombed barracks in Beirut in 1983. All I understood from the news was that "Arabs did it." This was supposed to suffice. Nowhere, until my class with Melissa and the fashion show, had I encountered any opposition to the myth.

Only now can I look back on my beliefs as a child and see them as layers of a self-renewing blindfold I had worn throughout my formative years. Why wasn't I taught the truth?

Peeling Away the Blindfold

Now my notebooks in college are filled with small phrases and my name, written in Arabic. As a child I wasn't even aware that those squiggles on the signs in the scenes of Middle Eastern violence were a language. I thought they were designs. No one thought to teach me otherwise. The time I've spent learning the Arabic alphabet is an effort to peel away the blindfold that warded off interest or understanding.

When scheduling the 1992 International Food Festival for my college in Florida, I called a mosque to ask when Ramadan began. I had only learned of this month of fasting a year earlier, just after the fashion show. How could someone be unaware of an event that shapes and defines the year for a fifth of humanity? Apparently no one in any of the schools I attended thought I needed to know. Yet learning of it enabled me to schedule our feast so that all, including a sizeable number of Muslim students, could participate.

The words in my notebook, the music I now listen to, the *debka* dancing I have tried, the beliefs I have learned to understand, the culture I have uncovered, the black hole in history which I am slowly beginning to fill, are all gems in a cultural collage of which I was ignorant for too long. Melissa gave me the first glimpse of this treasure the day of the fashion show. She took the time to tell me about things others dismissed as insignificant and irrelevant to my existence. Otherwise I would not have been given the choice. Our media-driven society would have chosen for me.

My participation in that fashion show did enable me to meet new people. It also opened my eyes to the richness and diversity of the entire Arab world. More importantly, by beginning to understand another culture, I came to understand more about my own culture and myself as a product of it. Of all the gifts I could wish for my fellow students, I could wish them nothing greater than the excitement of discovering such treasures for themselves. Perhaps my experience will help point the way. ✦

Christine Harland earned a B.A. at Rollins College in Winter Park, Florida, and an MBA at Rollins' Crummer Graduate School of Business. She spent the summer of 1996 as an intern in Oman and is now marketing manager for PaySys in Maitland, Florida.

Discovering the Victims Of U.S. Aid to Israel

By Eleni Katsoulakis

When I was a little girl with a serious illness, my mother made a pledge to Jesus that if I survived, I had to visit the Holy Land where He was born and light a candle in the Church of the Nativity. So, to keep my mother's sacred promise, I set out a few weeks ago to visit the path of Jesus and feel His agony.

Even before entering the Holy Land, I was startled by Israeli security. At John F. Kennedy Airport in New York I was detained in a private room and interrogated for four full hours! This was followed by a humiliating body search, while 400 Jewish passengers went through relatively quickly. All this was still on American soil.

Israeli security precautions in New York seemed minuscule, however, in comparison with the massive military and police presence on every street corner in Tel Aviv. Perhaps I would have become accustomed to it if I had not traveled to the West Bank.

There, despite warnings from local Palestinians that, after 6 p.m., no one was safe outside except the Israeli army, I walked one evening to a Christian church. Suddenly, a young Palestinian boy around 12 years old darted into the empty street and started to spraypaint an Arabic word on a wall. Later I was told that the word he tried to write was "Palestine."

He had not even finished one word, however, when armed Israeli soldiers appeared. The boy started to run away from them, but other soldiers appeared in front of him. Surrounded, he raised his hands in surrender, shaking terribly with fear.

As the soldiers shouted angrily at him, one of them came closer and then said something loudly to the other soldiers. In the next moment, before I could comprehend what was happening, the soldier shot the boy in the face, not once, but two or three times.

The defenseless Palestinian boy fell on the street, bleeding heavily from his face and screaming like a wounded animal. Several other soldiers then started to beat him savagely with clubs and fists, taking turns, for a long time, until the boy fainted. Then the soldiers pulled him to his feet, and held him as they continued beating him with extraordinary rage and hatred. When they let the unconscious boy fall again to the street, his tiny, bleeding body lay there, motionless.

Then a young soldier noticed me for the first time. I was standing only a few feet from the boy, but behind a building. I was too panic-stricken to move, but the soldier heard my uncontrollable sobbing. Pointing his automatic weapon at me, he yelled furiously, in a language which I did not understand. Then he pushed me violently against the wall. I was sure that, since I had just witnessed a horrible crime, he would kill me in order to seal my lips.

"I am American, I speak English," I said desperately.

"You are an American whore," he replied in an English accent made sinister by his hatred. "Only prostitutes feel sorry for Palestinians!" When he didn't shoot I fled, expecting a bullet in the back to bring me crashing down on the street next to the bleeding boy.

The next day, I heard that, in the hour that elapsed before an ambulance arrived, the soldiers pulled the wounded boy by his feet around the streets in order to terrorize the neighborhood. Torn between relief that I was alive and guilt that I had not been able to save the boy, I decided to stop visiting monasteries and churches. Instead I would go to the refugee camps of the West Bank and Gaza to see with my own eyes the reality of this unholy terror in the Holy Land. So the remainder of my visit was spent in the homes of families from among the more than one million Palestinians living today in the humiliating refugee camps of the Israeli-occupied territories.

In open disregard of international law, the Israeli authorities collect heavy taxes from some 1,800,000 Palestinians living under military occupation. These Palestinians, in turn, must seek but seldom get Israeli permission to dig a well, plant an olive tree, sell fruit in the streets, repair a roof, or build an addition to a home or business. The Israeli government does not provide even such rudimentary services as garbage collection in occupied areas, and restricts the sale or lease of land to Palestinians while half of the West Bank and most of its water has been confiscated by Housing Minister Ariel Sharon for the eventual use of Jewish settlements!

Tragic Tales

Every Palestinian I met had his own tragic tale to tell. A Christian Palestinian shepherd told me that in 1988, early in the intifada, he witnessed Israeli soldiers ordering three young Palestinian men to dig their own graves, in a bare field a few kilometers outside of his village. After a ruthless beating, the Palestinians were ordered to lie down in the graves. Then a bulldozer buried them alive. As the soldiers left, the shepherd, who had watched from a nearby hill, alerted nearby villagers who rescued the buried Palestinians. Later, when Israel's Shin Bet secret police learned the identity of the shepherd who had organized the rescue, they attacked him in the mountains and brutally broke his bones with stones!

A priest who was teaching in a church-sponsored school in the Old City of Jerusalem described for me another incident that took place in 1973, 14 years before the outbreak of the intifada. A little Arab boy of six or seven years wearing a green T-shirt and holding a tiny stone taunted some Israeli soldiers on patrol in East Jerusalem. The soldiers went after him, but the little boy disappeared in the side streets. The angry soldiers started searching nearby homes and stores, and stormed into the school.

In one classroom they saw a student wearing a green shirt. Although the student was 11 years old and had nothing to do with the little boy in the Old City, the soldiers grabbed the boy and smashed his head against the wall several times. Another unit of soldiers arrived and systematically began to beat the students in one classroom after another. Two hundred students were beaten, and three were critically injured.

When the priest tried to stop the frenzied soldiers, they seized him by his hair and pushed him down the stairs. He was seriously injured and hospitalized for more than a month. Later in the same day, the soldiers returned to the school and ordered all the students to kneel on the floor. They were terrorized for hours with guns pointed at their heads while the soldiers photographed them.

Such experiences, the priest told me, explain why hundreds of Palestinian children are suffering such post-traumatic pathological and mental problems as haunting fears, anxiety, phobias, insomnia, frustration, insecurity, prolonged depression, helplessness and aggressive antisocial behavior.

An 84-year-old West Bank villager showed me deeds to land he has occupied for his entire life and which, he says, has been in his family for more than 1,200 years. Now Israeli authorities have informed him that his property is being confiscated for a Jewish settlement.

I saw with my own eyes the bus stops and gas stations where desperate Palestinians gather looking for work. Israeli businessmen hire them for day labor at one-third of the wages paid to Jewish workers. When a job is completed some unscrupulous Israeli employers, instead of paying pre-agreed wages, report to the police that these workers have been working without permits, and have slept overnight on Israeli soil. As a result, the Palestinians lose their wages and may be jailed and fined.

I met a pretty little Palestinian girl, blinded by an Israeli plastic bullet. Some years earlier, a Jewish settler had attacked her father with a knife and gravely wounded him as he was returning from work. Israeli law provides little protection from such attacks. For example, if a Jewish settler kills a Palestinian, he may get less than six months in prison. A Palestinian killing a Jew can expect a life sentence.

A Vow of My Own

These are just a few of the things I saw before returning to the United States, my mother's pledge redeemed. But now I've made a vow of my own. Paralyzed by fear, I failed to act when I might have saved a life. But I won't fail again, while there are so many more lives still to be saved.

I ask, in God's name, is there any possibility that our government will guarantee $10 billion in loans to Israel to enable it to steal more lands from their owners, and destroy any Muslim, Christian or Jew who opposes the building of the Jewish settlements our own government calls "obstacles to peace"? Ten billion dollars from the taxes of decent Americans to carry out a morally reprehensible program in violation of every single human right and every moral tenet of my Christian beliefs? No, there is no such possibility, if I and the millions who share my beliefs have the courage to oppose it openly and not turn our backs on the troubles of our fellow human beings. There will be no more subsidies from moral American taxpayers for immoral Israeli purposes. That is my pledge to my God. ✦

Eleni Katsoulakis, a journalist in her native Greece, is a free-lance writer presently living in New Jersey.

Uncovering Congress' Dangerous Addiction to Pro-Israel PACs

By Andrea W. Lorenz

In the Jan. 25, 1993 issue of the *Nation,* Michal L. Sifry takes exception to some of the conclusions of a recent report by the Anti-Defamation League on "Anti-Semitism in America." "Criticism of Israel, it turns out, is no predictor for anti-Semitic attitudes," the Nation editor points out. "In fact, many critics of Israeli policy are well educated, follow foreign affairs closely and embrace tolerant, pluralistic attitudes at home."

Given such enlightened, and not at all uncommon, attitudes on the part of American Jews, why are so many members of Congress loathe to criticize Israel when it disregards international law and denies basic human rights to the Palestinians under its occupation? I found the answer only after I accepted an assignment to compile reports filed with the Federal Election Commission of exactly how much money pro-Israel political action committes (PACs) gave to candidates running for Congress in 1992.

As a new writer for the *Washington Report on Middle East Affairs,* I approached the assignment in March, 1992, with healthy skepticism. When dealing with any aspect of the Arab-Israeli issue, loaded as it is with emotion, one can only maintain credibility by not accepting what one is told on its face value and by constantly checking the facts. After all, I knew political action committees were a part of the American political landscape. They represent everything from ice cream manufacturers to the National Rifle Association. Teachers have PACs, gays have PACs, pro-lifers and pro-choice groups have PACs. Wasn't the issue of pro-Israel PACs wielding too much influence being blown out of proportion?

The importance of my research, according to Richard Curtiss's book *Stealth PACs,* in the fourth edition of which the figures I was gathering eventually would appear, is that federal law limits any one PAC to a contribution of no more than $5,000 to a candidate in a primary election and another $5,000 in the general election. Therefore, theoretically, no special interest could use its PAC to donate more than $10,000 to any individual candidate during a two-year election cycle. With 55 pro-Israel PACs actively supporting Israel, however, as was the case in the 1992 cycle, they would have the ability to outspend any other special interest.

But, I thought, if they had been doing this ever since 1978, as claimed in the book, wouldn't I have read about it somewhere else? I trekked down to the Federal Election Commission (FEC) and, with the help of a patient federal employee, I followed instructions left by my predecessor for collecting information from reports to the commission by 116 pro-Israel PACs listed in the book.

I discovered that only three of those PACs had names referring in any way to the Middle East. Names of the others referred either to good government, their geographic location in the United States, or both. Thus the author had dubbed them "Stealth PACs," and turned their innocuous names into an initial guide to identifying their true purpose.

The fact is that virtually no other kind of PAC adopts an innocuous name. After all, it is to any PAC's advantage to attract like-minded donors, and to be sure that the candidate knows why its campaign contribution was made. It struck me that there must be a reason for pro-Israel PACs to adopt such misleading names. Could it be to conceal from the public the existence of so many of them?

Still, I knew that not every innocuously named PAC existed to support U.S. aid to Israel. There was, for example, a PAC called "Emily's List" organized to support women candidates. How could I satisfy myself that the 116 PACs on the list, with names like Gold Coast PAC, Heartland PAC, and Badger PAC, were pro-Israel PACs? Why not call them up and ask them, just to be sure?

Since I already had discovered a new PAC, one not listed in the 1991 version of *Stealth PACs*, but which followed the donation patterns of those that were listed, I decided to start with it. I called the telephone number listed in Washington, DC for "Actionpac."

On my first call, I was told "Laurie" would call me back. After I left two more messages asking her to return my call, she did. She told me, however, that she was sorry but she could not tell me the purpose of Actionpac, or what kind of candidates it supported.

The spokesperson for only one of the several innocuously named PACs I called, Capital PAC, was candid about the PAC's pro-Israel stance. In that case, however, what he said was hardly news. I'd already seen Capital PAC described in Jewish weekly newspapers as one of the pro-Israel PACs.

In fact, election-year reading of such weeklies as *Washington Jewish Week* and the *Forward*, and the daily reports of the Jewish Telegraphic Agency, made clear which candidates the leaders of AIPAC and other national Jewish organizations were supporting. They were the same candidates to whom Actionpac, Capital PAC, and others on my list were donating.

How very effective all of this turned out to be is illustrated by political columnist Douglas Bloomfield, who wrote in the Jan. 14 *Washington Jewish Week*: "There is good news from Capitol Hill for pro-Israel forces..." He noted that 32 Jewish representatives had been elected to the House alone, and "Israeli defense and intelligence officials cannot help but be pleased with changes at the top of the two select committees on intelligence."

Bloomfield dubbed the eight Jewish Democratic and two Jewish Republican members of the House Foreign Affairs Committee a *minyan*, the Hebrew term for the quorum of 10 adult male Jews required for communal worship. Checking my list, I found that every one had received campaign donations from PACs on my "pro-Israel" list. Whatever the motives of the PACs, it was clear from Bloomfield's article that he, at least, had concluded that for these PAC-supported representatives Israel's interests would be placed above all others, including those of the United States.

So, a guide to identifying a pro-Israel PAC is not its name but its pattern of giving. Exceptions to that rule are "multi-issue" pro-Israel PACs. Multi-issue PACs give to Democrats but usually not to Republicans who are "right" on Israel. Their rationale is that in addition to support for Israel there are other issues equally important to their donors, such as support for abortion rights and opposition to prayer in schools. An interesting aspect of this pattern is that when faced with a pro-Israel incumbent and a pro-Israel challenger, as happens when a House member challenges a senator for the senator's seat, most pro-Israel PACs (but not necessarily the multi-issue PACs) give to the incumbent. This applies even if the pro-Israel incumbent is not Jewish, and the pro-Israel challenger is. Thus, when a member of Congress supports aid for Israel, the pro-Israel PACs will go all out to help that incumbent against all challengers.

In the course of my research, I noticed that the Hollywood Women's PAC donations in the current cycle did not follow the pattern of the "multi-issue" pro-Israel PACs, although in previous elections it had appeared to be one. When I called to check, they said they had decided that their first priority was to support women and pro-choice candidates, and that support of Israel was not as important. I therefore removed that PAC from the list of pro-Israel PACs active in the 1992 election cycle.

The final stage of my epiphany came when I had painstakingly entered all of the figures from individual pro-Israel PAC reports into the computer database and started adding them up. As the totals popped up on my screen, I could hardly believe my eyes— $108,000 in the current cycle to former Rep. Mel Levine (D-CA), who nevertheless lost in the Democratic senatorial primary election, and $382,630 since 1978 to Sen. Thomas Daschle (D-SD).

The 55 pro-Israel PACs that were active in the 1991-92 election cycle had contributed more than two and a half million dollars in critically important "early money" to pro-Israel candidates by June 30, 1992. By the end of the cycle, they had contributed $3,963,007 to 403 candidates, 281 of them Democrats and 122 of them Republicans.

This was an aspect of the U.S. political system that my history, political science and civics teachers had never explained. It began to dawn on me that many congressional candidates received from PACs enormous amounts of money for their re-election campaigns—enough to feed whole villages in the Third World for several months. Some of these staggering sums were listed in the daily newspapers.

However, one will not learn the true story about the pro-Israel PACs by reading most newspapers. For example, on June 8, *Washington Post* investigative reporter Charles Babcock reported the amounts contributed through March 31, 1992, by the nation's top 50

PACs. National PAC, the only pro-Israel PAC on his list, was 41st in his ranking of PACs by the size of their donations. Its then-total of $331,000 in donations put it below the PACs of the United Brotherhood of Carpenters and the United Steelworkers of America. That made pro-Israel contributions seem almost insignificant in terms of the big picture.

However, when I totaled donations to candidates by all of the pro-Israel PACs active by March 31, 1992, the figure was $2,020,983. That made the pro-Israel total nearly twice that of the heaviest hitter, the International Brotherhood of Teamsters, which had given $1,366,720 by March 31.

According to the FEC, it is not illegal for PACs representing the same issue to give to the same candidate, even though the savings and loan industry is the only other special interest to spawn such a proliferation of PACs, and they do not have deceptive names. What *is* illegal is for the direction of a group of PACs to come from one source. The American Israel Public Affairs Committee, Israel's Washington, DC lobby, denies providing donation guidelines to the pro-Israel PACs. Nevertheless, the giving patterns of those PACs—many of which were established by current or former members of AIPAC's board of directors—are remarkably predictable.

Do members of Congress who receive pro-Israel PAC money follow their consciences when it comes to decisions regarding Israel? It seems doubtful when they continue to vote the lion's share of U.S. foreign aid—close to half the total of U.S. bilateral aid worldwide—to Israel. In the 1992 fiscal year the U.S. gave nearly $1,000 for every Israeli man, woman, and child. Congress passed this legislation despite Israel's denial of basic human rights to more than a million Palestinians under its occupation and open Israeli disregard for international law.

What I learned from my research at the FEC is that whether or not pro-Israel PACs break the letter of the law, they certainly violate its spirit and intent. These donations of millions of dollars to candidates for Congress purchase appropriations of billions of U.S. taxpayer dollars to Israel. This money, in turn, subsidizes Israel's oppression of the Palestinians and the illegal appropriation of their lands for Jewish "settlements" in the occupied territories. Instead of holding Israel to the standards of a true democracy, such heedless U.S. government giving makes it possible for Israel to discriminate on religious grounds against people under its control.

Israeli human rights lawyer Lea Tsemel summed it all up best. In a recent interview for the Corporation for Public Broadcasting's "Frontline" documentary, "Journey to the Occupied Lands," she said: "The Palestinians envied the Israeli democracy. They realized that there is democracy in Israel and it exists mainly for Jews The feeling was that at least they will get some leftovers from that democracy table. And it took them, I think, like 20 years to realize that there is democracy over there, but there is no democracy for them." ✦

Andrea W. Lorenz is a writer, Arabist, and international business consultant who lives with her husband Pat Cunningham in Calgary, Canada.

VIII. FIGHTING BACK
1948-

AMERICANS ARE KNOWN for their sense of fairness and their support of the underdog. When, whether of Arab heritage or not, they learn the truth about the history and present-day realities of the Middle East, and the Israeli-Palestinian issue in particular, many of them "dare to speak out," in the words of former Congressman Paul Findley. The intensity of their commitment to a just solution in Palestine, and their tireless efforts to counteract the "mythinformation" served up by the American media, leave no doubt that they will continue to speak up and speak out until justice is a reality in Palestine, the Middle East, and in America.

Taking a Risk to Fulfill a Dream

By Farah Joseph Munayyer and Hanan Karaman Munayyer

In mid-1987, we ventured into the unknown. Against the advice of some of our closest friends, we decided to buy a collection of antique Palestinian national and bridal dresses brought to the United States from the Middle East to be sold. It bothered us that such a collection might be scattered. That would destroy a valuable asset belonging to a people who already have lost too much.

We took the tremendous financial risk of acquiring the whole collection to promote cultural awareness of Palestinian traditions. Since there was no time even to attempt to secure grants from Palestinian, Arab or American sources, we resorted to a home equity loan to finance this acquisition.

Each time we looked at the incredible beauty of the items in this collection, visions of the past swept into our minds. Born in the early 1940s, we had both lived through many episodes of the Palestinian tragedy. One of the worst began at midday in July 1948, in Farah's hometown of Lydda. The whine of bullets fired into the streets sent people rushing to their homes for shelter. The next day, we woke up to the noise of screaming and shooting. Peeking through the wooden shutters, we saw hundreds of people being herded along the street in front of our house by Israeli soldiers shouting, "Imshi ala Abdallah!" ("Go to Abdallah," then the king of the Hashemite Kingdom of Jordan). For many of the terrified families, it would be the last time they would ever see their homes.

Our Turn for Eviction

The next day, it was our family's turn for eviction. A group of Israeli soldiers armed with Sten submachine guns broke into the house and told us to be on our way "to Abdallah" in 10 minutes or risk being shot.

As we started out, I asked my father: "Why are these people lying on the ground?"

"They are sleeping," he answered. Only years later did I connect the people "sleeping" in the streets to the shooting and screaming of the day before.

On the way to an uncertain future, we passed by a church located next to the mosque in town. There, we found some of our relatives and friends evicted a few hours earlier. The priest insisted that, since it was late in the afternoon, we should spend the night in the church and leave the next morning. Luckily we did.

The next morning, Israeli troops came by and found about 250 Muslims and Christians taking shelter in the church. Through the priest's mediation, all were allowed to stay. That moment changed our lives. We were among the very few Palestinians who remained behind to witness the systematic destruction of many villages. Only later did we hear the horror stories about what happened to the thousands of our compatriots who were forcibly evicted or who fled on their own to avoid the massacres befalling Palestinians in the neighboring villages.

Link to a Now-Vanished Past

The pitiless expulsion of the population, followed by systematic looting and eventual destruction of whole villages, left traces of the accompanying misery in our souls. That probably influenced our decision, nearly 40 years later, to risk our comfortable home in the United States to acquire this collection. In our minds and hearts, this treasure constituted an irreplaceable part of the history and heritage of our beloved homeland.

It is to the memory of those thousands of neighbors who walked under the relentless sun "to Abdallah," carrying their belongings on their backs and their infants in their arms, and wearing our traditional clothing, that we have dedicated this project. These dresses, draped on our couch, were our tangible remaining links to those Palestinian exiles from now-vanished villages.

We decided to produce a high-quality videotape that would be accessible to both individuals and libraries and that would complement our own presentations of these costumes. Using professional filming crews and attractive young Palestinian models trained by Ms. Rima Nashashibi in California, we edited hours of footage into a 35-minute costume demonstration. Back in New Jersey, many more hours of close-ups of stitches, patterns and accessories were filmed at a professional studio. This resulted in an additional 30 minutes of edited videotape. These two parts were combined in a 70-minute videotape entitled "Palestinian National Costumes: Preserving the Legacy." Maha, our teenage daughter, narrated the tape in English.

We also produced a photographic portrait of 10 girls, each wearing a different dress, representing a different area of Palestine, and printed the first of a series of greeting cards, showing the famous Bethlehem "malak" or "royal" dress.

The tape was first displayed by the United Nations in December 1987, during the International Solidarity Week with the Palestinian People. Since then, it has been acquired by such institutions as the New York Public Library, the Cambridge Public Library and the Fashion Institute of Technology in New York.

To further promote the project, Farah made a series of presentations to Palestinian audiences in Israel and the West Bank in May of 1988, and we were encouraged to translate the script into Arabic.

After we did so, Kuwait National Television put considerable effort into adding background footage, and provided an eloquent young Palestinian announcer to narrate the Arabic version of this documentary. This new version was later edited in the United States to 60 minutes.

Hanan spent two years documenting the evolution of our traditional dress in Palestine, dating back to 2000 BC. In addition to the first collection acquired in 1987, we've bought two additional collections. At present our collection totals almost 200 dresses and numerous accessories and has become one of the largest and best in the world.

In 1989, we produced a condensed version of the existing English tape, "Palestinian Costumes and Embroidery: A Precious Legacy." It contains a new five-minute segment showing the origin of the art of embroidery in Palestine and the Near East and containing photographs of surviving pieces of ancient textiles from the Middle East in European and American museums. It examines the costumes in Palestine through the different epochs, from antiquity through the Greek, Roman, Byzantine, Arab and Ottoman Turkish periods up to the early 20th century. A distinct series of resemblances emerge linking present-day Palestinian costume to Canaanite spinning, weaving and dyeing traditions that evolved in the Greco-Roman period into a generalized Mediterranean style.

This style was influenced in Byzantine times by the Mesopotamian-Persian love of opulent decoration. It was further refined during the period of Arab Omayyad rule in Syria and Palestine. These embroidery motifs and weaving skills were subsequently passed on by the Omayyads from Moorish Spain and Sicily to the rest of Europe. Paintings by European masters from the 12th century frequently displayed embroidered Arabic calligraphy in costumes of wealthy Europeans.

When European and American missionaries first arrived in Palestine in the 19th century, they were amazed at the rich embroidery, which they attributed to the influence of the Crusades. However, the influence was in the opposite direction. European costumes at the time of the Crusades were unadorned. Contact by the Crusaders with the weavings and embroidery of the Near East popularized these arts in Europe.

Each time we see the glimmer of pride in a Palestinian child's eyes as we display this heritage, or feel the excitement of an American audience upon viewing and discussing a little-known aspect of the history of art, we know that we are one step further on a long and arduous, but immensely rewarding, road. ✦

Farah Joseph Munayyer and his wife, Hanan Karam Munayyer, are both Palestinian-American graduates of the Hebrew University of Jerusalem. Farah is a research pharmacist and Hanan is a molecular biologist. There three daughters—Maha, 16, Mona, 2, and Randa, 6—are pictured, left to right, at the beginning of this article in Palestinian dresses from the Munayyer collections.

A Lonely Battle for the Palestinians

By Marian Fitch

Looking back, it doesn't seem that there was ever a time when I did not hear about Palestine and Palestinians. Probably it was because, although I was a U.S. citizen with an American father and British mother, I grew up in England, a colonialist country when Lawrence of Arabia was still a national hero. There were always students at my school who jingled lovely foreign bracelets and spoke wistfully of Arab *souqs* and Indian hill towns or—magic name!—the Khyber Pass with its fierce watchers, guns at the ready, not at all averse to firing on unwary travelers below them.

With relatives in Spain and Alexandria, Egypt, I was drawn inevitably to the Mediterranean, although I was not to meet a Palestinian for many years and, in fact, when I started on my travels I went first to Poland. But the Palestinians were struggling for their rights, twice proposed and twice betrayed (as the Poles were betrayed at Yalta), and they were very much in my mind when I was working in New York in 1948. I had been incredulous when, the year before, it was settled by one power, the United States, acting for another people, the Israelis-to-be, that Palestine was to be divided, the larger and more productive half going to Jews who were mainly European.

The third people, the Palestinians, who were the most concerned, were to be dealt with as envisaged by Britain's Lord Arthur James Balfour when he said in 1919: "In Palestine we do not propose even to go through the form of consulting the wishes of the present inhabitants of the country, though the American Commission has been going through the form of asking what they are...Whatever deference should be paid to the views of those living there, the Powers in their selection of a mandatory do not propose, as I understand the matter, to consult them."

Later, working at the U.S. Embassy in Rome, I had to learn to keep my mouth shut although the news from Palestine was worse all the time. In 1967 I was allowed to appeal, through the embassy news sheet, for medical aid and blankets for Palestinian refugees, but only one other person answered my call. The rest of the embassy staff sent their aid to Israel.

Luckily, English traveler Freya Stark put me in touch with an English couple stationed at the British embassy in Amman who were the founders of Medical Aid to Palestinians.

Jordanian Airlines helped me get supplies through to the refugees. But I felt this was far from enough.

When I left government service under early retirement, therefore, I went back to Rome and found a job with a new office being opened at the Vatican whose purpose was to help the Palestinians and others in the Middle East. They had already set up offices in Beirut, Amman and Jerusalem and I was sent off to visit them and their dedicated staff members who were operating them against all odds. It was an enlightening experience and, fortunately, for every horror tale there was a good one of projects continued, food and medicine brought in, or children protected.

Those also were the days when Romans (and citizens throughout Italy) demonstrated long and hard for Palestinian independence, easily getting 10,000 people to fill the great piazzas. Amongst those demonstrators were large numbers of Palestinian students. Political leaders and PLO representatives (Italy had recognized the PLO) gave grand speeches and we chanted *Siamo tanti, siamo qui, siamo tutti OLP* ("We're many, we're here, we're all PLO").

During the same period, Israel was making Europe its battleground for the hunting of Palestinian intellectuals, shooting them down as terrorists whether or not they even knew how to use a gun. We lost several in Rome and out came the crowds. Meanwhile, of course, we organized fund-raising events and sent help however we could.

Archbishop Hilarion Cappucci, ex-prisoner of the Israelis, held a big meeting at his titular church of Santa Maria in Cosmedin, down by the Tiber, and I was mortified to find that all the Palestinians and Italians could sing "We Shall Overcome" but I, an American citizen since birth and now one of the few Americans present for the Archbishop's meeting, didn't know the song except as a name.

It was this feeling of being out of touch that helped motivate me to return to the States. There I found an astonishing change, from all the previous brief sojourns on leave when I had found no one who would listen to me describe the plight of the Palestinians. I first found my way to the American-Arab Anti-Discrimination Committee (ADC), whose staff showed me all that they were doing. Then ex-Congressman Paul Findley, to whom I had written from Rome, introduced me to the grand duo who had turned the *Washington Report on Middle East Affairs* into something unique on the American scene. From then on, it seemed that everyone I met had something to do with Palestinians, their rights and needs, and justice and peace for them, and I didn't need to feel out of step with my countrymen anymore.

Of course, I was hardly back before I went off to the Peace March in Jerusalem in 1989. Our plane was delayed, perhaps deliberately, and we weren't even allowed to go into the city, where we were told the Israelis had been savagely beating the marchers for three hours. Next day I discovered what had happened to the 800-strong Italian delegation and to all of the other brave ones who had started out to serve peace among peoples and had found one side that had no intention of being peaceful. I found many friends, dejected or hurt, but did not know until later that the couple who had helped me from the British Embassy in Amman had been among the marchers.

It was a sickening beginning for our visit, which showed me how much worse things had become in the Holy Land itself. We stayed with Palestinians in Gaza and, to our eternal shame, ran from Israeli soldiers throwing gas bombs while Palestinian women came to their doors and waited calmly to give help where they could.

In the night we were awakened by Israeli soldiers stomping into the room to demand our passports. Alas, mine was in the pocket of a friend in another house. I had some qualms but must have frightened off the soldiers with a "stony British stare" because, after waiting interminably to see my friend's passport, which she offered *slowly*, with her head turned from them, they "forgot" to ask again for mine. You can imagine the chagrin of our colleagues in the next house who had no such adventure, but I was secretly glad it had not ended in an Israeli jail cell.

There is no space left to tell of the kindness of all we met on that journey among the Palestinians. Since this was a "wake up" trip for the others, they were especially determined to "tell all," including the hostile treatment at Tel Aviv airport where the men were strip-searched, had their film taken away, etc.

It merely confirmed me in my own effort to keep on working until our government recognizes that Palestinians, too, are human beings who also have an inalienable right to life, liberty and the pursuit of happiness in their own country. There still is a long way to go, but I believe that if we hold together and keep speaking out by every means to our fellow citizens and those in government, we shall yet see a Palestinian state in being.

Someone once wrote that the Poles, in their spiritual endurance, stand alone. I have seen, however, that the Palestinians share that capacity, and it is up to those of us in the United States who know the truth about the Israeli theft of the Palestinian land to help make sure that all the deaths and sacrifices have not been in vain. No matter how long it takes, we can do no less. ✦

Twice retired from U.S. government and Vatican service, Marion A. Fitch now is a resident of Washington, DC, and a full-time activist for peace with justice for Palestine.

Making the U.S. System Work

By M. Jawaid Sultan Khan, M.D.

No two immigrants to the United States have come for exactly the same reasons. For some of us it was a matter of irresistible attraction, like iron filings to a magnet. For others it was a matter of being pushed by events at home. For most, it is a combination of individual factors. For certain, however, those of us from Pakistan do not come for purely economic reasons. There are places closer to home where we could make money faster, if that were our only goal. Nor have we come for religious reasons, since strict observance of the tenets of Islam tests our determination to integrate into an economic system and to raise children in a culture where days are not structured around the five prayers, weeks around Friday services, nor years around the Holy month of Ramadan.

We live, nevertheless, in harmony with our Christian and Jewish neighbors with whom we enjoy legal equality under the American system of separation of church and state. Those of us who remain in America have concluded that in this dynamic society and richly varied culture we can retain our own values while striving for personal fulfillment and a secure future for our children.

Of course I understood little of this when I left my home in Rawalpindi for medical studies abroad and a career as a pharmacist in a New Jersey suburb of New York City. Although my first goals were educational and professional, by the time I had satisfied those concerns I was deeply interested in the American political system. Many of my fellow Muslim immigrants were disillusioned by what they perceived as an irrational American bias against Islam. I am political to my fingertips, however, and I found it challenging that a system which, from afar, had seemed the ultimate in open democracy, with the citizens involved at every level, was perceived by American Muslims as closed to them.

There are perhaps historical reasons, but I believe that most of them go back no more than 40 years to the establishment of Israel and the resulting struggle within the American domestic political arena. Although Pakistanis are not Arabs, we and all American

Muslims are concerned about the unresolved Palestine problem and, of course, the fact that we are routinely slandered in the American Congress and media because of a political dispute between the Israelis and the Arabs overseas. I can do nothing about the history of the problem, but I think we all can contribute to the solution. After all, didn't the Jews—the other major non-Christian minority in America—once have similar problems? And yet my fellow Muslims were telling me it was the astonishing influence of Jews in American political parties and the media that now is locking Muslims out of the system.

I read a great deal about the subject in the *Washington Report on Middle East Affairs*, which seemed to have reached the same conclusions I have about U.S. Middle East policies. No matter whether you are Muslim, Christian or Jewish, if you examine the Arab-Israeli problem objectively, you reach the conclusion that a Jewish state will not be secure until there is a second state in the Holy Land for the Palestinians. Therefore the problem is one of educating the American media, Congress, and eventually all Americans. When the latter understand the problem, they will do the right thing and, when Americans finally do the right thing, there will be peace in the Middle East.

I contacted the *Washington Report*'s executive editor. He described the hard work, single-mindedness, and organizational discipline that had given between five and six million American Jewish citizens such a powerful veto on U.S. foreign policy that it was spilling over and hurting Americans like me, whose only offense was to be from the countries that oppose Israel overseas.

We Muslims are well organized, but not for political purposes. However, we brought this editor to speak to our annual banquet in the tri-state area of Connecticut, New York and New Jersey. He told an audience of several hundred indigenous Muslims and new Americans from Turkey, Iran, Afghanistan, Egypt, Syria, and other Islamic states as far apart as Morocco and Indonesia, that there are somewhere between five and nine million American Muslims, another two million Christian Arab Americans, perhaps a million Americans like him with extensive personal experience in Middle Eastern and Islamic lands, and one, two or perhaps more millions of activist Americans—Christians and Jews alike—in peace groups, trade groups, and other organizations for whom Middle East peace is a primary concern. All are potential one-issue voters if that issue is to create secure homelands for both Israelis and Palestinians in the land they must share in peace, and thus save American lives in the Middle East.

"If we together number 9 to 14 million," he challenged us, "and our message is not on behalf of special interests here or abroad, but only that Americans should act in the Middle East to support American interests and in accord with American traditions of self-determination, human rights and fair play—that's not a very difficult program to sell to the American people as a whole."

Of course he received a standing ovation, and I know many people congratulated him on his words. But I decided to concentrate on deeds instead. Specifically, how I would put the faith he and I seem to share in the American political system to the test in my own New Jersey community, if his organization would provide logistical support.

"First start to do it, using your own funds," he said. "Then write an article that will help others who want to do some of the same things in their own communities. In return, we will put our office and publications behind your effort."

That is why I am writing this article. The bargain I offered him is this: If I increase his subscriptions to between 800 and 1,000 in my congressional district, his publication will interview the district candidates about their specific views on how to attain Middle East peace two months before the 1988 general elections. I believe 1,000 subscriptions can influence 5,000 votes, enough to decide a tight race.

To start my part of the bargain, I first found out what towns are included in my congressional district. Then I asked the local telephone company for a telephone book for each town. I took out and marked the yellow pages listing churches and clergy, local newspapers, radio and television stations, public libraries, and political and religious organizations. Of course I included a list of local mosques and Islamic centers and organizations, since there are many of them in my district. The *Washington Report* has a gift subscription rate applicable to all of those categories. I sent a page each of zip code maps and locality abbreviations and $1,000 to cover subscriptions, to be selected from those lists. They in turn promised to send sample copies of the *Washington Report* even to institutions not selected, in hopes that some of them would subscribe on their own. I also sent lists of elected officials on the city and state levels which I obtained from the League of Women Voters. It has offices in almost every large city. Where there is no such office, I believe such lists could be obtained from the office of a city councilman or state assembly representative.

I went through the white pages of the same telephone books and marked the Muslim names and mailed those to the *Washington Report*. I paid special attention to Muslim names in the yellow page listings of physicians. These are busy professionals, but they are in contact with many people daily. The support of such Muslims, who are highly respected by non-Muslims, is essential to any educational effort aimed at the American public as a whole. There are a great many Muslims in my district, and I cannot donate subscriptions for all of them, of course. I believe, however, that when they receive introductory issues, many will subscribe on their own. All of them will receive the issue in which my article appears. Perhaps a few will offer to help me and my friends finish the job in my district, or will send this article to a friend or relative who might start the work in an entirely new locality.

Here is the tally so far in my district. There were about 30 *Washington Report* subscribers in the district before I became involved. I had provided an additional 50 gift subscriptions earlier, and most of these can be counted upon to renew their subscriptions on their own. Now there are an additional 200 new clergy, media and library subscriptions I have purchased at a special very low rate, and I am confident that another 50 institutions which I located will subscribe on their own. That's 330 subscribers virtually certain by the end of the year. Sometime before then I will start telephoning each, asking that they contribute one gift subscription of their own, and that they show the *Washington Report* to neighbors and relatives. Meanwhile, non-Muslim friends already are trying to arrange, or donate, group subscriptions for church and secular organizations to which they belong. Fellow Muslims are now contacting the Halal (Muslim) meat shops in the district, asking them to put issues of the *Washington Report* on display for sale. Arab Americans and Turkish, Iranian and Pakistani Muslims have obtained agreement from several Middle Eastern restaurants in the district to do the same.

I can see already that in our concern for peace in the Middle East, we Muslims are not alone. Our interest is to see the United States, our new country, loved and respected again in our former homes, which encompass one billion people in 45 countries. It was that love and respect that attracted those of us who grew up in the Islamic world to America. We want our children to be as proud of it as we once were when they visit the lands from which their parents came. Most of all, we want our children to be respected for and proud of their Islamic heritage in this new land in which they have been born.

I believe we will have the requisite *Washington Report* subscribers in our congressional district by the 1988 election. If so, I think it will indicate that I have "seen the light" about how purposeful and energetic people with no hidden agenda can secure their niche in the American political system. And, if I am right, I am certain of one other thing. At least two candidates contending in 1988 to represent this district in the House of Representatives will "see the light" on U.S. interests in the Middle East. For the first time they will be able to speak like good Americans from conviction and common sense, instead of from fear of an extremist, insatiable, and ruthless pro-Israel lobby. I believe that instead of outbidding each other with promises of more money and more deadly weapons for Israel, we will hear candidates from both parties telling the voters in my district that the best security for Israel is to end 40 years of bloodshed between Arabs and Jews on terms acceptable to both.

There was an Islamic golden age in history when Jews, Christians and Muslims lived together in harmony and produced one of the truly great world civilizations. We who regard Moses and Jesus along with Muhammad, peace be upon them all, as prophets who brought God's message to mankind, know that there can be such a golden age again. God willing, it will be realized, with our help, right here in our country, America. ✦

M. Jawaid Sultan Khan, M.D., is a pediatrician practicing in New York City.

A Personal Crusade Against Media Bias

By Gip Oldham, Jr.

My first view of the Middle East was from the cockpit of a World War II aircraft. At that time I was not interested in politics, and my university degree in mathematics had supplied no knowledge of Middle East history. I flew into Palestine several times, however, and a few months after I had been in Jerusalem's King David Hotel, the British headquarters for the area, it was dynamited by Menachem Begin's Irgun Zvai Leumi Jewish terrorist organization, with the loss of 91 Arab, British and Jewish lives.

My base was Cairo. An acquaintance in the British military police there told me not to believe all I heard from either his or my own government blaming Egyptians for terrorist acts there. In fact, the 1944 assassination in Cairo of British Governor General Lord Moyne was the work of Jewish assassins of Lehi, the Stern Gang, led by another future prime minister of Israel, Yitzhak Shamir.

My military service in Cairo ended in 1946, but in 1951 I returned to the Middle East as a commercial aircraft pilot based in Saudi Arabia. I flew in and out of every Arab country. On our vacations, my wife Virginia was able to visit them as well.

Half-Truths and Lies About the Arab World

As a result, we became aware of distortions, half-truths and lies about the Arab world in the U.S. media. On vacation in the U.S. in 1956, we saw Jewish organizations generate, through the media, such outrage over the sale of U.S. tanks to Saudi Arabia that longshoremen refused to load them on ships. Not once did we see it explained that the 50 tanks were part of the agreed lease price for the use by the American Air Force of the Saudi air base in Dhahran, then a vital link in a network of U.S. military bases and communications facilities on the periphery of the Soviet Union.

After Virginia and I returned to the U.S. from 18 years in the Middle East, we found time to challenge distortions of Middle East events. We wrote letters to newspapers. Our first letters concentrated on domestic issues and the changes that had taken place in our own country while we were overseas.

Then, in February, 1973, the Israelis shot down a Libyan commercial jetliner, killing all 108 aboard, when it strayed over occupied Sinai while seeking to land at Cairo airport. We wrote our first letters on the Middle East at that time, criticizing the manner in which our "free press" unquestioningly followed the Israeli propaganda line in an incident strikingly similar to the more recent shooting down of a Korean commercial flight by the Soviet Union.

Concerted Personal Attacks

Our letters attracted angry replies attacking us personally, rather than addressing the facts we presented. To us that meant we were doing some good, so we continued.

In the summer of 1974 there was a concerted drive against us personally in the Letters column of the *Dallas Morning News*. Afterward, every letter printed was altered in some way, and the number printed dropped drastically.

We began to write other newspapers and the same pattern followed. After an initial better-than-average success, letter attacks started and out-of-town papers informed us that they had changed policies and would only print letters from their own circulation areas.

After a west Texas paper printed 12 of our letters in one year, the first three on non-Middle Eastern subjects, a local doctor accused the paper of giving us an editorial column once a month. To make his point he enclosed copies of all 12 of our letters.

We found our main problem, however, was in reducing the relevant facts to the space generally alloted for letters to the editor. Whole paragraphs are needed to refute such catch-phrases as "our only reliable ally" or "Arabs have started all Middle Eastern wars," so popular with the media and politicians. Arab and Palestinian actions against Israelis were headlined, but covert actions against Arabs and Palestinians were not reported, or were described as "Israeli retaliation." "Pre-emptive strike" became the description of what the rest of the world saw as an overt Israeli invasion of Egypt and Syria in 1967, and of Lebanon over and over again in the 1970s and 1980s.

Support Too Late

Recently we attended the 50th reunion of my high school class in the same west Texas town whose newspaper had for a time printed our letters. At least 20 of my old classmates came up to say they had enjoyed our letters "before you stopped writing in our newspaper," and to note that my wife and I had "predicted a lot that is happening now."

All I could say was, "I wish you'd said that to the editor at the time we were under attack, instead of to us now. We never stopped writing. The paper was just too frightened by its advertisers to continue printing what we wrote." ✦

Gip Oldham, a retired commercial pilot, is an activist who resides in Dallas, TX.

POSTSCRIPT: *Virginia and I started writing letters to the editor of the* Dallas Morning News *in January, 1970. By April, 1974, each of us had had 100 letters printed, of which* about 50 were Mideast-related. We expanded efforts to other papers. As of November 27, 1990, we have a combined total of 1,246 'things' printed (that we know of for sure) in some 45 to 50 different publications. Seventy-five percent have been on the Middle East or related subjects. We had to struggle all the way because of media control. We should have learned from our experience with my book manuscript.

In July 1970 I wrote a 600-page manuscript about our 17½ years in Saudi Arabia. Covered were my Ten Thousand and One Desert Landings: Adventures and Misadventures of flying all around the Arab world, on ARAMCO desert operations. The book dealt with flying, oil exploration, drilling and producing, not to mention housing, commissary, laundry and health facilities. It also touched on vacation travel to some 30 countries, and daily living and social life in a foreign land.

Queries were sent with sample chapters and explanation that the book "was not political" but did show Arabs in a light different from that generally portrayed by the major media in the U.S. "The subject is not commercial" was the general rejection from 15 major publishers. Then a manager of a major 'aviation book club' (some 300,000 received its book list) agreed to read my manuscript. He said if he could use it he would send it to a major publisher from whom he bought many books, with a guaranteed minimum order. In October, 1971, I received word from a senior editor who had received the manuscript. In January, 1972, she returned the manuscript saying I should cut out all non-job-connected material, bring it down to less than 100,000 words, and resubmit. I 'did and did' and in February she had 275 pages. I inserted a self-addressed postcard at page 100 and a note asking her to please mail, with or without comment, when she reached that point. In June, after two inquiries, the manuscript was rejected with the usual "subject not commercial." The rewrite had never been read. The postcard was right where I had placed it. It is stored away.

In 1984 I wrote an ongoing series during and after the election campaigns, 10 parts total, for a weekly paper with a small but widely distributed circulation, titled The Best Congress Money Can Buy. In 1986 Virginia said, "Let's publish the series as a booklet." We budgeted a loss we could ill-afford and it became a 56-page booklet. We gave 325 away to people we knew would use the information and distribute extras and sold some 1,400 copies at our per copy cost. In 1988, the writer Philip M. Stern published his hardback, 325 pages, entitled The Best Congress Money Can Buy. It was then we learned one cannot copyright a title, only contents. And Stern's book on PACs certainly did not use any of my material, which was all on the Israel lobby and their PACs. Pro-Israel PACs were about the only PACs Stern did not mention. Hollywood and publishers engineered the "title" law change in 1978.

Over the years we have donated some 125 Mideast books to college and public libraries. Through friends we also were responsible for placement of nearly 200 copies of AET's program distributing Assault on the Liberty by James Ennes.

Thanks to AET programs we have given subscriptions to a dozen or more area 'opin-

ion molders.'

The conditions described in my "Seeing the Light" have not changed. Sometimes a change in a paper's editorial page editor allows 3 or 4 of our letters to be printed before 'something' causes another stoppage.

Virginia has averaged writing 5 or more letters to the editor per week for 20 years. Mine are fewer in number but more in word total. Even if too long to print as a letter, someone may read it. I usually add, "Check it out" and give several reputable references if not contained therein.

In January, 1994, Virginia and I copied 11 albums of our letters to editors, essays and articles we have written AND WERE PRINTED. We ended with some 1,200 pages and 1,376 items. We then recopied and had them bound hardback in five volumes, three for GDO Jr. and 2 for Virginia L. Oldham. At least 75 percent pertained to the Middle East. This five-volume set is now in a research section of a university library. Since that January, we have another 75 or more toward a sixth volume.

During the Gulf War I wrote 20 articles/essays on current news items. None were printed and so I set them aside. In 1995 I got them out and put into book form and we 'published' 15 copies in hardback. Five are now in university libraries.

Ours has been a decades-long struggle on the Mideast, seven days a week, reading, collecting information and spreading it around to 'activists' who still get printed, besides our own writing. Mostly it has been a very lonely battle. American Educational Trust and the Washington Report on Middle East Affairs *are the best things to happen in our cause. And so we continue our efforts.*

Peace Activist Sees Priority in Changing U.S. Middle East Policy

By Stephen Zunes

Iwas born not long after the creation of modern Israel and the expulsion of the majority of the Palestinian population. Like most Americans of my generation, I grew up with a rather romanticized view of Israel. This did not come from my parents. Indeed, since they were graduate students at Duke Divinity School in the early 1950s, they had held serious reservations about Israeli policies. By the late 1960s, they had become committed anti-Zionists.

Still, the naively idealistic view of the Jewish national homeland permeated American society when I was growing up. It was difficult not to sympathize with what was portrayed in the U.S. media as a small, progressive democracy threatened by militaristic, authoritarian neighbors attempting to wipe it off the map.

For a native Southerner growing up in the midst of the civil rights struggle, issues of justice and social responsibility were hard to ignore, particularly as I witnessed my parents' courageous activism against racism. Indeed, once a young Southerner concludes that prevailing community attitudes about race are false, it is easy to start questioning the conventional wisdom. Nor did being part of the Vietnam generation discourage my skepticism of establishment perspectives on the world.

The 1967 Mideast war, therefore, shattered my youthful image of Israel. It became apparent to me that the conquest of Arab lands was not a temporary military expedient, but an expansionist land grab.

Perhaps I realized this sooner than many other Americans my age because my father was faculty adviser to the Arab student organization at the University of North Carolina. I got to know Arabs as individuals, and as a result the stereotypes which enabled many Americans to rationalize Israeli militarism did not blind me to the fact that gross injustices were being committed against the Palestinians. It also became clear to me that the United States was a party to these crimes. A visit to Egypt, Lebanon and Syria with my parents five years later crystallized what I saw as the dangers of U.S. military involvement in the region.

Still, the Middle East was not my primary political concern. In college and in subsequent years, I became involved in a variety of causes, including movements opposing nuclear power, the arms race, apartheid, and U.S. intervention in Central America. In my graduate work at Cornell University, I did not take any courses on the Middle East.

It was only after receiving my doctorate and while teaching political science at Ithaca College in upstate New York and, subsequently, at Whitman College in eastern Washington, that I became increasingly involved with Middle East affairs.

While taking a pro-human rights stand in the Middle East was a natural outgrowth of my personal stand on Central America and South Africa, I observed that this was not the case with many prominent liberals in Congress and in public life who rationalized Israeli repression. Similarly, it seemed both the churches and the peace movement demonstrated much less vigor in addressing the Middle East than in critiquing U.S. foreign policy elsewhere.

It bothered me that I could go to a rally against U.S. intervention in Central America and march side-by-side with a mainstream/liberal Democrat and a Marxist radical, but when it came to the Middle East these erstwhile colleagues were at polar opposites. I felt inspired to help end this polarization among socially conscious Americans that paralyzed efforts to change U.S. Middle East policy.

At the same time, I had trouble identifying with the positions of the far left or others who identified with the Arab cause. I was aware that there were many Jews who considered themselves Zionists who were also sincerely committed to peace and justice in the Middle East. In addition, as a result of frequent visits to the Middle East, I was painfully aware of human rights abuses in Arab countries as well. I oppose U.S. arms transfers to Arab states as well as to Israel.

A watershed event for me was my participation in a visit by student peace activists organized by the Fellowship of Reconciliation, an inter-faith pacifist organization, to Jordan and Iraq just prior to the Gulf war. We were on one of the last flights out of Baghdad before the bombing began.

Afterward, I took a leave of absence from teaching to embark on a 40-city speaking tour. During those travels I discovered that, in large part, both supporters and opponents of the Gulf war were profoundly lacking in even the most basic information regarding the Middle East and U.S. policy there. This was even more apparent when the discussion moved to the Israeli-Palestinian dispute.

A Contribution to Make

The need for the kind of peace education to change U.S. Mideast policy, and the inevitability of another Middle East war if no such change is made, convinced me that I had a contribution to make. I founded the Institute for a New Middle East Policy (INMEP) in the summer of 1991. The goal is to encourage a U.S. Middle East policy based on support for human rights, international law, self-determination, and non-military resolution to conflict. Located just outside Seattle, INMEP reaches a nationwide constituency including scholars, the religious community, peace and social justice activists, and the general public through articles, public speaking, and appearances in the media.

An important element in my current work is acknowledging that both Jews and Arabs have been oppressed historically. Therefore special sensitivity is required of those seeking to help them establish peace. Rather than solely criticizing Israel, I emphasize that some Israeli government policies, and U.S. support for them, ultimately are in no one's interest. Being of neither Jewish nor Arab background, I emphasize that I am simply pro-peace and pro-justice.

The decision to leave a secure faculty position at a good liberal arts college was difficult. I am convinced, however, that working to change U.S. Middle East policy, particularly regarding Israel/Palestine, is the most important thing I can now be doing, particularly with the Clinton administration at times taking positions to the right of even the Israeli government. Rather than simply blame the pro-Israel lobby for America's short-sighted policy, we must see it within the context of our government's longstanding pattern of bankrolling violations of human rights and international law by its allies. These policies were altered only when mass movements rose up to challenge them. We must build just such a movement today. ❖

Stephen Zunes, Ph.D., is assistant professor in the University of San Francisco's Department of Politics.

Replacing Campus Racism With Informed Debate

By Dima Zalatimo

For Palestinians living under occupation, seeing the light comes by virtue of birth. For those in the diaspora, it is individual experiences that help mold our psyche and shape our political state of mind. Born in Kuwait to Palestinian parents and raised in Illinois and Saudi Arabia, I grew up with a thorough sense of my Palestinian identity. My childhood was a period of inquiry and discovery; I was never actually compelled to defend or justify my heritage.

This changed when I attended the University of Michigan. In Ann Arbor, I found myself confronting the racism from which my parents had long sought to shelter me.

My awakening began when, in a speech class, I attempted to persuade fellow students that our government should cut aid to Israel. Classmates exhibited an intolerance for alternative views on the Middle East by deliberately disrupting my speech. As a result of this and numerous incidents to come, I became aware of what being Palestinian in this country actually entails.

As a Palestinian at such an overwhelmingly pro-Israel campus, your identity is constantly assaulted. The uninformed and misinformed are very comfortable making overtly racist comments to your face. Any challenge to their views is met with hostility and even violence. The experience can be quite demoralizing.

The Perils and Rewards of Speaking Out

I remember being booed by an auditorium full of students when I pointed out the falsity behind an Israeli guest lecturer's claims of Israeli democracy. I found the speaker's astonishment at me and my comment particularly disturbing. Since the University of Michigan has historically been friendly to Israel's supporters, he was taken aback by the presence of a vocal Palestinian in his audience. Ironically, at the end of the lecture an Arab student thanked me for speaking out when she had long been afraid to do so.

This incident had a catalytic effect on my political development. I came to realize the importance of challenging my opponent and articulating this opposition. The fact that there were other Arab-American students experiencing the same tide of racism made confronting the situation easier.

A fellow student was once spat on by a young woman during a bucket drive to raise money for Palestinian refugees in Lebanon. I wondered to myself why any woman would react so viciously to a humanitarian effort. Did she not believe Palestinians suffering in refugee camps were worthy of our fund-raising? Did she doubt that Palestinians lived in refugee camps? Or was it that she didn't want to acknowledge the suffering of Palestinians? I was bewildered by this woman's reaction.

As troubling as the incident was, it brought the Arab-American students together and made us stronger. The stronger we became, the more hostile and irrational our opposition became.

As a result, we learned to struggle on campus both as individuals and as a collective body. An injustice against one was viewed as an injustice against all. We realized that the ability to mobilize and respond to particular incidents was essential to our effectiveness as concerned Arab-American students.

Taking the Initiative

Increasingly, pro-Israel activists found themselves reacting to our initiatives rather than creating their own. Dr. Israel Shahak, an Israeli professor of chemistry and a Holocaust survivor, who is an outspoken critic of Israeli policy, was harassed and told to go back to Poland when he spoke on campus. A talk by another opponent of Israel's policies, Jewish theologian Marc Ellis, was delayed due to a bomb threat.

In the meantime, I found that many students were able to overcome their skepticism and listen with open minds. Thus, I learned the importance of outreach. A large percentage of the students and faculty members were not as dogmatic as I had initially perceived them to be.

As a group, Arab-American students built broad-based coalitions with other groups fighting for human rights in South Africa and Central America. Thus, when it was time to mobilize around an issue, we were able to rally mass support.

The culmination of Arab-American student activism at the University of Michigan was our work at the school newspaper, the *Michigan Daily*. Recognizing its importance as a medium for educating the campus about the Palestinian cause, a number of Arab-American students began writing for the newspaper. I became a news reporter.

We began by educating staff members about the Middle East and found many of the Jewish students especially receptive. Having established support among the newspaper staff, it became easier to publish editorials representing a Palestinian viewpoint. The issues we addressed became increasingly controversial. Our editorials became the focus of heated campus debates.

As a news reporter, I covered campus events related to the Palestinian-Israeli conflict. The articles I wrote were fair and accurate (I take issue with the word "objective"), and highlighted controversial points other reporters normally overlooked due to self-censorship or lack of knowledge.

Attempts at Intimidation

My reporting caught the attention of the local Hillel director. He and many other Israel supporters persistently complained that my coverage of events regarding the Palestinian-Israeli conflict could not be "objective" due to my background. These people would never complain about an African-American covering minority affairs, or a woman reporting about sexual harassment, or a ballplayer writing for the sports page.

The controversy surrounding our work at the *Michigan Daily* received national and international publicity. A pro-Israel student protest of alleged anti-Semitism at the *Daily* received coverage in *The New York Times* and the *Jerusalem Post.*

When political intimidation failed, our opponents resorted to violence. Vandals spray-painted "Jew haters will pay" and "PLO Daily" on the walls of the student publications building on campus. Jewish editors who had supported coverage of pro-Palestinian speakers and presentation of both sides of the Israeli-Palestinian dispute received death threats. Naturally, these events did not reach *The New York Times* or the *Jerusalem Post.*

By this time, I was thoroughly prepared to challenge whatever opposition I faced. I had discovered the importance of speaking out, reaching out and educating. I am thankful for my experiences at the University of Michigan. As troubling as they were, they made me a stronger person and a more determined Palestinian. I have redirected the light I see into a beam of future hope. ❖

Dima Zalatimo is a former director of English-language programming on the Arab Network of America in Washington, DC.

A Handbook for Successful Negotiations With a Hostile Librarian

By Tom Refai

G etting the *Washington Report on Middle East Affairs* into a public or school library's periodicals collection (PC from now on) is, in my opinion, one of the most important things any citizen can do to make available objective, and therefore largely unreported, information on the Middle East. Many American libraries have collections consisting largely of periodicals that purposely circumvent serious examination of Israel, U.S. policies dealing with it, and the international consequences for American credibility.

With library collections the major source of serious information on the Middle East for both adult general readers and students working on class projects, most *Washington Report (WRMEA)* readers would be willing to donate a subscription to their local public library. However, this may involve more than just dropping a note into the library's "suggestion box."

I learned this from personal experience. I also learned, however, that with some diplomacy, and a persistent "carrot-and-stick" approach, even an initially biased librarian can be persuaded to do what thousands of U.S. libraries already have done—provide a space for America's best, and most widely circulated, journal of Middle East affairs.

An account of my ultimately successful four-month campaign to add the *WRMEA* to my suburban township public library's PC may provide some encouragement to others whose first effort to donate a subscription has been rebuffed by a librarian who has allowed personal prejudice to override his or her professional obligation to the public's right to know.

In mid-January of last year, I dropped a note in my local library's "suggestion box" requesting the addition of the *WRMEA* to the library's PC. Within two weeks I received a one-and-a-half page letter rejecting the request on grounds that the *WRMEA* "was not objective," "would not add to the comprehensiveness and balance of the library's PC," "did not have any public demand," and "was not indexed." The librarian who drafted the letter obviously hoped that such a "shotgun" approach would intimidate me into inaction. Wrong!

I immediately set up an appointment with the library director. In the three-week interim, I did some personal research into the library's PC as it stood then. I found that its only regular Middle East coverage was provided by three "mainstream" news weeklies, *Time, Newsweek* and *U.S. News and World Report.* (The latter is a magazine with sometimes outrageously pro-Israel leanings.) There also were two other shamelessly pro-Israel, anti-Arab and anti-Muslim periodicals. These were *Commentary* (a rigidly "neo-conservative" monthly published by the American Jewish Committee—a group hardly representative of the diversity of American Jewish opinion) and *The New Republic* (whose owner-publisher's pro-Israel fanaticism has been the subject of continuous journalistic legends dating back 26 years to his previous publication, *Ramparts,* flagship of the "New Left" of the 1960s).

I also made a list of the many non-indexed periodicals in the library's PC. With copies of the *Washington Report* in hand, I met with the library director and respectfully pointed out the lack of balance in the Middle East reporting represented by the library's existing PC.

To make my case, I had prepared photocopies of various articles from *Commentary.* One purported that the 1982 massacre of hundreds of Palestinian refugees at Beirut's Sabra and Shatila refugee camps was due entirely to "Christian Arabs." (In fact, even the Israeli government's Kahane Commission concluded that Israeli Defense Minister Ariel Sharon bore "indirect responsibility" for the massacre.)

I also pointed out that thousands of U.S. libraries, including those of the two major universities in my state, already carry the *WRMEA;* that there is public demand which I would be willing to document by circulating a petition; and that lack of indexing does not preclude inclusion of a periodical in his own library's PC. (I also told him that I was confident that the *WRMEA* would be indexed in the very near future, which it since has been.)

The upshot was that after that first interview the library director withdrew his denial and said he would "reconsider" my request. He also asked if I would leave the copies of the *WRMEA* I had brought with me for the library's reconsideration review. (This, of course, made it clear that he had not really reviewed the magazine in the first place, before sending me the "shotgun" letter of denial.)

I did not point this out, however. Instead, since I was not prepared to let go of my own current *WRMEA*s, which I use constantly as reference material for letters to local editors, I told him I would get some other copies to be dropped off to him within two weeks.

This gave me a chance to prepare a small note attached to each of three different copies citing articles relevant to the discussion we had had. One item I cited was a Rachelle Marshall letter to the editor, printed in the April 1991 issue, entitled "Confusing Criticism of Israel With Hostility Toward Jews." When I delivered the three issues to the library, I included a two-page letter detailing my personal goal (i.e., a mutually acceptable peace between Israel and its Arab neighbors), and pointing out that this goal, along with supporting human rights throughout the Middle East, were reflected in every issue of the *WRMEA.*

A Diversity of Backgrounds

I also pointed out the diversity of backgrounds of WRMEA writers (e.g., Christian, Jewish, Muslim, Israeli, American, Arab and more). Additionally, I politely addressed in my letter each point raised in the libarian's original denial, saying: (1) insofar as there is information in the *WRMEA* not found anywhere else in the library, it would certainly add to the comprehensiveness of the library's collection; (2) insofar as magazines such as *Commentary* and *The New Republic* are included in the PC, the *WRMEA* is needed to give the library balance and objectivity; and (3) there certainly is a public demand for the magazine, which I was demonstrating with a petition.

Four weeks after I dropped off the letter, notes and duplicate copies of the magazine (which, with a simple phone call, I obtained from the wonderful people in the American Educational Trust's Washington, D.C., office), I made another appointment with the library director to see how the reconsideration process was proceeding. He attempted to obfuscate the purpose of the meeting by bringing up totally unrelated issues.

He did say, however, that the library was "taking a look at re-evaluating the entire periodical collection." He mentioned a quarterly periodical on the Middle East that the library was considering, and said he could "not say yes or no to the *WRMEA* yet."

I agreed that the quarterly he mentioned is objective, but pointed out four issues per year of one quarterly could hardly offset 104 issues of two highly biased weeklies, *The New Republic* and *U.S. News and World Report,* and 12 issues of the monthly *Commentary.*

Taking a "cup is half-full" attitude toward his comments, I therefore suggested that the library also consider *Tikkun,* a dovish and liberal Jewish magazine that I personally find to be worthwhile reading, to add a totally different Jewish perspective than that provided by *Commentary* to the PC.

After this second meeting I wrote a one-and-a-half page follow-up letter to the library director thanking him for meeting with me, expressing my appreciation for the library's encouraging step forward, and my confidence that the library eventually would add the WRMEA to balance its offerings. I also mentioned that I would contact his secretary in the near future for another follow-up meeting, to which I would like to bring some local Arab Americans so as to establish rapport between the library and this "important subgroup." Since I knew I was being stonewalled, I adopted a firm tone in my letters, establishing a written record of my good faith efforts, but kept them courteous and not at all antagonistic.

During the six-week period between the second and third meeting with the library director, I collected more than 30 signatures from residents of the township served by the library on a petition with a preamble stating: "We, as residents and taxpayers of XYZ township, request, in the strongest terms possible, the addition of the *Washington Report on Middle East Affairs* to our library's periodicals collection."

Getting the signatures was not that difficult. Since both of my parents are Arab-American medical doctors, I started with some of their professional colleagues, who enjoy enough community standing and financial independence to take a public stand on a free-speech issue like this one without worrying about retaliation. I made copies of the signature sheets (with the preamble included), and gave some not only to the medical professionals but also to other personal friends of my generation who understood my concern, believed strongly in free speech, and were willing to collect signatures and addresses from others. While doing this, I left recent copies of the *WRMEA* with everyone involved so that all signatories could make fully informed decisions.

To my surprise, I found that about half of the Arab Americans I contacted already were familiar with the *WRMEA* and highly supportive of my efforts. I had thought, like Christopher Columbus, that I had "discovered" it all on my own.

The entire effort to document public demand, a powerful argument to back up my case, was much easier and more rewarding than I had expected.

Nevertheless, I also contacted an acquaintance at a local newspaper to inform him of the potential story if a public library blatantly denied such a legitimate and well-documented public request. It was not as difficult as I had expected to find a local reporter willing to expose efforts to stifle legitimate public debate, a subject of concern to all journalists, not just those familiar with Middle Eastern issues.

Though this aspect of my efforts turned into a "non-story," in light of the fact that my library eventually acquiesced to a legitimate and well-documented public demand, it helped to know I had a "stick" at my disposal to wield if my rights as a taxpaying citizen were rebuffed.

Even while making journalistic contacts in case of a refusal, I was making different arrangements in hopeful anticipation of a final acceptance by my library. Two friends, a physician and his wife, both of whom were subscribers to the *WRMEA* and signatories of my petition, agreed to host the library director and a guest of his choosing to "an evening of dinner and casual conversation," as a good will gesture when the *WRMEA* was accepted.

All this turned out to be more preparation than was necessary. I believe that a true act of kindness sometimes elicits a corresponding response, even from those who have come to regard people of different backgrounds as "the enemy."

My Final Meeting

When I arrived for my final meeting with the library director, I was happily surprised to hear him immediately accept, on the library's behalf, "a gift subscription to the Washington Report." (To circumvent any "nit-picking" over the library's budgetary concerns, I early on had assured him that a pool of XYZ township residents would donate the subscription if the library did not have funds of its own.) He offered his acceptance even before I could hand over a *copy* of the petition. (I'd kept the *original* signatures in hand in case more sticks were necessary.)

Although it wasn't needed, it is worth mentioning that I had attached a covering letter to the petition stating, politely but firmly, that if the library refused our request, we taxpaying petition signers would demand a meeting with the entire library board of directors. Just below that statement were two more. One said that if the library accepted our request, "we would like to thank the library director personally for his efforts," and the second invited him to the aforementioned evening at my friends' home.

In the end, it took four months of persistent, diplomatic efforts to have America's premiere magazine on Middle East affairs added to my hometown library's periodicals collection. But I don't begrudge a moment of the time spent.

The young ladies and gentlemen, mostly high school students, whom I've seen doing research in my library on current events will have access to critically needed background on Middle East events. They will learn that these events touch their lives and affect their futures far more than they would ever have realized without my intervention and that of my supporters. And all of the good, but misinformed, Americans in my part of the world will finally have a library that gives them a fair shot at "seeing the light."

Meanwhile, I have 30 friends I now know are willing to stand up and be counted. I admire every one of them for it. I believe the feeling is mutual, particularly since I suspect that some of them really didn't think my campaign was going to be successful in view of the initial hostility of a library director with an "attitude" about the Middle East.

Now, at the end of a long hard day, any of us can get a lift from just driving by the library and knowing that we've had a role in exposing its patrons to the knowledge that, someday, will make our country's Middle East policies truly "even-handed." ✦

Tom Refai is pursuing his M.D. degree at Wayne State University in Detroit, Michigan.

Laying a Foundation in Ohio for National Muslim Political Empowerment

By Mahjabeen Islam-Husain

ortunately I arrived several minutes before the program "The Presidential Election—What Every Muslim Should Know" was to begin. This was at the ISNA (Islamic Society of North America) convention this past Labor Day weekend, in Columbus, Ohio. Soon the room was filled and people were sitting on the floor. My friend Dr. Samina Hasan had to sit on the floor, too.

The discussion began with Suhail Khan, who is employed by Congressman Tom Campbell, followed by Richard Curtiss, editor of the *Washington Report on Middle East Affairs,* and concluded with Dr. Agha Saeed, president of the American Muslim Alliance.

I have always felt that politics was really dubious business and, consequently, always kept a respectable distance. This meeting however, changed that in a flash. My mind suddenly understood that this was not your regular politics, but the destiny of Muslims in North America that we were dealing with, and that shaping that destiny was not such a utopian or remote concept, but rather a practicable and foreseeable one. Richard Curtiss and Agha Saeed made it seem so simple!

I left the room elated and thought I was the only one (I am wont to get enthused rather easily when Islam is the cause). Imagine my joy when I found that Samina also felt the same way!

After some hurried promises from the speakers to come to Toledo, we excitedly spoke about involving some other families, many of whom were at that lecture. We returned from the convention on Monday and the following Friday had our first meeting. The ones who came to that meeting questioning, left committed. We had formed an organization with representatives from all five mosques in Toledo—two Sunni, one African-American and two Shi'i. We had decided to hold our event on Sept. 22, 1996, having Richard Curtiss and Agha Saeed as the speakers, with introductions of the Democratic and Republican candidates for national, state and local offices, some remarks from Ohio Congresswoman Marcy Kaptur, and concluding with short speeches by myself, Dr. Zakir Husain and Samina.

Having only two weeks to prepare for the event, we were fairly frantic. Visions of facing an empty auditorium and other permutations of the same "daymare" were common in the following days. Obtaining mailing addresses, computerizing them and then mailing the flyer were tasks that seemed insurmountable but, *alhamdulillah,* did get done. Much was deputized to our youth, and they were troopers indeed. The sound system, the food, the equipment, organization of prayer, arrangements for voter registration, etc., etc., all were completed.

The day arrived—bright and sunny. My nerves, though, refused the vacation. Prior to the event the local newspaper had been informed, and stated it would cover the event on that day. The religion editor, whom I have known, sounded very excited when I was giving her some basic information. In order to help her get a better idea I faxed Richard Curtiss' *Washington Report* editorial on the potential power of a bloc Muslim and Arab-American vote. Two days prior to the event she called and wanted photographs of Samina and myself. I tried to get her to include all the individuals of the organization we had formed, United Muslim Association of Toledo (the acronym, UMAT, means followers of the Prophet Muhammad in Arabic), in the photograph. Although the photographer took pictures of everyone, they featured only Samina's and mine, to our embarrassment. To top it all, they printed an "advance story" in the Sunday paper on the morning of the event. By this point my nerves were fraying.

Alhamdulillah the event was a great success. Some 300 people attended, *salat ul-Asr* and Maghrib prayers were held, and Dr. Agha Saeed and Richard Curtiss enlightened everyone. At least 50 voters were registered. Dr. Zakir Husain discussed the reasons for some Muslims not getting involved in the political process. Having a captive audience of Republican and Democratic candidates as well as a congresswoman was not an opportunity I was going to let go unexploited.

I spoke (vehemently) about the bigoted portrayal of Muslims, the "Judeo-Christian-Islamic" heritage with which political candidates should familiarize themselves, and the unconstitutionality of the anti-terrorism bill. The congresswoman asked for a copy of my speech and Samina's. Muslims in the audience were delirious and the political candidates somewhat aghast.

Riding the crest of recognition by non-Muslims and appreciation by Muslims is indeed very gratifying. Our task ahead is very daunting, however. Getting Muslims to agree to come in large numbers to vote, to try and vote as a bloc and to arrange for an exit poll, makes pulling teeth sound so easy!

Commendation and Criticism

After the UMAT event of Sept. 22, we received a great deal of feedback from Muslims and non-Muslims alike. Much of it was commendation, some of it criticism.

The five mosques of Toledo coming together, especially individuals who had been conducting a "cold war" within the community, was something that was discussed repeatedly. That one event could melt away the differences was something these very individuals could not get over.

The night of the UMAT event, Dr. Agha Saeed had nominated Samina and me as American Muslim Alliance chairpersons for the state of Ohio. We were reassured that if we could put together an organization and such a well-attended event in such a short time, opening a chapter/chapters would not be difficult at all.

We yielded to the gentle coercion, thinking simplistically that the mundane status quo of life would resume. Chapter opening was like a very distant mirage, and (our subconscious hoped) would most certainly fade away when the time came. WRONG! Everywhere Samina and I went we sensed expectations. (Yikes! Great Expectations!) Many had multiform ideas about the future of UMAT and welcomed its local presence. But a lot more hoped to make a national difference, especially politically.

A meeting of the UMAT Founding Members was held on Sept. 29, and feedback regarding the occasion and whether or not to affiliate with the AMA was discussed. Overall, everyone reported that the event was very well received. Affiliating with the AMA was decided on by essentially a consensus vote. It was decided that UMAT was to be a local, unifying organization, holding events related to religious, social, educational and perception issues, whereas the AMA chapter would take over the political aspects of UMAT.

Needless to say, when informed of this, Dr. Agha Saeed was very happy and promptly sent all the required material. In light of the closeness of the November election, it was decided to set an AMA chapter on Oct. 4.

A full-time medical practice, my home, three young children and the derivative chauffeuring responsibilities, and my great interest in playing tennis, already had made my life's train run a little too fast most of the time. Now, with the commitment to these new organizations, my days go by like visions in time-lapse photography.

On the day prior to the AMA chapter opening I pored over legalese, trying to decipher the bylaws of the AMA and making up a format to speak. I did not do any Power Point slides or even overhead projector ones. Feeling maternal to *necessity,* I wrote my presentation in point form on an artist's flip-pad made of recycled paper. The pad was hung up on an easel and the AMA was introduced in a sequential method, keeping the format interactive.

Success again! Forty-four members were enrolled, and a congressional chapter, which must have 30 members, was inaugurated. Interestingly, there was representation from throughout the community. On a sectarian basis, there were both Sunni and Shi'i Muslims. On the basis of national origins there were both South Asian and Middle Eastern immigrants and their descendants, African-American Muslims, and Muslims of European ancestry.

The League of Women Voters had invited Samina and me to talk about our organization on Oct. 14. Again on the artist's pad I wrote in point form an introduction to Islam and then described the formation of UMAT and the AMA. We were very well received.

We were supposed to talk for half an hour, but ended up speaking for two hours.

The agenda for our next AMA meeting is to install an executive committee, work out schedules to transport Muslims to vote on election day, and to discuss which candidates and which local issues to back. My personal hope is to pass along as many of my responsibilities as possible to the four members of the Executive Committee, so that I can get back to my sufficiently stressful normal routine.

Interestingly, practically all my patients, and in fact some physician friends of mine also, believe that I have significant political aspirations. My sole aim, however, is to work toward getting the Muslim voice heard across the United States in a loud crescendo chorus. The squeak of Muslim political action committees, and/or the squawk of individual power-seeking Muslims is simply not adequately serving the future of Muslims in North America. My vision is to have an individual voter-funded organization, like the AMA, in the major cities of all states in the U.S. by the year 2000. Outlandish and idealistic? It certainly sounds so, doesn't it? But then who could have thought that two women could have set up two new organizations, one event, and one meeting in the space of only one month. ✦

Dr. Mahjabeen Islam-Husain is a practicing family physician in Toledo, Ohio. Born in Karachi, Pakistan, where she received her M.D., she interned in Toledo before setting up her own medical practice there. She became an American citizen in 1989.

INDEX

Abbas, Abul, 200
Abdel-Shafi, Dr. Haider, 210, 212
Abraham, ii, 26, 158, 184, 224
Abraham's Rock/Rock of Abraham's Sacrifice, 6
Abu-Lughod, Ibrahim, 46
Achille Lauro, 154, 220
Actionpac, 231
Aden, 198
AET Library Endowment, 29
Afghanistan, 148, 242
Africa, 35, 36, 143, 159
Agnosticism, 6
Ajami, Fouad, 142
Al Da'wa, 132
Al-Assad, President Hafez, 198, 200
Al-Ghabisiyya, 213
Al-Haq, 214
Al-jabr wa'l muqabalah, 170
Al-Khowarizmi, Mohammed Ibn-Musa, 171
Aladdin, 157
Aleppo, 26, 170
Alexandria, Egypt, 238
Ali Baba, 157
Allenby Bridge, 116, 138, 153, 197, 215
Allied forces, 1, 219
Altar of Burnt Offerings, 6
Amari refugee camp, 187
American Air Force, 245
American-Arab Anti-Discrimination Committee (ADC), 19, 54, 149, 154, 186, 210, 239
American bias against Islam, 240
American Bible Lands Tour Group, 115
American Cancer Society, 193
American Colony Hotel, 21
American Community School, Beirut, 23
American Educational Trust, ii, 29, 43, 75, 168, 173, 196, 248, 257
American Friends Service Committee, 48, 82
American hostages, 77, 134
American Israel Public Affairs Committee (AIPAC), 50, 92, 198, 233
American Jewish Committee, 102, 256
American-Jewish community, 59, 108
American/U.S. media, 12, 30, 49, 70, 88, 90, 99, 110, 114, 126, 134, 154, 156-57, 161, 163, 173, 180, 191, 216, 234, 242, 245, 249
American military and economic aid to Israel, 163
American Movement for Israel (AMI), 211
American Muslim Alliance, 260, 262
American Muslims, 241-42
American political system, 241-42, 244
American pro-Israel bias, 198
American public opinion, 43, 178
American School in London, 136
American University, The, 55, 143, 162, 196, 225
American University in Cairo, ii, 196
American University of Beirut (AUB), 55
Americans, i, ii, 11, 20, 23-24, 26, 29, 32, 36, 40, 42, 48-53, 55, 57-58, 62, 69, 70, 72, 75, 88, 91, 96, 99-100, 107-108, 110-112, 114, 118, 128-129, 131-133, 143, 146, 148-149, 152, 155-158, 160, 162, 164, 166, 172-173, 175, 180, 189-190, 194, 196, 208, 212, 216, 218-221, 228, 234, 239, 242, 244, 248-250, 259

Day of the Destruction of the Temple, 7
Dayan, Israeli Gen. Moshe, 37, 78
"Days of Rage," 151
Dead Sea, 95, 137
Debke, 138
Deborah, 65
Declaration of Independence, 107
Declaration of Principles of Peace, 213; signing ceremony, Sept. 13, 1993, 164
Defense Department, 76
Deir Yassin, 16, 34, 46, 50, 61, 94, 97-98, 128
Demjanjuk, John, 42
Denmark, 108, 118
Department of Commerce, 149
Descartes, 171
Desert Storm, 221
Dhahran, Saudi Arabia, 23, 203, 245
Dine, AIPAC Executive Director Thomas, 50
Dir Kifa, 169
"Disappeared," 151
Doar Hayom, 8
Dome of the Rock (*Qubbat Es-Sakhra,* "Mosque of Omar"), 6, 184
Doxa, 130
Druze, 166
Dubrovnik, 176
Duke Divinity School, 249
Dulles, Secretary of State John Foster, 31

Earlham College, 55
East Jerusalem, 39, 44, 69, 118, 141, 202, 215, 228
East-West Center, 156
Eastern Europe, 25, 202
Eaton, Charles LeGai, 145
Eban, Israeli Foreign Minister Abba, 38
Egypt, 16, 44, 63, 77, 106
Egyptians, 41, 152, 224, 245
Eichmann in Jerusalem, 143
Eichmann, Adolf, 65, 143
Eilat, 23
Ein Karem, 192
Eisenhower, President Dwight D., 16, 26-27
El-Amine, Bilal, 169
El-Buraq, 7
Elborz Mountains, 112
Ellis, Marc, 253
Ellsworth, Oliver, 49
"Emily's List," 231
Encyclopedia Americana, 127
Encyclopedia Brittanica, 127-28
Encyclopedia Judaica, 47
England/Great Britain, 1, 17, 22, 34-35, 138, 238
English newspapers, 12, 28, 40, 47, 53, 56, 59
Ennes, James, 247
Epps, Frank, 118
Eridu, 25-26, 28-29
Euclid, 171
Europe, i, 1-2, 22, 25, 27, 30, 34, 37-39, 45, 56, 66, 75, 79, 83, 96, 99-100, 107-08, 117-19, 124, 145, 151, 154, 159, 171-72, 179, 181, 202, 211, 214, 220, 237-39, 262
Europe, Eastern, 25, 117, 202
Europe, Western, 2, 25, 171
Exodus, 49, 60, 74, 78, 92, 99-100, 151
Ezrat Nashim Hospital, 85
Ezrat Nashim Jerusalem Mental Health Center, 84

Far East, 25
Farsi, 25, 112
Federal Bureau of Investigation (FBI), 162
Federal Election Commission, 230-31
Fellowship of Reconciliation, 86, 250
Fernea, Elizabeth, 217
Ferraro, Rep. Geraldine, 133
Fertile Crescent, 26, 224
Findley, Paul, 75-76, 234, 239
Finkelstein, Israel, 36
First Amendment, 88
Flapan, Simha, 176
Florida Today, 21
Foreign Assistance Act of 1961, 186, 188
Foreign Service Institute, ii, 25-26, 29
Forrest, A.C., 118
Forward, 231
Franjieh family, 166
France, 1, 16
Frank, Anne, *Diary of,* 220
Frankel, Viktor, 86
Freij, Mayor Elias, 38, 201
Friendly, Alfred, 36
"Friends of the Arabs," 14
"Frontline," 233

Galilee, 95, 213
Game of Nations, The 60
Gandhi, Mahatma, 125, 152
Garden of Eden, 26
Gaza, 16, 31, 39, 44, 50, 82, 93, 138, 140, 148-49, 151, 162-63, 176, 178, 183, 185-188, 190,
     192-98, 200-02, 227, 240
Gemayel family, 166
Geneva Convention, Fourth, 188
Geneva Convention, Third, 39
George Mason University, 57, 148
Georgetown University, 57, 73, 137-38, 162
Georgia Institute of Technology, 164
Germany, 1, 22, 67, 124, 129, 134, 147
Gershom, Rabbi Yonassan, 85, 120, 123
Gershon Agron Road, 33
Ghana, 35
Gilgamesh, 26
Golan, 39
Golan Heights, 44, 53, 95, 99
Gold Coast PAC, 231
Golding, Louis, 34
Good Samaritan, 141
Grand Mufti of Jerusalem, 9-10, 14
Greater/Eretz Israel, 50, 66, 79, 175
Greeks, ancient, 171
Greening, Thomas, 86
Gulf countries, 63
Gulf crisis, 200, 202, 210
Gulf war, 210-11, 250
Gun and the Olive Branch, The, 151

Ha'aretz, 36
Ha-Am, Ahad (Asher Ginzberg), 47
Habash, Dr. George, 60, 159
Habib, Amb. Philip, 101
Hadassah, 31, 61

77, 113; hostage crisis, 89, 117, 166
Iran-contra affair, 133
Iraq, 1, 5, 24-26, 28, 72, 91, 101-02, 130, 146, 164, 190, 198, 200, 202-03, 205-09, 221, 250
Irbid, Jordan, 167
Irgun Zvai Leumi, 1, 16, 50, 61, 94, 127-28, 245
Isaac, 159
Isabella and Ferdinand, 130
Ishmael, 159
Islam, i, ii, 3, 5-6, 26, 37, 71, 136, 138, 145-46, 148, 167, 190, 217, 224, 241, 260, 262
Islam and the Destiny of Man, 145
Islamic Society of North America (ISNA), 260
Islamic Spain, 130
Israel and the Arabs, 46
Israel Defense Forces (IDF), 16, 187
Israel lobby, 57, 198, 244, 247, 251
Israel's Fateful Hour, 202
Israel, 1948 "War of Independence," 16, 41, 198
Israel, State of, i, 16-17, 22, 37, 42, 44-45, 63-64, 89-90, 99, 106-07, 124-26, 129, 167, 175, 177, 179, 199, 202, 213, 220
Israel-Arab Reader, The, 151
Israeli bombing of Iraqi nuclear reactor, 101
Israeli consulate, 218
Israeli death squads, 213
Israeli Embassy, 162
Israeli invasion of Lebanon, 1982, 90, 93, 100-02, 104, 106, 110, 114, 136, 173, 176, 178, 220,
Israeli lobby, 143, 196
Israeli militarism, 249
Israeli military, 79, 83-84, 87, 92, 94, 118, 129, 138, 141, 175-76, 178, 201-02, 211, 213
Israeli military courts, 140
Israeli Ministry of Foreign Affairs, 33
Israeli Ministry of Tourism, 56
Israeli reprisal raids, 46
Israeli settlements, 153, 175
Israeli siege of West Beirut, 18, 23, 90, 102
Israeli-Lebanese border, 92
Israelis/Israelites, ii, 16-18, 20-23, 26-27, 30-31, 35-37, 39, 41, 46-47, 49, 55-56, 58-59, 62, 64-65, 69, 78, 80-82, 84-85, 92, 95, 97, 99-100, 110, 118, 124, 127-29, 144, 147, 149-50, 152-55, 163, 168, 175-77, 180, 185, 192, 194, 198, 200, 212-14, 217, 238-39, 242, 245-46
Israel-Palestine dispute, ii, 234
Istanbul, Turkey, 35, 162
Italy, 1, 239
Ithaca College, 250

Jabalya refugee camp, 149, 163
Jabotinsky, Vladimir, 8
Jackson, Rev. Jesse, 133
Jaffa, 114
Japanese Americans, internment of, 210
Java, 190
Jay, Jeffrey, 86
Jean Christophe, 2
Jeddah, 136
Jehovah's Witnesses, U.S., 148
Jelazoun refugee camp, 118, 183, 187
Jenin, 149
Jericho, 138, 141, 182, 184, 192
Jerusalem, 3-4, 6-8, 11-18, 21, 30-34, 37-39, 50, 58, 60, 65, 69, 78, 84, 90, 93-96, 98, 104, 107, 114-15, 118, 122, 128, 136-38, 141, 143, 149-51, 170, 183, 191, 197, 202, 213, 215, 227-28, 237, 239, 245; Old City/Muslim Quarter, 3, 96, 115, 141, 183-84, 227-28
Jerusalem Film Festival, 39
Jerusalem Post, 32, 60, 150, 254
Jesus, 6, 35, 38, 69, 195, 224, 226, 244

173, 176, 183-84, 186-87, 190, 192, 195, 201, 227, 253, 256
Renaissance, European, ii
Reuter News Service, 35-36
Revolt, The, 46
Rivlin, Moshe, 104
Riyadh, 203
"Road to Peace, The: Israelis and Palestinians," 217
Rodinson, Maxime, 46
Rolland, Romain, 2
Roman Catholics, 126
Romans, 124, 239
Rome, 6, 36, 58, 173, 238-39
Roosevelt, Kermit, 60
Roosevelt, President Franklin D., 176
Rosenbaum, Richard, 147
Rosh-Hashanah, 65
Rubinstein, Danny, 102
Russia, 34, 37, 39, 47, 148, 173

Sabra and Shatila refugee camps, 1982 massacre, 90, 102, 106, 113, 162, 173, 180, 198, 256
Sadat, Egyptian President Anwar, 63, 77, 159, 161
Saeed, Dr. Agha, 260-62
Safad, 13
Said, Edward, 46, 79, 151
Salam, Saeb, 61
Saleh, Peter, 61
Saudi Arabia, 23, 52-53, 136-37, 160, 178, 200, 203, 210, 245, 247, 252
Savings and loan industry, 53, 233
Schachter-Salomi, Rabbi Zalman, 123
Scud missiles, 204
Sebastopol, 34
Security Council, U.N., 35, 67, 102, 164
Seder, 78, 122
Senate Foreign Relations Committee, 101
Senegal, 36-37
Senghor, Senegalese President Leopold-Sedar, 36
Separation of church and state, 241
Serbs, 152
Shah of Iran, 112-13
Shahak, Dr. Israel, 110, 253
Shakaa, Mayor Bassam, 118
Shamir, Israeli Prime Minister Yitzhak, 1, 34, 36, 42, 50, 67-68, 94-96, 98, 107-08, 127-29, 178, 201, 245
Sharon, Israeli Defense Minister Ariel, 37, 42, 67, 96, 106-08, 175, 184, 227, 256
Sheehan, Vincent, i
Sheikh Suleiman Alamuddin, 61
Shi'i, 142; Lebanese, 24, 56, 260, 262
Shin Bet, 91, 201, 227
Shur, Chaim, 85
Sifry, Michal L., 230
Sinai, 16, 23, 26, 31, 38, 44, 53, 64, 67, 99, 144, 246
Sindbad the Sailor, 144, 157
Six-Day War of 1967, 44, 49, 55, 63, 65, 78-79, 99, 109, 112, 150
Solomon's Temple, 6-7
Somalia, 146
Sorbonne, 35
South Africa, 33, 35-36, 38-39, 89, 147-48, 151-52, 250, 253
South Asia, i, 25, 30
South/southern Lebanon, 39, 56; Israeli buffer zone, 142
Southeast Asia, 55, 109, 262
Soviet Jews, 73, 151
Soviet Union, 16, 26, 37, 245-46

Vietnam War, 55, 87, 109
Vis, 176
Voice of America (VOA), 26, 203
Vorster, Johannes, 36

Wadi Al Arabah, 23
Wadi Qilt, 182
Wailing Wall/Western Wall ("Ha-Quotel ma-Aravi"), 7-9, 11, 15
Wall Street Journal, 102
Washington, 19, 25, 28, 30-33, 39-40, 50, 57, 62, 70, 75, 80, 102-05, 108, 110, 113, 136, 161-
    62, 164, 180, 182, 185, 189-91, 211-12, 220, 225, 231, 233, 240, 250, 254, 257
Washington Jewish Week, 231
Washington Post, The, 36, 101, 232
Washington Report on Middle East Affairs, i, ii, 29, 33, 75-76, 85, 88, 143, 145-46, 158, 160,
    182, 211, 220, 230, 233, 239, 242-44, 248, 255-58, 260-61
Wasson, Thomas, 31-32
Watergate, 63
Watson Foundation, Thomas, 170
Weisel, Elie, 86, 108
West Bank, 16, 30, 35, 39, 44, 49-50, 53, 82, 95, 118, 128, 138, 140, 149, 151, 153-55, 165,
    170, 172, 174, 178, 183, 185-86, 190, 192-93, 197-98, 200-02, 212, 214-15, 226-28, 236
West, the, ii, 2, 18, 30, 35, 63, 66, 97, 145, 161, 166-68, 207-08, 220
White House, 178
Whitman College, 250
Who Knows Better Should Say So, 24
Whose Land Is Palestine?, 118
Williams, Walter, 148
Witztum, Dr. Eliezer, 85
Woman of Nazareth, A, 18-19
Women's International League for Peace and Freedom, 48
Woodrow Wilson International Center for Scholars, 190
Wooster College, 28
World Vision, 135
World War I, 1
World War II, ii, 1, 198
Wounded Knee, 128
Wright, Dr. Edwin M., 25-29

Yale University, 49
Yalta, 238
Yarmouk University, 167
Yemen, 10, 52, 198
Yeshiva University High School of Brooklyn, 174
YMCA, Jerusalem, 31-32
Yom Kippur War of October, 1973, 63, 66, 99
Yugoslavia, 151, 176
YWCA, 138

Ziegler, George & Elizabeth, 198
Zionism, political, 8
Zionism/Zionists, 2-11, 13-15, 17, 24, 31, 33-34, 37, 42, 4747, 49, 59, 66, 75, 78-7978-79, 85,
    92-93, 98, 100, 102-04, 103, 128-30, 143, 149-5151, 174174-75, 198-99199, 213, 214-15,
    249-50
Zionist Organization, 7, 8